City Lives

Cathy Courtney and Paul Thompson

City Lives

The changing voices of British finance

Methuen

First published in Great Britain in 1996
by Methuen London
an imprint of Reed International Books Ltd
Michelin House, 81 Fulham Road, London SW3 6RB
and Auckland, Melbourne, Singapore and Toronto

Reprinted 1997

We are grateful to the National Life Story Collection and
the British Library National Sound Archive for their permission
to use the interviews cited in this book, which are all
deposited in the oral history collection of the British
Library National Sound Archive

A CIP catalogue record for this book
is available at the British Library

ISBN 0 413 67890 3

Typeset in 10 on 13 point Times
by CentraCet Ltd, Cambridge
Printed and bound in Great Britain
by Clays Ltd, St Ives plc

Contents

List of illustrations

The photograph of Lord Rothschild is by Gilbert Adams.
All the others, with the exception of Gwilym Lewis,
Lord O'Brien of Lothbury, Lord Benson, Sir Kenneth Kleinwort,
Jane Partington and Nick Durlacher, are by Cathy Courtney.

Foreword

There have been many accounts, cursory and detailed, of how the City of London works and of its history both in times of order and of crisis. This volume, however, which deals with a unique period of financial and institutional transformation, is unique also in its approach.

With the help of modern technology, unavailable to previous generations, it draws on the oral accounts of what happened during what were unforgettable days in City history. The accounts are those of participants in the daily operations of the City, not of eye witnesses or of outside commentators; and for this reason they carry with them a very special sense of authenticity. Each participant perceived of what was happening, of course, in the light of his previous experience as well as of his present knowledge and his place in the operational pattern. This is history both from above and from below, history that carries with it a sense of immediacy. It will be read with interest both inside the City and outside.

As Chairman of the National Life Story Collection I am proud to be associated with this project and to write this foreword. It is the task of our small but lively organisation to use the advantages of tape (and of visual) recording in the interests of posterity. What has previously been lost will now be saved. Our previous studies include the steel industry on the eve of fundamental changes. The City of London provided a different kind of challenge. The City is still changing, and it has undergone further crises since the volume was assembled. For this reason alone this book will be far from the last word.

Asa Briggs

Introduction

The success of the City of London in maintaining its pivotal role as one of the world's financial capitals has been an astonishing achievement. In the last fifty years it has stood out as a rare victory against the odds, with first the British Empire's worldwide political and trading network, and then its home base in the domestic manufacturing economy, crumbling around it. It was a success which demanded a radical transformation of the City's financial techniques and culture: a transformation from the old slow-moving system based on the mutual trust of a gentlemanly British élite, to an incessantly demanding struggle with the ruthless instabilities of today's open global markets.

This book is unique in presenting that transformation from the inside, in the words of the working generation which has shaped and experienced it. The power of the City silently influences the pockets and politics of every household in Britain. Yet most people have little understanding of how the financial City works, and what kind of people run it.

There have of course been plenty of commentaries of one kind and another on the City. There are a handful of books which explain clearly how the City functions or used to function technically, and a very small number of histories of particular banks or other institutions. But none of these give much sense of the City's working culture and its people in the twentieth century. There is a surprisingly thin and usually barbed line of novels about the City. Dr Johnson was exceptional among writers in his remark, which Boswell duly noted on 27 March 1775, that 'there are few ways in which a man can be more innocently employed than in getting money'. Novelists from Anthony Trollope's *The Way We Live Now* (1875) and George Gissing's *The Whirlpool* (1897) to J. B. Priestley's *Angel Pavement* (1930) and Margaret Drabble's *The Ice Age* (1974) have seemed eager to focus on how fortunes could be made or lost quickly through booms and crashes, manias and frauds, but none of them has really understood finance. More informed journalistic accounts of the City's culture have also targeted its fashionable weaknesses: shifting in the post-war years, as Anthony Sampson's successive editions of the City chapters in *The Anatomy of Britain* illustrate, from the problems of the over-protective old boy network to those of unregulated fraud. And astonishingly few long-term City financiers have ever broken into print themselves with autobiographical evaluations of their working lives. It is symptomatic that the autobiographical market has been scooped in exposé form: by *Liar's Poker: Two Cities, True Greed*, whose young American author, Michael Lewis, worked for Salomon Brothers in New York and London for a mere two years in 1985–7; and most recently, in the confessions of Nick Leeson, *Rogue Trader*, on his role in the fall of Barings.

It was because of this extraordinary neglect of inside accounts of the transformation of the City that, when we set up the National Life Story Collection at the British Library's National Sound Archive to create through interviews a living record of the life experiences of both the eminent and ordinary men and women in Britain, we immediately recognized this as a prime gap. The result was our 'City Lives' project, which was led for the first two years by Paul Thompson and from 1990 by Cathy Courtney. The project had to be and was sponsored primarily from within the City itself. We immediately gained crucial and perceptive support from Sir Nicholas Goodison and Sir Robin Leigh-Pemberton, then Chairman of the Stock Exchange and Governor of the Bank of England, and later on we have been particularly helped by Sir Kenneth Kleinwort and by the Esmee Fairbairn Trust. A full list of all who sponsored interviews, the one hundred and twenty-two men and women whose life stories have been recorded and deposited in the National Sound Archive, and of those who interviewed them, is printed at the end of this book. It would have been impossible without the support and time which they gave to the project, and we are grateful to them all.

It seems appropriate that the 'City Lives' project has taken on a coherent shape partly precisely because of the way in which it was funded through sponsorship. Essentially, the project has created a collective portrait of the most successful men of their working generation, born between 1920 and 1950, who held senior posts in the City at the end of the 1980s. They gave us a remarkable amount of time, with typically over six hours of interview recorded; and their life stories are the heart, both of the collection at the Archive, and of this book.

Ideally we should have liked to have been able to expand the project, both backwards and forwards in time, and also socially, even though the resulting material could have hardly been squeezed into this book. We were unable to secure funding for this except fragmentarily. We were able to record a few interviews with the older generation, already retired, who had started work in the City between the wars. Most of these were recommended by our core group, and to an extent seen as former mentors, so that they fit well into the same frame. But it would be fascinating to record a wider cross-section of this older generation of former City leaders while there is time. We were also able to include a small number of interviews with the generation born in the 1950s and 1960s, focusing especially on those, such as women or ethnic outsiders, who were new to the old City culture, and so experienced it from a different perspective. A wider cross-section from this generation too would be well worth recording, and we hope in time to be able to undertake this.

Lastly, of course, the City does not just consist of financiers who get to the top. Even within the financial City, there are far more who stay at a lower level, or who fail disastrously; and there is a range of crucial support workers from clerks and typists, messengers and cleaners, to barbers and preachers, spouses and therapists. And there were, and to a lesser extent are still today, the other branches of City activity outside finance: the press, the law, the food markets, shipping and so on. The City of London is an extraordinary mosaic of separate but interacting worlds, each with its own living history, most of it slipping quietly into oblivion. We see the history which people carry in their life memories as a crucial part of our heritage, as much as the objects and buildings to which they are complementary – and on which we spend infinitely more money. So for us, the 'City Lives' project is a start: a first shaft in this historical gold-mine.

Human memory is well known to be fallible. Eyewitnesses will have different memories of a car crash even minutes afterwards. And people sift, select, discard and rearrange their memories over time, depending on where they have arrived. Just as an account of a marriage by a person who is still married rarely has the openly bitter tone of one divorced, so a working career is viewed much more positively from its apex than after a forced redundancy. (For this reason alone, even before the constraints of libel are taken into account, this book could not have been a hot source on recent City scandals.) Hence historians, like lawyers, argue ferociously about the value of remembered evidence, or 'oral history', and its strengths and weaknesses are discussed at length in Paul Thompson's book *The Voice of the Past*. Here it will suffice to make three comments.

Firstly, it has been shown that memory is on the one hand especially unreliable as a narrative of events, and worse still on chronology; cautions which need to be borne in mind in interpreting the pages which follow. On the other hand it has proved relatively trustworthy on everyday patterns of working practices and relationships in earlier life, and since these are rarely recorded at the time, memory can provide a unique and invaluable source for understanding them.

The second is that memories do not have to be true to be interesting or important. Indeed, the very selections or distortions with which people recount the past can be especially good clues to how they think about the world. For all of us, even those who write off history as irrelevant, memory is the essential frame for knowing who we are and what we need to do. Thus what we believe about the past is crucial. When City financiers talk now about whether Siegmund Warburg lied to Hugh Kindersley in the street during the British Aluminium Battle in 1958, it does not matter whether he lied or not, but that they see the battle as an epic struggle, a turning point, and still recount it. For the old City order, Warburg's victory was as welcome as King Billy's on the Boyne was to the Ulster Catholics. In the City as in Ulster, our view of the past provides myths we live by in the present.

Lastly, each life is a single thread. That means that memories are very good at showing the connections between different spheres of life: for example, between family, education and training, and work. This is why the earlier parts of this book draw on a limited number of testimonies, making the connections observable. Life stories are also good at evoking the immediate context, whether at home or work. But because they are from a single, individual perspective, they can rarely convey how a system works as a whole. They need to be put in context.

Although the City of London has been a centre of banking and finance since the middle ages, the Square Mile has only become predominantly a financial centre during this century. On the eve of the First World War less than a tenth of the City's work-force were in banking or stockbroking; that is, half the number who were in other professions, or in manufacturing; a third of those in the food and mineral markets. London was then one of the world's greatest ports, and Britain had the largest share of the world's shipping fleet. Even in 1939, a quarter of the City itself was occupied by warehouses. They lined the river front, barges and lighters loading on the mud, while porters carried fish into the Billingsgate market and coal was traded immediately behind it under the elegant cast-iron dome of the Coal Exchange.

London is no longer a port, Britain no longer a maritime nation, and city centres have become too inconvenient for wholesale commercial markets. This has transformed the City's landscape, so that three-quarters of its buildings have become offices, and also its functions. Billingsgate fish market has closed, the Coal Exchange is demolished, the meat market at Smithfield only hangs on as an anomaly, and the only physical trades which really matter in the City any longer are in gold and diamonds.

This means that it has proved very difficult for the City to hold on to most of the trading exchanges which originally developed as part of a real physical market, even when in principle they could be traded on the basis of samples only, or as 'futures' based on expected later production and distribution. Since 1939 more City markets in commodities have in fact been lost than either retained or created. Not only coal and fish, but corn, wool, tea and cotton have gone. Of the old trading floors, the London Metal Exchange proved the most resilient, set up in 1882, which went on battling for world primacy with New York, holding on to copper, lead and zinc, and opening up new markets in aluminium and nickel. The City also developed a new trade in oil futures from the 1970s, setting up the International Petroleum Exchange; while the newly organized London Commodity Exchange (FOX) won significant trades in futures in sugar, coffee and cocoa. Nevertheless it is now clear that London lost immense opportunities in the international futures markets by failing, in contrast to Chicago, to develop means of trading futures *between* commodities by bringing them all under a single roof, or of hedging currency instability after the freeing of exchange rates in 1972–3. In the previous period of fixed rates London had found a valuable growing market in 'counter-trade', the organizing of barter in exchange for non-convertible currencies. But the London market in currency 'swaps' did not emerge before the early 1980s. Hence by 1980 Chicago already had more than two-thirds of the world's futures trading, and ten years later, after the London Inter-national Financial Futures Exchange (LIFFE) had opened its doors, London's share was less than a tenth.

The City had also developed other more specialized functions around London's role as the hub of an empire and a worldwide shipping network. In the mid-1950s the Baltic Exchange was still handling two-thirds of the world's ship chartering business. But by the 1980s, with too many of its members slow to adapt, it had become an elegant but defunct fossil. Lloyd's, on the other hand, had depended primarily on marine insurance, of which it was the world centre, but its members showed much earlier imagination, switched into motor and air insurance from the 1930s, and above all developed a speciality in reinsurance. Lloyd's also became heavily involved in the American insurance market. As a result, although growing less fast than the world insurance market as a whole of which it has a shrinking share, Lloyd's did expand strongly in the post-war decades, and its membership, under two thousand five hundred in 1948, has risen forty years later to thirty-three thousand five hundred.

Historically, the City had pioneered fire and life insurance in the eighteenth century, and some of the biggest insurance companies, such as the Prudential, still keep their headquarters there. But their organization and culture have long been altogether different from the City, institution-ally characterized by large-scale paternalistic bureaucracy and calculated caution rather than by market dealing and individual risk-taking. Most of their work-force has been scattered across the provinces, and many of their head offices have become largely symbolic presences. The changes which they have experienced through the opening up of the finance markets are another story, which we can only hint at here. The same is true of the two other leading client service professions, law and accounting. The lawyers remain nationally entrenched in the mediaeval Inns of Court, again a different world; but there have long been specialized City firms. Accountants are a somewhat newer breed, but of rapidly growing post-war significance as specialists in bankruptcy and merger investigations. Both City lawyers and accountants have increasingly linked up with overseas counterparts, so that once-small leading firms now count their staff – and some even their partners – in thousands.

The interlocking institutional system of the City as a financial centre up to the 1980s was also a legacy which had fused earlier domestic and imperial needs. On the eve of the First World War London was the world's prime centre both for raising long-term capital and for dealing in short-term credit.

The Stock Exchange had risen primarily as a market for long-term government stocks, expanding into local municipality and foreign government loan stocks, and joint stock companies for constructing railways, telephones, gas and electric supply, both at home and overseas; and later more generally into trading and merchandising enterprises. The Edwardian Stock Exchange was truly international: more than half of its trade was in foreign securities, at a time when a third of Britain's assets were calculated to be in foreign investments. But from the First World War onwards it went into a slow decline. Although London has a crucial international role in the cross-border trading of securities, this increasingly bypassed the Exchange. It was initially unable to deal in Eurobonds. By the 1980s both the New York and Tokyo exchanges, based on much more powerful domestic economies, had daily volumes of trade ten times greater than that of London's Stock Exchange. Its membership was restricted to British nationals, and falling from five thousand five hundred to under three thousand five hundred by the 1960s. There was a traditional sharp division between the brokers, who handled clients, and the jobbers, who actually bought and sold, and there were fixed commissions, which were off-putting to the biggest corporate investors. Consequently its business shrank to simply trading in British-based securities – and by the early 1980s it was even losing some of this trade to New York.

In the Edwardian era the Bank of England, although still a private corporation, issued sterling as the world's prime currency, and kept a watchful eye over the other banks, whose head offices clustered around it.

These were of two types. The first were the clearing banks, with their branches now not only in high streets throughout Britain but also in the bigger cities through the Empire and in Europe. They had to keep a proportion of their money liquid rather than on long loan in order to meet crises, and the best place for putting short-term money to use was London. The clearing banks were consolidating into giant slow-moving pyramidal corporations rather like the big insurance companies.

The discount houses and merchant banks, by contrast, were small but specialist. Discount houses had originated as sellers of one month's or three month's credit notes, or 'bills of exchange', for immediate cash at a discount. The merchant banks had developed this system which eased domestic transactions into a key instrument for financing international trading, operating through webs of contacts across the world, sometimes strengthened – as with Hambros – through cross-ocean marriages and cousinages. Later some of the merchant banks such as Kleinwort and Helbert, Wagg became specialists in international currency dealing, for which London was the principal centre between the wars. Others developed the techniques of raising money through the creation and issue of new securities and using their contacts to place them with buyers, as opposed to offering them on the stock market. 'The secret of an issuing house is distribution,' one former merchant banker has written, and then, as now, 'The traditional Old Boy Net still played its role, in shifting large blocks of shares.'[1]

From the First World War onwards the experience of a progressively weakening British economy, compounded by the 1929 Wall Street crash and the Depression years which followed, led to a much more defensive and restrictive system. The Accepting Houses Committee set up in 1914 became a closed ring through which the Treasury sold government bonds to the discount houses, who in turn sold them on to the clearing banks, taking up the liquidity. The Bank, nationalized immediately the Labour government came to power in 1946, guaranteed the system as the ultimate source of loans, but insisted that the clearing banks keep over a quarter of their deposits liquid. This was good for the domestic economy because it helped to keep the pound stable at relatively low interest rates, but it rigidified the established finance system.

No doubt this partly explains why the City finance houses in the 1950s seemed so irredeemably conservative in their ways. As always, however, the City was made up of a mix of types. The division between brokers and jobbers on the Stock Exchange was based on the social disdain between stockbrokers, who needed gentlemanly airs to deal with rich individual clients, and energetic loud-voiced dealers, who might indeed turn out to be the mythical ex-street market barrow-boys made good. Similarly, in the foreign money markets the more cultivated merchant bankers would have felt ill at ease with the dealers on the market floor itself, which one observer described in 1940 as 'the nearest thing to Bedlam that I know – half a dozen men in a little room, shouting in incomprehensible jargon into telephones, pushing switches up and down all the time in response to the flashing indicator lights'.[2] But in fact most young merchant bankers had to try their hand at dealing, and some of them relished it. They also had the energy and enthusiasm for the tough travelling needed to re-establish or win foreign markets in the post-war years. It was young men like these who began to open up key new finance markets from the late 1950s onwards.

The first crucial move was the creation of a market in Eurodollars and Eurobonds (loans in dollars for the developing European Community's institutions), in London rather than in New York. Although Warburgs had already started in Italy, the London market was initiated from 1957 by Hambros with the connivance, but outside the control, of the Bank of England.[3] In the 1970s this was followed by the development of trades in OPEC petrodollars, which after the first oil crisis were lent to Third World and Communist banks, and in direct international inter-bank loans. The inter-bank loans were based on a new financial instrument invented in the 1960s, the sellable certificate of deposit (CD), which enabled banks to lend to each other without any ultimate collateral to guarantee the loan.[4] And finally London reasserted itself in international currency dealing, from the early 1980s creating alongside it a market in currency swaps, enabling the hedging of bets against fluctuating exchange rates by balancing risk and return.

All this was uncontrolled: indeed, much of it had come to London simply because New York was more strictly regulated, and the smaller European finance markets still more so. Paradoxically, although part of London's appeal was its reputation for trust and political stability, it was at the same time functioning as an offshore banking centre between Europe and North America. Before long, indeed, it also became clear that time zones gave London an additional advantage in its position between Tokyo, Hong Kong and New York. These new markets proved explosively prosperous, and new foreign banks and finance houses flooded in to set up their London branches.

The new money markets were the City's most dramatic post-war success: but they were also the undoing of the old City. By the 1980s there were essentially two finance capitals on the Square Mile. There was the old regulated domestic City, still under the benign supervision of the Governor of the Bank, its 'headmaster, whose frown could terrify grown men and whose handshake could launch a career', who had headed off the threatened 1974 bank crash by summoning the top bankers and insisting that they funded 'lifeboats' to rescue the victims.[5] If the Governor now seemed less frightening, he kept up his style, his office guarded by tail-coated attendants and furnished with paintings and furniture like a country house drawing-room, with scarcely a symptom of modern technology. On his wooden desk were still 'twin crystal pots of black and red ink' and a silver handbell to summon assistance.[6]

Yet now, side by side with the old City but outside the Governor's domain, was the new international finance City. By the mid-1980s there were over five hundred foreign banks operating in London, most of them as multi-purpose finance houses. They were rapidly attempting to extend the technique of worldwide dealing by computer-backed telephone calls, which had been established for currency dealing, into bonds and equities, futures and options. At the same time new ways of raising money were being developed, such as 'junk bonds' in take-over bids and 'securitization' against the value of companies, house mortgages and commercial property – and ultimately, in the case of some bluffing tycoons like Peter Clowes, on sheer ability to generate a flow of money. Once the credit boom burst in the late 1980s it emerged that some of them had never had the resources they claimed, but were simply recycling credits faster and faster through unregulated channels. It should have also been obvious, especially to the large banks whose fingers had been burned by the property crash of the early 1970s, that credit based on the assumption of ever-rising property prices was bound to be unsafe.

The walls between the two Cities were demolished by the Thatcher government. Exchange controls were completely lifted in 1979, so that major companies and pension funds could invest on a global market. Most of the key subsequent reforms, such as of the building societies, were intended both to open up their own territories to outsiders and to free them to compete in the most attractive current markets. 'Big Bang', the reform of the Stock Exchange negotiated by its chairman Sir Nicholas Goodison with the government in 1983 and carried out three years later, which abolished the demarcations between banking and finance, and between brokers and jobbers on the Exchange itself, symbolized the optimism with which both the old and the new City embraced deregulation. It was characteristic of these years that in 1980 the Exchange had already set up a new market in 'unlisted' securities for newly established firms; and that when it opened a giant new trading floor with electronic screens displaying share prices in 1979, few anticipated that within six years the historic floor would be empty of dealers because the new technology made it easier to trade from one's own office, or that many of the leading members of the old club would have been taken over by giant national or international finance houses and sent out to grass. As the epic moment of hope which preceded doom, 'Big Bang' still symbolizes the earlier eighties, just as the ignominious failure in 1993 of Taurus, the Stock Exchange's long-overdue attempt to develop a wholly computerized system for dealing, may come to stand for the nemesis of the nineties.

The deregulation of the 1980s, the explosion of credit, the take-overs of so many old City landmark companies, and the subsequent implosion, collapse of confidence, and large-scale redundancies, marks the end of an era, the culmination of the progressive logic of post-war change, as well as the last working years for many of the generation we have recorded here. At the time when they were interviewed it was not yet clear whether in the leaner City of the 1990s the merchant banks like Barings or Rothschilds or Hambros, or stockbrokers like Cazenove's, who resisted takeover in the boom years, could continue in their leading roles, providing the institutional threads between past and future which had so characterized the old City. The more recent collapse of Barings in 1995, and almost simultaneous take-over of Warburgs, makes such an outcome now seem even less likely.

Certainly in the 1980s, history had looked increasingly irrelevant in the new global finance market. 'It was a young people's world, for global dealing and hustling needs stamina and optimism. Older bankers who remembered earlier crashes deplored the hype, the rash loans and the short horizons' – but were ignored while the money flowed in. 'Just to dip a fingernail into the stream generated super-profitable commissions.' The yuppie became 'the cultural hero of the eighties, the embodiment of the "go for it" enterprise culture'.[7] The illusion was created that dealers were 'somehow free of the constraints of organization', when they were in fact overloaded human flashpoints in the highly sophisticated technological and institutional system through which 'the vast global pot of financial assets restlessly surges'.[8] Michael Lewis's *Liar's Poker* well conveys the atmosphere of this 'modern gold rush' at its worst, the trading floor 'a jungle' of gambling and obscenities, 'a minefield of large men on short fuses waiting to explode'.[9]

Such traders certainly had no time for reflecting on the past. But it is important to remember that the atmosphere of the 1980s was certainly not a new experience for the City's finance markets. Thus in the first Baring crisis of 1890 the Bank of England did decide to bale out the merchant bank, then threatened by Argentinian debts. But a contemporary bemoaned that they were but one of many victims of over-optimism: 'We are run over with rotten liability companies, flooded with swindling "bucket shops", crashes and collapses rain upon us, and the "promoter" and the "guinea-pig" still and ever enjoy impunity.'[10] And in the aftermath of the bursting of the 1980s credit bubble, for which we are all still paying, who can deny, on reflection, that there was some wisdom in the caution urged from the experience of those 'older bankers'?

Having said that, let us hasten to add that our purpose in editing this book is not to provide financial instruction, for which we have neither the intention nor the competence, but to select from the rich and extensive collection of interviews at the National Sound Archive a range of intrinsically interesting extracts which we have edited from the memories of the City's older generation. Above all, they vividly convey the changing culture of the late twentieth-century City. These are mostly confident voices, which speak for themselves without the need for explanations from us. It will suffice to add a few more preliminary comments.

We open with a small number of 'ancestral voices'. Bagehot observed in *Lombard Street* in 1873 of bankers that 'the calling is hereditary. The credit of the bank descends from father to son: this inherited wealth soon brings inherited refinement. Banking is a watchful but not a laborious trade.' Immediately after the Second World War the merchant banks were not only typically still headed by family members, but many of them were ageing men 'in their early eighties or late seventies': for 'age was a good deal more fashionable then than now'.[11] Thus Alfred Wagg, Lord Kindersley, Chairman of Lazards, and Lord Bicester, Chairman of Morgan Grenfell, had been active young men under Queen Victoria. Hence the working generation financiers who were young after 1945, seeking to revive a City which seemed still half wrapped in mothballs, felt an especially strong need to wrestle free from the past and to distance themselves from it.

The images which they convey of earlier City 'characters' are thus not of models to admire, but of cautions: counter-myths. Among these ancestors are men portrayed as doing little work and making little effort: rode downhill to the office, read cattle herd books rather than bank accounts, refused to converse with other partners, and left for home in the early afternoon. They uttered adages such as 'Buy something and sit on it', or 'Never read a balance sheet . . . Look at the board'. Those who were not born gentlemen pretended to be. In these recollections one man stands out especially as an exception, Siegmund Warburg, 'an upsetter of the existing Establishment' who seriously wanted change. He was said to run his bank in a 'truly Prussian' style, with every conversation and telephone call monitored.[12] Warburg was a reviled outsider, ridiculed by the Establishment for his foreign accent and his lack of a sense of humour, dismissed as 'a squirt, an upstart'. But his was the ancestral voice which heralded the future.

The next two chapters provide glimpses of our main generation's childhood family backgrounds and the paths through which they reached the City. The diversity of these is obvious. The commonest background, however, is the 'ordered world' of a securely well-to-do home. All such families had servants, and some of them a substantial staff: Sir John Baring recalls a cook, kitchen maid, scullery maid, butler, footman, housemaids, lady's maid, and governess. And most often such childhoods led to schooling at Eton. The special place of Etonians at the top of the City remained notable even at the end of the 1980s.[13] However, the City was not then a favoured direction for top school or university leavers. Harry Ree remembered being told at Shrewsbury that 'only shits go into the City'. The result was that for this generation, before recruiting campaigns began to change the image of a job in finance, only those who already had some personal associations with the City were likely to consider it as a life's career. Hence these sons of comfortable families typically found their way to the City after leaving their public schools through family connections, direct or indirect. There were also, however, a smaller number from similarly fortunate backgrounds who got straight to the top of the City much later on, having made their name outside it in politics.

There were two other less typical routes. The first was meritocratic, from rather humbler middle-class homes through the education system: provincial grammar-school boys who went on to university and professional training. It was possible to reach the City directly through the administrative hierarchy of the Bank of England, whose lower reaches were organized on the competitive civil service model, which gave a better chance for less successful public-schoolboys.[14] Alternatively they could climb up through the much vaster bureaucratic structures of the clearing banks or insurance societies, beginning at provincial branch level.

The rarest path to the top was from the poor working-class homes in inner London which provided most of the City's messenger boys and a few of its successful dealers. It was difficult even for a successful dealer to win through to the upper level. 'It's all right having barrow-boys doing the dealing – they're good at it, it's what they understand,' one senior banker explained recently, 'but higher up, you've got to have people who are at ease in industrialists' drawing-rooms.'[15] Nevertheless, some did succeed. Among them was Leonard Toomey, whose only family connection with the City was that his father, an Irish stonemason, helped to reconstruct the Bank – 'There's a lot of stone in that' – but was so frequently unemployed that his family could never afford a proper meal.

These routes brought with them different underlying attitudes to the purpose of work. In upper-class households it was not the custom for fathers to discuss money matters with their wives or children, and they were in any case more often than not away. For a boy, going shooting thus provided one of the few chances of being close to his father; and later too, if he followed him into the City, it was often in a spirit of 'fun'. A very different atmosphere was imbibed by Sir Brian Corby in his lower-middle-class Methodist family, which, by contrast, imbued him with a 'respect for other people and prudence'; he carried this, appropriately, into the Prudential, but to an extent, with changing times, he has tried to shed it. Leonard Toomey, on the other hand, found his first job at Lloyd's through a tip-off when he was a West End club page-boy, and worked his way up there, always fired by his fear of slipping back into the poverty of his childhood: 'The terror of ever reverting back to it, nothing else ... It marked me. It's marked me for the rest of my life.'

The social range is equally diverse among the younger generation, born in the 1950s and 1960s, even though the balance of social origin may have been changing. Thus among the women, Valerie Thompson was the daughter of an East End market greengrocer and pub singer, and herself started into City business as a telex operator; while Philippa Rose first fell in love with the City through visiting her father's office and gazing at all the important-looking marriageable men in suits. And just as in the 1940s Sir Kenneth Kleinwort was taken to see the family bank vaults and 'fascinated to try to lift a gold bar', so a quarter of a century later Ms A was 'taken to see the gold' as a child visiting her father's office at the Bank of England.

There is a much more marked contrast between the generations in the precise mode of entry. For our main generation, not only was the door opened through family connection, but the process of admission was surprisingly perfunctory. Very few competed for advertised jobs, many were not interviewed at all, and those who were interviewed remember discussions which steered well clear of finance. Michael Verey's father talked Alfred Wagg into employing him at a dinner party. This style lingered on. Even in the 1970s Ross Jones was interviewed as a potential banker about cricket, while Michael's son David Verey got into Lazards after discussing T. S. Eliot with its Chairman, Oliver Poole. The first person we interviewed who had entered the City itself through a deliberately organized interview focused on professional potential was Ms A for a job in 1981. The first to reach the top through a mailshot was David King, who after working for more than seven years as an accountant for Arab firms sent out his self-description to a hundred companies in 1987, and eventually landed as Executive Chairman of the London Metal Exchange.

Even then, when David King joined the Exchange, he was the only one of the senior staff with a professional qualification. The service professionals at the fringe of the City always had to become qualified, but our main generation did this while on the job: Lord Benson, Sir John Craven and David King as accountants, Sir Brian Corby as an actuary, Hugh Peppiatt as a solicitor. They stand out from the true financiers we interviewed, none of whom had any formal qualifications. More remarkably, in contrast to the younger generation among whom there are several who shone in their education as mathematicians, Corby is unique with his Cambridge mathematics degree. When John Wolff left school in 1958 to join his family business on the Metal Exchange, starting at the bottom as a message boy, he was sure 'there wasn't anything I could study which would have helped in the trading', and even when Ross Jones became a banker in the late 1970s, 'three A levels was considered overqualified'. For a long time, in the banks the system of learning continued to be through circulating from department to department, staying in each for long enough to grasp its workings.

The reason for this approach was that neither of the main aspects of successful work in City dealing was thought to depend on formal skills. The two key arts were in finding and retaining clients, and in dealing. In talking about their work, some City men tried to explain the techniques required for effectively handling clients. Thus Siegmund Warburg emphasized the inter-personal skills of listening to them and feeding back their own ideas; Lord Benson the centrality of good communication in clear written English. Most said they picked up the techniques on the job. Gwilym Lewis recounts his discovery that Americans would talk business any time, unlike the British: 'playing golf, anywhere'. Conversely, Americans who came to work in London banking, like Charles McVeigh in the 1970s, would gradually realize that over the double-length English lunch, even when business was not being mentioned, opportunities were likely to be sized up. Eating well could be good for the firm as well as for the digestion.

Direct dealing, on the other hand, always depended on a thrusting personality combined with an ability to calculate very fast. This was how dealers made money in exchange telephone dealing in the 1950s. In just the same spirit, when Ms A was set to sell securities for a Japanese house in 1985, 'I was just given a telephone.' Valerie Thompson, who was given her chance to deal in millions by Salomon Brothers, had left school without passing any exams: but she had always shone at maths. She learned the art of dealing through selling apples at her father's market stall. 'Trading apples and oranges is not too dissimilar from trading securities: the principles are the same as in the City.'

Dealing also demanded genuine physical stamina. The old face-to-face trading floors could be quite rough. The Stock Exchange was regarded as a 'hurly-burly' unsuited to women, while on the Coffee Futures Market in the late 1950s, where 'we all stood in a ring and shouted ... the atmosphere could get quite tense and fist fights sometimes happened'. Telephone dealing removed the danger of physical fights, but the strain was no less. With the new communication technology allowing worldwide trading right round the clock, dealers had to work increasingly long hours, hunched over the telephone, sometimes without even a pause for lunch. Above all, it was a job demanding resilient nerves. When Valerie Thompson began trading Floating Rate Notes for Salomon in the 1980s, 'I was totally soaked in sweat. I was dripping, my skirt and everything.' She summoned the guts to go on from 'all my pent-up anger against men and life that came from my childhood, I could express in trading'.

Because most of the lives we present here are the success stories of people who have played active parts in the post-war transformation of the City, much of their testimony traces their innovative roles, in developing the Eurodollar, pension fund and local authority securities markets; in special investigations; in systematizing office practices and recruiting techniques; in negotiating their once-small firms through mergers into giant internationals. Much of what they had to say is interesting precisely as their own view of how such innovations came about.

Almost always, however, they place their own careers within a subtle double time perspective. On the one hand there is the sense of progress, pointed up by descriptions of inefficient past ways. Thus Leonard Toomey in the 1950s contrasts himself – 'a grafter, I worked' – with his old-style semi-alcoholic boss who never did a day's work. Similarly Haruko Fukuda describes the 'scruffy' office of Vickers da Costa in the early 1970s, crowded with 'robust' stockbrokers who 'followed their intuition more than reasoned argument, they were jumping around, always going out for long lunches and coming back having had five brandies', and drinking again late into the evenings. There is an underlying irony when David Verey describes the 'splendid atmosphere' of the all-male Private Clients' Department at Lazards in 1972, headed by Lord Tryon, with its dim lights, dark furniture and whiff of large cigars. Other merchant bankers contrasted the serious new business-lunch style favoured by Warburgs with the 'languid country house luncheon', with no talk of business, which persisted at Hambros.

This view of change as progress is expressed concurrently, however, with a nostalgia for the City world which has been lost. Much of their comment on changing technology, for example, conveys this double reflectiveness. On the one hand there are memories of dusty Dickensian offices with handwritten ledgers. We can trace the laggardly introduction of adding machines and calculators from the 1950s; more sophisticated computing and data processing from the 1960s; telex dealing in the 1970s; and electronic screens in the 1980s. These innovations were certainly crucial to the City's success, just as had been the introduction of the world telegraph system in the 1870s or the first telephone networks at the turn of the century: and they are recognized as such. But at the same time there is some wistfulness for what is lost. Stockbroking 'was fun' but has 'become electronic and lost its personality'. Previous skills have become redundant. In the 1950s a banker would balance his firm's daybook by casting straight down with mental arithmetic: pounds, shillings, pence. Their minds became almost as fast and reliable as calculating machines. But such abilities no longer tell as they did. As another merchant banker put it, 'the back of an envelope is not popular now'.

This comes across very strongly when they consider the shapes of their careers. Once they had entered work in the City, with very few exceptions – most notably Sir John Craven – our main generation not only stayed working in the sector, but remained for long years loyal to the same firms. Seven got to the top as chairman of the firm which they had originally entered at the start of their working lives in the City, and scarcely any moved more than twice over forty years. They are quite different from the competitively footloose young of the 1980s, like Ms A, who worked for four different firms in five years. Up to the 1970s, partly because trading was so personal, it was regarded as unacceptable to take one's clients to a new employer. But in return for long-term loyalty, firms then offered secure and lasting jobs. When Hugh Peppiatt was articled to his father at Freshfields in 1953, he was not just training to be a solicitor, but already had his feet firmly 'on the ladder in a system which you could regard as pretty well assuring yourself of a lifetime's job'. Freshfields were typical in thinking that for a man who was doing well, it was 'slightly bad form to go off and do something else'; but the converse of this was that they would not push out a weaker partner. The same old attitudes to loyalty underlay the dismay with which Dundas Hamilton watched the demise of his stockbroking firm after its take-over at 'Big Bang' by County NatWest: the extraordinary way with which the staff was suddenly first doubled, and then halved by sacking both the competent and the incompetent, after a history of one hundred and thirty steady years in which they had never made a loss, and 'we never had a redundancy ... It was a real tragedy'.

Such intense loyalties were characteristic not only of the smaller City firms. A similar spirit permeated a big corporation like the Prudential. Sir Brian Corby believes that it may have been 'too paternalistic' in its concern with staff, and too reluctant to take on new outside specialists: 'When I started work you very much grew your own timber.' But if today the Prudential has become a tougher organization through shedding 'the concept of lifetime employment that we used to have', something important has also been lost with 'the concept of the Prudential family': of a great firm to which employees could commit themselves for life because it would 'look after them in a positive way'. Ms A conveys the most extreme contrast with her experiences of the ethos of the new multi-national finance houses. The first was a Japanese firm, a cockpit of 'warring men, all stabbing each other in the back', the second an American bank, which set its employees to compete with each other. 'There is nothing to encourage you to work as a team and you are discouraged from sharing information.' This is a system of wood-fired power which stakes all on short-term gain, with no thought of timber for the future.

These changes are reflected in differences in the nature of commitment to work. The successful men of our main working generation certainly worked long hours, which gave them relatively little time for either family life or leisure. Peter Spira describes merchant banking as 'very disruptive of domestic life, it's jolly difficult to have children and see much of them'. The newly married Leonard Toomey 'used to sit in bed reading balance sheets; it's not been very pleasant for my wife'. These experiences are echoed in Haruko Fukuda's description of how in the 1980s, 'I was up often all night dealing, and brokers from Tokyo used to ring at midnight and I talked to them from bed'; or Ms A's of 'working nearly a hundred per cent of the time'.

The crucial difference is that Ms A saw her private life as entirely separate from the City, and eventually decided to get out in order to protect it. The successful men of our main generation, by contrast, sought, at home and from their leisure, reinforcement for their commitment to work. Traditionally, bankers would mix at the opera, stockbrokers shoot or fish together. Wives were not expected to understand high finance – or men concern themselves with the petty figures of household budgeting – but to stand by with psychic succour at crucially stressful moments. And to be social assets, 'a credit to the firm'. Hence, as Laurie Conner recalls, 'In my day you went and asked your senior partner's permission to get married.'

This kind of whole-hearted commitment also made retirement from work potentially very painful indeed, because it can mean losing an entire social world. Dundas Hamilton took a warning from watching his own father, after retiring in 1948, 'gradually disintegrating because he had no other interests'. Many of the stockbrokers forced out after Big Bang are reputed to be similarly lost souls, 'utterly miserable now'. But there are also important differences in attitudes to retirement among continuing City institutions. Thus when Hugh Peppiatt retired as a senior solicitor in

1990, the break was absolute: 'No sooner did you walk out that evening and you're no longer a partner. It was actually a very traumatic way of doing things.' In accountancy, by contrast, Lord Benson enjoyed a second career as a consultant after his first retirement at sixty-five, and still kept his office at Cooper's. And as an insurer, while Gwilym Lewis 'ceased to be active day to day', he still 'kept up my relationships, lunching at Lloyd's ... I'm ninety-three now, just an old fossil. I'm the oldest member of Lloyd's.'

The notion of 'personality' as part of work, indeed of membership, was fundamental to this generation's working experience. It also infuses their interpretation of the two very striking aspects of change with which this book concludes. They are the decline of trust, and the opening of the City to outsiders. The two are organically connected.

The City finance work-force immediately after 1945 was not only white and male, but in the wake of victory more proudly 'English' than it had been earlier. George Nissen describes how Smith Brothers were frozen out of the gilt market because 'they were strongly Jewish and regarded as rather spivvy ... They were regarded as outsiders'. Siegmund Warburg, 'that shower', offended doubly. He was not only Jewish (tracing his line back to an Andrea del Banco in seventeenth-century Pisa), but also German, 'Prussian'. It seemed to be conveniently forgotten that many of the founders of the City's other major merchant banks had been Jewish. As the impact of wartime nationalism faded, over the next few decades City attitudes were to soften. Americans were welcomed quickly, and in time Europeans, including Germans, could be admired. The Japanese were harder to digest, however; and it has remained very unusual for British Asians or blacks to enter the City.

The most spectacular breach of the walls has therefore been by women. Michael Verey recalls how 'women were totally disregarded when I started in the City. They were typists or bookkeepers, there was no question of them becoming partners or any nonsense of that sort.' He still feels that they are a worse 'long-term bet ... because they would marry and have babies'; and many other City men continue to think in the same way. Some institutions like the London Metal Exchange specifically excluded women by their rules from membership. Hence it was not easy for women to win their entry into the City in the 1970s. Resistance was predictably strong at the Stock Exchange, many of whose male membership felt 'passionately ... that it was quite inappropriate for women to subject themselves to the rough and tumble of life on the floor', the 'scramble' in the 'hurly-burly' crowd. Some of the brokers did indeed make life very nasty for the pioneers, sticking things on their clothes, assaulting them with sexual innuendo and cruel nicknaming. But these young women fought through, and their presence has irrevocably changed the texture of the City's working culture. The recent closing of the Gresham Club can thus be seen as symptomatic of a wider change. For even though women financiers may come from similar homes to their masculine peers, their arrival means that the City can no longer operate in the old club style.

For work in finance, the greatest strength of the old club style is that it allows easy trust. Fraud and crime were not big issues in the City of the 1950s. Many memories symbolize this. You could leave a car unlocked outside your office with rugs in it, you could carry gold bars wrapped in newspaper on a bus, you could get your membership of Lloyd's without having the figures for your assets checked. This was not just because there probably was less crime on the streets as well as in the offices, for the contrast with the present can be exaggerated. There is plenty of evidence that insider dealing, for example, which was not then illegal, was widespread, and indeed even accepted provided it was kept quiet within the City's élite. As Sir Martin Jacomb put it, 'There was plenty of dishonesty in the old days among the old guard, most of it smothered in a smear of respectability so it never came to light.'

The crucial point was that there was order. This was possible because the City was made up of enclosed circles where most people knew each other well: a series of networks of different 'clubs', with only narrow doorways in the social walls between them: 'Bankers used to despise stockbrokers ... Calling on a stockbroker was absolute anathema ... Jobbers – you didn't even know jobbers.' There were also more personal networks, often of old schoolfriends, like Peppiatt and his cousins, 'all at Winchester together and three of us in the City together'; but especially of old Etonians.

It was not just a matter of connections, however. Within each club the old City motto, 'My word is my bond', was enforced through blackballing those who failed to conform. 'Good Etonian standards means a total trust,' as Michael Verey put it. 'During my time in the City, those who hadn't been to Eton were striving for Eton standards and the Eton ethos dominated from Kim Cobbold, Governor of the Bank of England, downwards.' At the heart of the City was the 'inner circle' who 'saw that everything was properly run and orderly and if anyone misbehaved, they got rapped'. If there was a crisis, they simply 'rang each other up and fixed everything'. Although it was a system, Russell Taylor reflects, which was 'in many ways unfair to individuals, who might have been imaginative rather than crooked, it was a cheap and effective method of enforcing investor protection'.[16]

He speaks for many in this regret for the securer foundations of the City's old reputation. As Corby comments, 'the Prudential's reliability is absolutely crucial'. London did win part of its money, in the post-war decades, through trust, as well as through its unique combination of specialist expertise. It will need both in the future. In short, if these memories intertwine satisfaction with wistfulness, each has its justification.

Paul Thompson

Notes

1. Russell Taylor, *Going for Broke: Confessions of a Merchant Banker*, Simon and Schuster, New York and London, 1993, p. 47 (he was at Robert Benson, Lonsdale, in the late 1950s); Anthony Sampson, *The Essential Anatomy of Britain: Democracy in Crisis*, Hodder and Stoughton, London, 1992, p. 91.
2. O. R. Hobson, *How the City Works*, News Chronicle, London, 1940, p. 71 (cited in Ranald C. Michie, *The City of London: Continuity and Change, 1850–1990*, Macmillan, London, 1992).
3. Taylor, p. 64.
4. Russell Taylor attributes this to the London branch of New York Citibank in 1961: p. 64.
5. Sampson, p. 92.
6. Jeremy Paxman, *Friends in High Places*, Penguin, Harmondsworth, 1992, p. 271.
7. Sampson, p. 89; Leslie Budd and Sam Whimster, *Global Finance and Urban Living*, Routledge, London, 1992, p. 2.
8. Budd and Whimster, pp. 2, 5.
9. Michael Lewis, *Liar's Poker: Two Cities, True Greed*, London, 1989, pp. 11, 42, 57.
10. E. A. Vizetelly, introduction to Emile Zola, *Money*, 1894 (Michie, p. 1).
11. Kathleen Burk, *Morgan Grenfell 1838–1988: the Biography of a Merchant Bank*, Oxford University Press, Oxford, 1989, pp. 94–5.
12. Taylor, p. 55.
13. In 1990, of the seventeen members of the Court of the Bank of England, four were Etonians; so were the heads of five merchant banks, and a third of the directors of Barclays, Hambros and Kleinworts (Paxman, pp. 270–5).
14. Paxman, p. 275.
15. *Ibid.*
16. Taylor, p. 55.

Textual Note

The National Life Story Collection's 'City Lives' project contains over a hundred and twenty detailed recordings to date. The interviews were made as a unique national resource and were not done specifically with this book in mind. Many different accounts could have been compiled from the City Lives archive and it has, inevitably, been necessary to focus on a few key areas to represent the period under inspection in this one. A wealth of material remains in the collection at the British Library's National Sound Archive for those wishing to research other aspects.

Whilst it has been essential to edit the transcripts in order to ensure continuity and 'readability', the greatest care has been taken to distort the spoken word as little as possible and in all cases to keep to the spirit in which it was said. It should be remembered that the interviewees were responding to questions put to them by the NLSC team.

The book falls into four parts. The first commemorates some of the City personalities from the past, whilst the second part looks at the background, attitudes and careers of twenty-six individuals representing differing generations (the eldest was ninety-three when he was recorded, the youngest, twenty-six) and a variety of financial sectors. The third part examines ethical and social issues. All these extracts are taken from the main recordings made with the interviewees for City Lives, undertaken by the NLSC between 1988 and 1995. The events in the City during 1995 and 1996 have been dramatic, and the fourth part of the book is formed from follow-up recordings documenting each person's response to more recent events.

George Nissen and Leonard Toomey were kind enough to help with the glossary, and all the contributors to this book have been responsive to our need to check details with them. Brief biographies of the speakers follow this Textual Note.

Both Paul Thompson and Cathy Courtney have worked on the NLSC's City Lives project; the bulk of this book has been edited by Cathy Courtney and the introduction has been written by Paul Thompson.

We would particularly like to thank Jean Rigby, the NLSC's Co-ordinator, for the steady and vital help she has given us throughout the work on this book, and Geoffrey Strachan and Mary Chamberlain of Methuen for their advice and encouragement.

Cathy Courtney and Paul Thompson

Biographies

Hermann Abs (1901–94) At the time of his recording was the Hon. Life President of the Deutsche Bank. He first visited the City of London in 1924. NLSC recording made in 1990.

Lord Benson (1909–95) Joined the accountancy firm Cooper Brothers & Co. in 1925, where he was a partner between 1934–75. He was an adviser to the Bank of England 1975–83. NLSC recording made in 1988.

Sir Timothy Bevan (b. 1927) Joined Barclays Bank Ltd in 1950 and was Chairman 1981–7. NLSC recording made in 1993.

John Castle (b. 1911) Began his City career with William Brandt as a junior in the bank in 1926. Joined the Drapers' Company in 1931 as a junior, Beadle 1948–76. NLSC recording made in 1989.

Sir Brian Corby (b. 1929) Joined the Prudential Assurance Company Ltd in 1952, and was Chairman of the Prudential Corporation plc 1990–95. NLSC recording made in 1988.

Sir John Craven (b. 1940) Worked in Clarkson Gordon & Co., Chartered Accountants 1961–4; Wood Gundy, Investment Bankers 1964–7; S. G. Warburg & Co. 1967–73 (Director 1969–73); Group Chief Executive of White Weld & Co. Ltd 1973–8; Vice-Chairman of S. G. Warburg & Co. 1979; Chief Executive of Merrill Lynch International Ltd 1980; Founder and Chairman of Phoenix Securities Ltd 1981–9. He became Chairman of the Morgan Grenfell Group plc in 1989. NLSC recording made in 1991.

Nicholas Durlacher (b. 1946) Has been a Member of the Stock Exchange since 1970. He was a partner in Wedd Durlacher 1972–86, has been a Director of BZW Ltd since 1986 and became Chairman of BZW Futures in 1992. He has been a director of LIFFE since 1984 and was Chairman 1992–5. NLSC recording made in 1995.

Haruko Fukuda (b. 1946) Joined the stockbrokers Vickers da Costa in 1972 and in 1974 moved to James Capel, where she became partner in 1980. In 1988 she joined the board of Nikko Europe, an unprecedented appointment for a woman in a Japanese institution. She became Vice-Chairman of Nikko Europe in 1995. NLSC recording made in 1991–2.

Sir Roger Gibbs (b. 1934) Worked in Jessel Toynbee & Co. Ltd 1954–64, where he became a Director in 1960, and joined de Zoete & Gorton, later de Zoete & Bevan, 1964–71, where he became a partner in 1966. He was Chairman of Gerrard & National Discount Co. Ltd 1975–89 and has been a Director of Gerrard & National Holdings plc since 1971. He was made Chairman of the Wellcome Trust in 1989. NLSC recording made in 1992–3.

Sir Nicholas Goodison (b. 1934) Joined H. E. Goodison & Co. in 1958 and was Chairman 1975–88. He was a member of the Stock Exchange Council 1968–88 and Chairman of the Stock Exchange 1976–88. In 1989 he became Chairman of the TSB and is now Deputy Chairman of Lloyds TSB Group plc. NLSC recording made in 1988.

Dundas Hamilton (b. 1919) Former Senior Partner of Fielding, Newson-Smith. Deputy Chairman of the Stock Exchange Council 1973–6. He published *Stockbroking Today* in 1968 and *Stockbroking Tomorrow* in 1986 and has also written plays. NLSC recording made in 1988.

Francis Holford (b. 1937) Worked in the Information Department with the Corporation of Lloyd's before joining the accountancy firm, Goddard & Co. in 1959. Joined Rudolf Wolff in 1967, where he was Chief Financial Officer. He was Managing Director 1976–91 and Chairman 1982–91. NLSC recording made in 1992.

Sir Martin Jacomb (b. 1929) Practised at the Bar before becoming a Director of Kleinwort Benson (1968–85); Deputy Chairman of Barclays Bank plc 1985–93; Chairman of Barclays de Zoete Wedd 1986–91; Director of the Bank of England 1986–95; Deputy Chairman of Commercial Union Assurance Company 1988–93; Chairman of PosTel Investment Management Ltd 1991–4; Chairman of the British Council since 1992; Chairman of Prudential Corporation plc since 1995. NLSC recording made in 1993–5.

Ross Jones (b. 1959) Joined the discount house Gerrard & National in 1977, where he is now Chief Executive of Gerrard & National Ltd. NLSC recording made in 1992.

David King (b. 1945) Trained as an accountant and initially worked abroad. Joined the London Metal Exchange in 1987, becoming Chief Executive in 1989. NLSC recording made in 1992.

Sir Kenneth Kleinwort 3rd (1935–94) Joined Kleinwort Sons & Co. Ltd in 1955; Director of Kleinwort Benson Ltd 1971–6; Director of Kleinwort Benson Group 1976–94. NLSC recording made in 1990.

Gwilym Lewis (b. 1897) Member of Lloyd's of London; joined Sedgwick Collins in 1919, where he became head of the American Non-Marine Department. Former Chairman of Arbon Langrish. NLSC recording made in 1990.

Charles McVeigh III (b. 1942) Joined Salomon Brothers in New York in 1971, and came to work in their City office as Vice-President in 1975, becoming Chairman in 1987. NLSC recording made in 1993–4.

Sir Jeremy Morse (b. 1928) Deputy Chairman of Lloyds Bank 1975–7 and Chairman 1977–93. He has been a Non-Executive Director of the Bank of England since 1993. NLSC recording made in 1988.

George Nissen (b. 1930) Joined Pember & Boyle in 1953, Senior Partner 1982–6. Director of Morgan Grenfell Group 1984–7. Member of the Stock Exchange 1956–92, Member of the Stock Exchange Council 1973–91, Deputy Chairman of the Council 1978–81. Chairman of Gilt-Edged Market Makers Association 1986–92. Chairman of IMRO 1989–92. NLSC recording made in 1991.

Lord O'Brien (1908–95) Former Governor of the Bank of England. NLSC recording made in 1988.

Jane Partington (b. 1956) Trained as a nurse. Became a Blue Button in 1975 and was one of the first women to go on to the floor of the Stock Exchange. She joined Phillips & Drew in 1986, where she is now Research and Marketing Manager. NLSC recording made in 1992.

Hugh Peppiatt (b. 1930) Joined the firm of solicitors, Freshfields, in 1954, Senior Partner 1982–90. NLSC recording made in 1992.

Philippa Rose (b. 1958) Joined Kleinwort Benson in 1979 and later worked for the recruitment consultants, Crone Corkhill, before establishing Philippa Rose and Partners, an executive search firm, in 1981. NLSC recording made in 1992–3.

Lord Rothschild (b. 1936) Member of N. M. Rothschild & Sons 1956–76, partner 1964; Chairman of St James's Place Capital plc (formerly Rothschild Investment Trust and J. Rothschild Holdings plc) since 1971. NLSC recording made in 1996.

Jack Spall (b. 1930) Joined the East Indian merchants, Wallace Brothers, in 1947 and moved to Merrill Lynch in 1961. Joined Sharps Pixley in 1970, where he became Deputy Chairman before retiring in 1988. NLSC recording made in 1991–2.

Peter Spira (b. 1930) Joined S. G. Warburg in 1957, where he became Vice-Chairman. He spent eight years as Group Finance Director of Sotheby's before joining Goldman Sachs International as Vice-Chairman 1982–7. Deputy Chairman of County NatWest 1988–91. NLSC recording made in 1991–2.

Lord Swaythling (b. 1928) Chairman of Samuel Montagu & Co. Ltd 1970–73; Chief Executive of Orion Bank 1974–9; Director of J. Rothschild Holdings plc 1983–9. He was a member of the Board of Banking Supervision, Bank of England 1990–95. He has been Chairman of Rothmans International plc since 1988. NLSC recording made in 1993.

Valerie Thompson (b. 1956) Joined Hitchens Harrison in 1971 and moved to Vickers da Costa as a telex operator. She joined Salomon Brothers in 1973, where she became a successful trader before leaving in 1987. She now runs her own company, Euromarket Trading Consultants, and in 1996 published her first book, *Mastering the Euromarkets*. NLSC recording made in 1993.

Leonard Toomey (b. 1924) Went to work at Lloyd's of London as an office boy in 1939. Formerly Chairman and Active Underwriter of A. B. Dick-Cleland Underwriting Agencies Ltd. NLSC recording made in 1989.

David Verey (b. 1950) Joined Lazard Bros in 1972, becoming Chief Executive in 1990 and Chairman in 1992. NLSC recording made in 1993.

Michael Verey (b. 1912) Joined Helbert, Wagg in 1934 and was Deputy Chairman of J. Henry Schroder Wagg & Co. Ltd 1966–72, and Chairman 1972–3. NLSC recording made in 1992–3.

Davina Walter (b. 1954) Joined Cazenove in 1974 and moved to Henderson Administration in 1985. She joined Morgan Grenfell as a Fund Manager in 1995. NLSC recording made in 1992–3.

John Wolff (b. 1940) Joined Rudolf Wolff in 1958. In 1990 he left to set up his own consultancy business, John Wolff International. NLSC recording made in 1992.

Jeremy Wormell (b. 1943) Was a gilt-edged market analyst 1969–87 and Head of gilt-edged research at Pember & Boyle 1975–85. He was a Director of Morgan Grenfell Securities Holdings 1986–7 and has been a Director of National Provident Institution since 1993. He is currently writing his third book, *The History of the National Debt 1900–32*. NLSC recording made in 1991.

Part One

Ancestral Voices

Ancestral Voices

Sir Martin Jacomb (b. 1929)

My grandfather, Reginald Jacomb, gave up being a solicitor and took over the control of the family wool-broking business and made a success of it. He had other interests in the City and was a minor but perfectly respected City gent. Some people say he was the model for Soames Forsyte because he knew Galsworthy. He ended up as President of the London Life Association, then a big mutual life insurance company.

Like everyone else, he would have worn a black coat and black waistcoat, black and white striped trousers and a watch chain – I've still got his gold watch. He would have worked assiduously but relatively short hours. There were no expense accounts or company cars. He would have lunched at the City Club in Old Broad Street every day, which is exactly the same now as it would have been then.

Jeremy Wormell (b. 1943)

The City Club, opposite the Stock Exchange, is a grand-looking Georgian building with huge great lamps in front and probably a hundred-and-fifty-foot, white-painted frontage. One of my partners at Pember & Boyle was Robin Bevan, whose family firm was Barclays Bank, of which his brother, Tim, was Chairman and his forebears before him. Robin's great-grandfather believed 'A gentleman never ate except at his own table', so he bought the premises of the City Club, which was then just a huge private house. He kept it fully staffed with a good cook. The wealth that you must have had to buy premises like that to eat there each day must have been seriously untold.

George Nissen (b. 1930)

Boyle, of Pember & Boyle, was killed in the South African War. There was a Boer War Memorial in the Stock Exchange which showed people bending over, comforting the sick, and it was always said that one of them was Boyle robbing the dead.

Lord Swaythling (David Montagu) (b. 1928)

My great-uncle, Lionel Montagu, was always known as 'Cardie' because he used to play bridge a lot. His father, who was a great patriarch, sent for Cardie and said, 'The time has come for you to become a partner in the bank.' Cardie said, 'What does that involve, sir?' – you called your father 'sir' in those days. His father said, 'To start with, five per cent of the profits.' Cardie said, 'Can I have two and a half per cent and leave at lunch-time?' It so shocked the old man that he agreed to it.

Sir Kenneth Kleinwort (b. 1935)

My grandfather, Sir Alexander Kleinwort, not only had the place in Sussex, which was very substantial, but he had a not insignificant house in Curzon Street and another down at Eastbourne on the coast. He never learned to drive and was always taken everywhere by chauffeurs. In the summer he would often be driven up and down from Sussex by day and it was said the policemen on duty on London Bridge could set their watches by [him,] 'Three-thirty, there's Sir Alexander going home', because his car would always cross the river at that time. When the weather permitted he drove with the car's hood down, sitting in the back with a fur-lined leather coat which went down to his ankles, a helmet on his head and his long white beard flowing in the wind. When he got to Sussex, he walked into the house and his coat and helmet would be taken off for him and then he would go into the gents, fill the basin with hot water and wash the smuts and the dust off his beard with soap.

Sir Alexander had an elder brother, Herman Kleinwort, who was a sleeping partner in the bank and never came into the office. The two didn't see eye to eye and it was virtually agreed that HGK, as he was known, would stay clear and Sir ADK would run the show with his cousin, Herman Andreae, and 'the boys', my father, Ernest Kleinwort, and his brother, Cyril. Herman lived in an enormous house on the east side of Belgrave Square, which is now an embassy. On a Saturday morning he would call for his coach and horses and be driven to the City to have a look at the bank from the outside and make sure it was still there. Then he would go back to roast beef and Yorkshire pudding in Belgrave Square.

Sir Martin Jacomb (b. 1929)

Alexander Kleinwort loved fast motor cars and the tradition has it that his chauffeur had to get from Haywards Heath to Fenchurch Street within one hour and if he didn't, he was sacked. I'm told there were a dozen pensioned-off chauffeurs at the time of his death.

Mr A (b. 1932)
Cyril Kleinwort used to make a great thing of the fact that he rode to work
on his bicycle every day. Indeed he did, but what was not known to
everybody was that he lived in Hampstead and that Hampstead to
Fenchurch Street was basically a free-wheel and that on a Friday night his
chauffeur was told to gather together five bicycles, put them in a van and
take them back to Hampstead for the following week. He had a bicycle
for every day in the same way that my grandfather had a strop razor for
the seven days of the week.

Sir Kenneth Kleinwort (b. 1935)
My father always said, 'Your best investment is your backside. Buy
something and sit on it.' He also told me, 'Never be greedy. Never try and
buy at the bottom and sell at the top. Always let somebody else have the
final ten per cent. In the long run, that'll pay you and you can let the
greedy wolves cream off the top of the milk.'

Sir Martin Jacomb (b. 1929)
Cyril Kleinwort taught me to be more patient than I naturally am, not to
rely on one's immediate judgement but to wait a little bit to check. He
taught me that events move much slower than you think they're going to.
He taught me never to fear having top-quality subordinates and to go out
of your way to surround yourself with them and get them to do the work.
You must never underestimate the amount of help you need. Cyril didn't
go out of his way to teach me, it was just there by clear observation.

Lord Benson (b. 1909)
Louis Franc was a Belgian who became a partner in Samuel Montagu. He
had one of the quickest minds as an arbitrageur that I've ever come across.
He built up an enormous business at Montagu and an enormous private
fortune. He made a remark which left a lasting impression on me. He was
looking at the portfolio of his investments and he said, 'Henry, I'm living
on the income of the income of the income.' That was a considerable
achievement.

Peter Spira (b. 1930)
Ernest Thalmann of Warburgs was a very grave man. He took to me and
one morning asked what my Christian name was and then said in his
baleful voice, 'You may call me Ernest.' This was an accolade that had
never been granted to anyone. Even Eric Korner wouldn't call him 'Ernest'
– they called each other Korner and Thalmann. It was extremely difficult
for me ever to do it, but one day I plucked up courage and called him

Ernest in public. You really could have heard a pin drop. The place was stunned by a shattering silence.

Michael Verey (b. 1912)

There was a fellow in the cash department who had a wife and two children and had been out of work for two years. He got a job at Helbert, Wagg and for the rest of his working life he caught the train before the train he needed to catch in order to guarantee that he would not be late for work so there could be no possible reason for sacking him. He was just frightened; it was so appalling being out of work that he could never run any risk at all. He stayed for thirty years.

Lord Swaythling (David Montagu) (b. 1928)

My father used to go to Samuel Montagu's every day. He and his labrador would be picked up in the Rolls by the chauffeur and driven from Grosvenor Crescent to the beginning of the park, precisely three hundred yards, where he would get out and walk the dog to Admiralty Arch where the car would pick him up again and take him to the City and the labrador home.

I thought he must be a great banker to have to go off to the office every day. In point of fact what he used to do when he got there was his herd books or answer letters from the English Guernsey Cattle Society. I don't think he ever took much part in the bank. I went there to lunch once or twice as a child. There were two founding families, the Montagus and the Franklins, and they didn't talk to each other. They were permanently at war, so much so that there was a round table at lunch and a 'dumb Alice' – a circular thing – because if you were a Montagu, you couldn't bring yourself to say to a Franklin, 'Pass the salt', so you swizzled the dumb Alice instead.

Michael Verey (b. 1912)

Kit Hoare was a splendid pirate. If you said 'Kit' everybody knew you meant Kit Hoare, he was the only one. He was a very good, tough stockbroker. He made a lot of money and he loved the City. He was also a terrific snob and a fair-sized name dropper with an eye to the main chance. He was always on the coat-tails of anybody who had been successful, but rather disregarding how they had got their success. He would have boarded any ship. He was a proper old boss and I'm sure he didn't delegate at all. If Kit said to anyone at Hoare's, 'You do this', whether they approved or disapproved, it was done and they were all beholden to him because his profits were marvellous. He was thoroughly good company, lots of stories and fun. What you just had to do was stand up to him.

Sir Martin Jacomb (b. 1929)
Kit Hoare was a lovely man and a bit of a rascal. He had free access to Kleinworts. I used to find him walking up and down the passages. The idea of a broker being able to gain unrestricted access to a merchant bank's Corporate Finance Department is ridiculous by today's standards – of course, he wasn't allowed to do this, he used to claim he'd lost his way! I'm certain he would make use of insider information but he was a skilful broker and never cut corners so fine it spoiled the business.

Mr A (b. 1932)
Kit Hoare was very irascible and so strong a personality that he made it difficult for some of his partners to assume responsibility and it skipped a generation. I remember Lord Airlie telling me about the first time Schroders were going to be the principal underwriters for an ICI issue – always in the past it had been Kit Hoare's cheque, handled entirely by Hoare & Co. Lord Airlie was at the far end of the room but he said, 'I've never heard a row like it.' So the old boy was pretty forceful.

I believe he got stuck in the lift in the City University Club. It was a lift with a cage and Kit was in there fulminating, all you could see was the top of his head. Somebody who knew him quite well went into the dining-room and got a bun and stuck it on the end of his umbrella, pushed it through the bars and said, 'Eat that you old bugger and shut up!'

Kit was still wandering around the office at the age of eighty-eight, making a nuisance of himself. We had to employ a chauffeur to carry him around and parcel him off in the afternoons to somewhere else. There's a terrible portrait of him in the room where I work even today, so I can't forget what he looked like.

Michael Verey (b. 1912)
Alfred Wagg was a star, a really original thinker. He was a dreamer and all his dreams came true. He was the lucky young man with a silver spoon and he wanted to do something for other people. With others, he started boys' clubs in the East End of London. He bought a property of 300 acres in the country and turned it into hutted dormitories, playing-fields, a swimming-pool, so that all the children from elementary schools in the East End could go for a fortnight at a time and do their lessons in the country and have swimming and games. He poured money into that. When he died, he left nothing, he had very sensibly given it away.

Michael Verey (b. 1912)

Lionel Fraser was the son of a butler and a housemaid and in the end he became Chairman of Helbert, Wagg. He had left school at sixteen and had been a clerk in a little merchant bank which Alfred Wagg bought, and just through sheer hard work he became an absolutely leading merchant banker. He was straight as a die. He took night classes to teach himself French. He was driven by ambition to make money, to live in Cadogan Square, to be a member of White's and the St James's Club. Very few people knew that he was a butler's son, most people thought he was an Old Etonian. He was distinguished looking, beautifully dressed – not overdone – and excellent manners. Most people regarded him as the *crème de la crème*, which he was.

Sir Timothy Bevan (b. 1927)

The old partners' room at Barclays Bank was dominated by two of the directors, Theodore Barclay and my fifth cousin twice removed, Emlyn Bevan. They were the two heavies. Dealing with Theodore was extremely frustrating. You had to write letters in a certain way. You couldn't write, 'Dear so and so', you had to send rather stiff, very formalized memoranda which used to annoy everyone you wrote to. They used to go through the copy letters every day criticizing what was wrong. It took some time to realize the simple answer was to have two letters, one which went with the copies and the one you actually sent off.

Theodore liked the place extremely cold and Emlyn liked it extremely hot. Emlyn used to get there early, find it cool, and wind up the thermostat. He would then go out to the National Provident, by which time Theodore would walk in, find it too hot and wind the thermostat straight down again. After a time he would go off to the Sun Alliance and Emlyn would come back and wind it the other way. It would go up and down like a yo-yo. We couldn't think what to do until we hit on the simple thing of cutting the wires of the thermostat so that the temperature stayed exactly the same. They both wound it up and down perfectly happily and all lived happily ever afterwards.

Michael Verey (b. 1912)

Arthur Villiers dominated the investment scene at Barings and was one of the shrewdest investors of all time. He always said, 'Never read a balance sheet, don't waste your time on that. All you have to do is look at who is on the board and if it's a good board, buy the shares, and if it isn't, don't.' I said, 'But Arthur, who tells a good board?' To which he replied, 'Ah', and crossed the street.

Arthur gave everything away to charity and was immensely admired.

He lived in the East End in a bedsit above a ghastly pub. He would invite you to lunch and say, 'Of course, the food's dreadful, you mustn't be particular about that. But we will give you something good to drink.' He had champagne for lunch every day.

Sir John Craven (b. 1940)
Siegmund Warburg was almost a psychologist in the way he could draw in a client and get that client to talk. He operated very quietly, just using the sheer force of his personality. He was not physically prepossessing, although I'm told women found him attractive. He was quite short and he had something of a hunchback and very sallow features. He was a one-to-one person. He always said, 'Let the client talk. Don't try to sell him what you've got to sell. Get him to tell you what his problem is and that will give you time to think about it. Try and give him the answer to his problem in his own words. He'll think, "How remarkably clever this man is, he's telling me exactly what I always intended to do anyway." Then you've got to impress him that you're the person who can implement the idea.'

Another tip Siegmund gave me was, 'Never leave a conversation with a prospective client without leaving something on the table that you can get back to him on. You don't say, "Goodbye, maybe we'll see each other in a year's time." You say, "Thank you for seeing me. I'll look up that book I referred to ten minutes ago and send you a copy."' You left the door slightly open so that you had a good, natural excuse to go back again.

Michael Verey (b. 1912)
I wouldn't have worked for Siggy Warburg. At Helbert, Wagg we were mixed in our views. We knew he was tenacious and cautious and all the rest of it but I don't think he regarded there being any other life but business and we regarded business as a means to an end. We wanted to have fun and crack some jokes. Jokes were not cracked at Warburgs – not more than once, anyhow. He was frightfully concerned about change and getting things properly organized, and most of us didn't give a damn about that. We took a bit of change in our stride but we certainly didn't want too much. He was an upsetter of the existing Establishment. He wasn't a member of it and he didn't like it and was trying to get rid of it. At the start, the Establishment was dismissive and he was regarded as a squirt, an upstart. Very few people would have regarded him as a personal friend. People took off his foreign accent.

Mr B (b. 1944)
During the downturn in the Stock Market in the 1970s, a senior partner of one of the City firms – a marvellously courtly old man and a great

womanizer – was appalled to find out that a couple of new partners had been made up in April and had no income since the firm had no profit. He called each of them in and said, 'I never want to hear about this again. I refuse to have any thanks. It is a gift. It is not a loan.' He handed them a cheque each for ten thousand pounds. Those were the days when ten thousand pounds was worth something, it would be about a hundred thousand now. When things looked up and they made lots of money, one of them made the mistake of saying, 'Can I repay you?' He said, 'No.' It was an extremely generous move by a paternalistic senior partner out of his own pocket.

Dundas Hamilton (b. 1919)

Frank Douglas was enormous, very generous, always showering people with presents. He was a man of great contrasts. He was a most awful snob. He was in the Royal Lodge of Masons and he hob-nobbed with earls and princes and peers yet he also had some extraordinarily unattractive moneyed friends. Everything about him was huge. He got his parachute-dropping badge after the age of forty, when he was about seventeen stone. He had both a Rolls and a Bentley and he always had a loader with three guns instead of two. He hated personal conflicts; if anybody had to be sacked, he wouldn't do it and always sent me to tell the chap. I dedicated one of my books about the Stock Exchange to him because of all that he'd done for me. He not only got me my career in the army, he got me my career in the City and really pointed me in the right direction everywhere.

George Nissen (b. 1930)

Dick Wilkins was a great big fat man and he drank a huge amount. He had six or eight racing cars and an enormous power-boat which he used to roar round in races. He was a grandee, a great friend of the Queen Mother's, and he lived in the Savoy, where he had the same table every day. He was always pulling people's legs and joking. He and George Reid of Pember & Boyle had a very close relationship and did a great deal of business together. They used to go to the Savoy and have these drinking sessions in the evening. Dick always believed that if he got George sufficiently drunk, he would find out the secrets of all the business he was doing. They drank a huge amount of kümmel and brandy and whisky and a decent amount of champagne. George got frightfully drunk but he prided himself on having a head like iron and never actually gave away any secrets.

Part Two

Life Stories

Early Days

Gwilym Lewis (b. 1897)

I was born in Birmingham. When I was five we moved to Croydon where I went to Whitgift Grammar School before going to Marlborough. We had a staff at home – a gardener or two, a chauffeur and, I expect, a couple of characters in the house, a cook and so forth.

Both my parents were Welsh. My mother's father was a lay preacher and headmaster of a ragged boys' type of school, and my mother was a very charming person. I had two sisters and two brothers. We were Presbyterians and Liberals, and father was a deacon in the church. My father was called Hugh Lewis and he started in the insurance business with the Northern Insurance Company and ended up at the top of the Liverpool London Globe. He was very much a City man. His brother was Sir Alfred Lewis, Head of the National Provincial Bank, now the National Westminster.

I left school in 1914. I went to London University on a crammers' course which probably corresponded to Matric. Then I went into the Royal Flying Corps. It was pretty tough work. It was either you or the other chap that was killed. My elder brother was killed. I went in a schoolboy and came out a man.

Lord O'Brien of Lothbury (b. 1908)

My father's family came from Bristol, but his mother died when he was young and his father, he always told us, was a master mariner, not much at home. My mother's family was numerous and varied and we saw more of them, but only in early life, our ways parted afterwards. My maternal grandfather was a bespoke gentleman's bootmaker in a village in Buckinghamshire.

I was born in 1908 and I had two brothers. My father had joined the educational department of the old London County Council and was allocated to an area close to Wimbledon, and my parents came to live in Southfields. Indeed, my wife also came from Southfields and we have lived in and around Wimbledon all our lives, virtually.

My father was an educationalist and extremely insistent we should pay attention and have a good education and I of course share his view that it's a vital factor: particularly if one doesn't start on the top steps. I went to the local elementary school at Southfields and then I went to Wandsworth School from 1920 to 1926. I didn't win a scholarship, my father paid the fees, which weren't very high. I am a totally unrepentant élitist and I believe that the grammars created an élite which was worth creating and it was in everybody's interests that it should be created. I really didn't have much contact with public-schoolboys until I came into the Bank of England, where I must say on the whole I found them extremely agreeable. I can only remember one boy from Wandsworth School who went to university, and he took inter-BSC, as I did. Like matriculation is the upper crust of general schools, inter-BSC is the upper crust of higher schools.

Lord Benson (b. 1909)

My maternal great-grandfather was Emmanuel Cooper, the great anti-slaver who worked for Wilberforce in the early 1800s. He had of issue thirteen children and four of those were the men who became the four partners in Cooper Brothers. (Not only were the Cooper brothers practising as accountants in the very early days of the accountancy profession but two or three of their sisters also worked in the firm and helped to keep it going.) The twelfth of Emmanuel Cooper's children, Francis, was my maternal grandfather. Francis married a girl called Ada Power, the daughter of a great eye surgeon, and they had four or five children, one of whom was my mother.

I know less about my father's family, but my grandfather came originally from Ireland and became a priest of the Church of England and was a vicar in Shropshire for some thirty years. My father left England and began to teach in South Africa before joining the British forces in the Boer War. After the war he became a clerk to a Mr Justice Leonard Bristow who had been sent out from London. Leonard Bristow was married to one of my maternal grandmother's sisters and in 1903 or '4 my mother went out to South Africa on a social visit to Mrs Bristow and in the course of that visit met my father. They were married in Pretoria in 1906 and remained in South Africa. My father practised as a solicitor in Johannesburg until he died, in harness, in 1931.

I had a happy childhood; we were by no means well-to-do, but we didn't suffer hardship at all. I was sent to St John's College in Johannesburg and later to Parktown High School, and I finished schooling there in 1925. I was just an average schoolboy. I had no distinction in mathematics. Mathematics is not at all important for accountants; it is the English language which is important for accountants. I say to any parent who asks my advice about his child going into the profession, 'Make him a master of the English tongue', because if you can speak and write clearly and you're of average intelligence, you must succeed. You can always get a brilliant mathematician on the staff if you want – but expressing oneself so that the public and the client understands what you're after is quite a different topic.

Michael Verey (b. 1912)

My grandmother Hasell, Lady Verey, was one of ten children and we have maintained contact with the Hasell cousins in Cumberland, a very ancient family who lived in the same house for over three hundred years. Grandfather Verey was a magistrate. He had a yacht, he hunted, he shot, he lived comfortably in the country with two or three gardeners, coachmen, horses. With the Great War it diminished, but for forty years he was very comfortably off. My mother's father was a judge.

My father went to Eton and then to Trinity, Cambridge. Then he became a solicitor. He and my mother met on a rowing occasion in punts on the Thames. I had an older brother and sister and we were brought up in London; my father was away in the war and didn't come back until 1919 so he didn't mean anything in our lives at that time. I was born into an ordered world and didn't think much about the future. I knew I would go to Eton because 'we' went to Eton and then, if I wanted to, I would go to Cambridge.

I was competitive, which came, I think, from being the younger son. I loved Eton and hated leaving. I did languages for the first two years at Cambridge, French and German, and Law for the last year. I wasn't an intellectual at all. I did the work because it paid me to.

Dundas Hamilton (b. 1919)

My father was the son of an Edinburgh stockbroker, who was also Honorary Secretary of the Edinburgh Stock Exchange. My mother was the daughter of a prosperous coal merchant and he was really the money behind my family. My paternal grandfather, who had died before I was born, had married a second time so 'Mama', as we called her, was in fact father's stepmother. She was a very small, enormously energetic lady who had been left a little money and had gradually materialized quite a decent fortune just by investing the income from a trust fund. She died at the age of ninety-six or seven. The great story about Mama concerned a company called Scottish Motor Traction that was the subject of a take-over bid. On her deathbed she said to the doctor looking after her, 'Have you got any Scottish Motor Traction, doctor?' And he, deciding he would be gentle and kind with the old lady who was almost passing away, said, 'You know, I don't think I have.' Mama is reported to have said, 'If you had, doctor, you would know!' And then she died. Those were her last words. She was very much into stocks and shares, having married a stockbroker and her children were stockbrokers.

My sister and I were born in a house just outside Woking and when I was about a year old we moved up to Hook Heath where we had a small house, which in due course we added to, with a big garden. My father was knee-high to a grasshopper and was called 'Wee Hammie' in the Stock Exchange. He would go off to the Stock Exchange on the early morning train and used to carry a bag. His feet got tired at the end of the day and he used always to carry a spare set of socks and a pair of more comfortable slippers to put on in the office. As a small child I thought the Stock Exchange was a place called 'The Stockings Changed' and I imagined him sitting in this enormous building doing nothing but taking his socks off and putting them on again. When I was older, I thought he was a thief and that the bag was for the loot. I used to watch very carefully and try and catch him out.

I went to prep schools and then to Rugby. From 1929–32 there was a bad slump and my parents had financial problems because the Stock Exchange was doing very badly. The cook, the maid and the housemaid had to go, we had one car instead of two, and the question was whether my sister and I would have to leave our schools. I think my grandfather probably came to our rescue. From Rugby, I got an exhibition to Clare, Cambridge. Once I'd decided on science being my line, I thought I was destined to go into the British Oxygen Company, where my cousin was chairman. In order to get the job I wanted in my cousin's firm, I had to get a First, so I worked hard and I was rather a tedious little swot at the time, very ambitious. At the end of the first year war broke out. I was exempted by being on the science side at university but I enlisted in the Royal Artillery. In a way I regret that I wasn't able to finish my time at Cambridge, but had it not been for Mr Hitler I would have been a research chemist and a more dreary job I can hardly imagine.

Leonard Toomey (b. 1924)

I was born at our home in Battersea. There were six children. One of the boys died when he was about six months old and I lost a sister, Eileen, when she was six years old; she had bronchitis and pneumonia, and you quite often died of that in those days. I had only one grandparent that was alive and that was my mother's father, who came to live with us until he died. He was a crochety old bugger and I didn't really like him.

My father was first-generation Irish and was a quick-tempered man, to put it mildly. He never had much to do with us kids at all. He was a stonemason. He helped build the Bank of England; there's a lot of stone in that. He'd got himself a job when he was thirteen and people like him had no chance of ever making any money. If there was bad weather and father didn't work, there was no unemployment money. Unless you were comparatively well off and worked on the railroads or were a postman, practically every family was in the hands of the money-lenders and you could never pay back the interest so you just got more into debt. That was one reason why in adult life I could never borrow a penny for anything.

We lived in a terraced street. There was no such thing as a bathroom; there was an outside toilet, where you had to walk with a candle. Most of the houses had a scullery and a cold tap. At one end of the street was the railroad and the other side of the street was the Gas Light and Coke Company. My mother was a cleaner at the War Office and used to go to work at five o'clock in the morning and then come home again during the day and go out to work again in the evening, so we never saw her. We had no meal as such. You had a bit of bread and scrape or bread and dripping. You never had any weight problems in those days! You bought your food at the corner shop and you ran everything up on the slate. Your mother would say, 'See if Mr Dawkins will let us have half a pound of ham.' You'd go to the shop and he would look down the list and sometimes he'd say 'No', because you'd run up too many debts on the slate and you'd have to slink out of the shop. It marked me. It's marked me for the whole of my life.

I was bunged away to my first school when I was three and a half. I have got every school report I ever had. When I first went to the school, out of I think there were forty-two boys, I came second in the class and after that, no one beat me. And I was the top athlete, I won everything pretty well. I've run on all the tracks in South London. I started at Battersea, I've run at Herne Hill, I've run at Crystal Palace, White City, Tooting Bec, you name them all, I've run there. There was a great deal of uproar when I left school because I should have stayed there, you see, and I left at fourteen. I had to make some money for my mother. I would have liked to have a full education. I read every night when I go to bed. And I'm not talking about fiction either, mostly. So I've had to educate myself, really.

I was determined to get to work to get some money. It was hard. I got a job eventually as a page-boy in the Overseas League in St James's in Park Place. I earned eleven and six a week, carrying luggage, cleaning shoes. I worked seven days a week and there were no hours in the hotel or catering trades before the war, you just worked. Sundays, I used to start at six o'clock. The first thing I had to do when I got there was clean about forty pairs of shoes. Then I used to finish on a Sunday at twelve, back again at four till ten. I was only there for six months and I used to look for other jobs.

Sir Brian Corby (b. 1929)

I was born in Raunds, a shoe manufacturing town in Northamptonshire. My father's father worked in an estate agency-cum-financial agency and my mother's father was the manager of the local Co-operative store. My father went to grammar school and left fairly early to start work as a clerk in one of the shoe companies and eventually became a director. My mother worked for the Co-operative Society until she married and after that she didn't work.

My sister and I grew up in a semi-detached house in a cul-de-sac which led to the factory where my father worked. Next door in the other half of the house lived my father's brother. I could go through the back of the garden, along a path, to where my father's parents lived and in doing so I would pass where my grandfather worked, so it was very close-knit. In the late thirties we moved to a detached house on the outskirts of town.

One's social life was very much the town and revolved round the Methodist chapel, and events like garden parties were important. To go to Northampton, the nearest large town, was quite an adventure. We were an archetypal lower-middle-class family of the time. We were able to have holidays every year at the seaside and a small car but we were never extravagant. There was a proper way to behave and one didn't question too much the established proprieties. We learned respect for other people and prudence.

It was quite a hard-working, non-conformist type of upbringing and education was given a high rating in one's order of values. Academically, my parents felt I had promise – I was always regarded as having a certain numeracy – and they clearly hoped I would benefit from being better educated. I went to the local school and, after the eleven-plus, to Kimbolton, where my father had been. Initially I was a day boy but I enjoyed school and asked to become a boarder which enabled me to take a greater part in school activities. I became captain of soccer, vice-captain of cricket and I was a prefect and head boy. In the last year at school I acted as housemaster for two terms as I'd already got my entrance to Cambridge and was waiting to do National Service. I taught myself Spanish for something to do.

I wasn't given an exhibition at Cambridge since I was going to get help from the state because of my parental situation. I read Mathematics. We worked hard and were anxious to get a reasonable degree and a reasonable job. Halfway through the second year I began thinking what would I do next, scratching around to see if there was anything that was a combination of academia and a business career. One of my friends was thinking of becoming an actuary and I decided I would find out what this was about. Arising from that, I took the first part of the Actuarial Examinations in my second year at Cambridge. I decided I was quite interested in this particular subject and would investigate companies to go to.

Sir Martin Jacomb (b. 1929)
My mother was born in 1890 and became a volunteer nurse in Serbia in the First World War and then went on to be a nurse in Cairo. It was at this time she met my father, an army officer on Allenby's staff, and my parents were married in Alexandria. I was born in 1929, in Surrey, the last of five children. By this time, my father had returned to work in the family wool-broking business.

Very early on, my mother had developed a tremendously strong streak of doing things for other people and this became totally dominant throughout her life. She didn't believe in private property or anything to do with material wealth. If you had too many toys, your toys got taken away from you and given to the children in the village. When our house in London was burgled, you could tell by the evidence of the search that the burgler must have been surprised that my mother didn't have any possessions in her bedroom – hardly any clothes even, and certainly not jewellery.

We went to live in London when I was seven. I went to a pre-prep school in Holland Park called Dr Gill's and then to St Aubyn's at Rottingdean. My closest friend there was Baldwin's grandson (who was later my best man) and I remember going to see Baldwin in his study just before we went back to school – an old gentleman with a pipe, sitting in a room lined with leather books – and that he gave us each half a crown. We then went to say goodbye to Lady Baldwin, who gave us five bob. Seven and six was far more than I had ever had before for a whole term at school.

During the war our house was bombed and we went to live in Haslemere. Some evacuees were sent to live with us and that certainly brought home to me the work my mother did trying to make life more bearable for the poorer people around her. I became more aware of the fact that even though I was not particularly well placed, I was a hell of a lot better placed than a lot of other people. One boy who was billeted on us hadn't eaten for a long time when he came to stay with us and I remember discussing hunger with him.

At the same time, I was conscious of the fact that a lot of people were much better placed than I was – that was the strongest influence Eton had on me. That realization creates a very strong urge to become a real individual who is respected by others and is able to do things and influence events. I went to Eton when I was twelve. It was a revelation to be treated as a grown-up. A large number of the boys who arrived when I did had come back from Canada where they had been evacuated. They were well into sophisticated life and had got girlfriends and knew what night-clubs looked like from the inside, things beyond my wildest imagination.

After Eton I did National Service and was sent to Singapore and Ceylon. I then went to Oxford, where I decided to read Law, a decision which dominated the rest of my life. After Oxford, I went into my father's wool-broking business, Jacomb, Hoare & Co., which was based in Coleman Street in the City. I found it extremely dull and gave it up after less than a year. I was the last surviving son (my elder brother had died of polio), so that marked the end of the Jacomb participation in the family firm.

I decided to become a barrister. Through my father's help, I was able to spend six or eight months in the Litigation Department of Slaughter and May, which was at that time based in a decrepit basement in Austin Friars. Through my work at Slaughters, I joined chambers as a pupil at New Square, Lincoln's Inn. You couldn't make a living at the Bar while you were a pupil, so I used to correct exam papers and I also wrote on tax for the *Financial Times*, which is how I met Nigel Lawson.

I got married when I was thirty, after about five years at the Bar. A lot of people have asked me why I stopped being a barrister in 1968. One reason is that I never had either the desire to become a judge or the confidence in my ability to get that senior. The prospect of being an ageing barrister was incredibly unappealing, even that far in advance. However, I had never made any plans whatsoever to deal with that situation.

George Nissen (b. 1930)

My father had died a short while before I was born. His father was a Norwegian who had gone to America in about 1849, got involved in the gold rush and then become a mining engineer. My father (who was also a mining engineer and who invented the Nissen hut) came to England before the First World War and became naturalized. My mother's parents lived in Scotland and her father was chairman of what he regarded as the most up-market of the many jute companies in Dundee. I have a brother five years older than me.

I went to the Dragon School, then to a school called Elstree and later to Eton. I made friends at Eton who played an enormously significant part in my life. For example, David Bewicke-Copley, who was a bit ahead of me. We moved through school together and when I went into the army he was my platoon commander. We both went to Cambridge, where we read Law, and when we left we both went into the gilt-edged market – he to Mullens and I to Pember & Boyle. We were both on the Stock Exchange Council when he became Government Broker. His death – he fell off a horse and killed himself – caused the Bank of England to call on my then senior partner, Nigel Althaus (another great friend who had also been to Eton), to become Government Broker and I became senior partner at Pember & Boyle. So my whole life, really, was intertwined with Lord Cromwell, as David later became.

Hugh Peppiatt (b. 1930)

I am the eldest son and have a brother, three years younger, who is now a Church of England minister. We lived, as the lawyers say, at all material times in Beaconsfield. The first house I lived in was quite small but my father built a substantial house on about two-and-a-half acres and we lived there in some middle-class comfort.

My maternal grandfather was at Thomas Cook and my father's father was a reasonably senior clerk on the Southern Railway. My father had two brothers and my paternal grandmother was a very ambitious woman; they struggled hard so that the boys could go to a good day school, Bancrofts, but my grandfather died young and, as they had no money, I think my father left school at sixteen. He went to work in a solicitor's firm and the First World War caught up with him. When I was about five, he decided he would like to come to work in the City and came to Freshfields, where he later became senior partner.

My uncle, Will, was killed in the First World War and one of my most poignant memories is meeting a tailor in the City when I was articled there. When I gave my name he said, 'Are you any relation of Captain Will Peppiatt?' I said, 'Yes, he was my uncle.' 'Oh,' he said, 'he died in my arms.' I was so moved by this that I immediately burst into tears and so did the tailor. The other surviving brother, Kenneth, went as a junior clerk into the Bank of England and progressed very fast up the Bank's hierarchy. He was Chief Cashier and older people remember K. O. Peppiatt as a name on a banknote and still say to me, 'Oh, Peppiatt who signed the banknote, any relation of yours?' He went on to be a director of the Bank. He was a nice, kind uncle. He and my father were very close. They were ambitious for their children (my uncle had two boys and a girl) and I think wanted to try to get for us what they hadn't had themselves. My two cousins, my brother and I all went to Winchester, so we were quite a block at that school. My elder cousin went to work at Mullens, the stockbrokers who got merged with Warburgs at the time of Big Bang. My younger cousin was a brilliant stockjobber who worked at Akroyd & Smithers, which became the market-making arm of Warburgs. Warburgs' chairman, David Scholey, once said to me, 'Why don't you come and work at Warburgs, Hugh, and we'll rename the place Peppiatts!' And so we were all very close friends, all at Winchester together and three of us in the City together.

I left Winchester in '48 and went into the army to join the Coldstream Guards and, with them, went to Africa. I came back to read Modern History at Oxford, and when I came down set about finding some way of going to the States with about equal motivation in wanting to pursue my interests in American history and wanting to put off earning a proper living. I secured a Fellowship from the Commonwealth Fund and went to Wisconsin, where I had a marvellous time studying and doing some teaching. I was offered an Associate Professorship at Berkeley University and I was very minded to take it – apart from anything, it paid fifteen thousand dollars a year and I could never have imagined as much as that. I was about to sign up when the man who offered me the job said, 'I don't think I'm going to take your answer. I think you should go back to England and telephone me from there.' He was a very wise bird. I came back on the *Queen Mary* and arrived in Southampton Water on a foggy day in October. After ten days I telephoned America and said, 'I haven't got the faintest idea what I'm going to do. I'm very unhappy to be back here. It's absolutely awful. It's cold, there's no fuel. But it's home and I'm going to stay.' And so there it was.

Peter Spira (b. 1930)

I was born in London in 1930. My father was a doctor. His father and mother were Polish and my father's early youth was spent in Antwerp before the family moved to France. My paternal grandfather was in the diamond business. In his late teens my father was sent off to America to learn to be a businessman; he took one look and his eyes filled with horror. He came to England shortly before the First World War and was naturalized as a British subject and qualified at St Thomas's. My mother's mother was widowed and my mother got a secretarial job in the City with Seligman Brothers when she was twenty-one and worked until she got married. By chance, Warburgs acquired Seligmans the year before I joined the firm.

We lived in Hampstead. Both my parents were of Jewish origin but we were a very agnostic house. My father was deeply fond of my sister and myself and was incredibly proud of anything we achieved. He had a pretty violent temper – verbally, not physically – and in later years I used to say I was grateful to him because it enabled me to cope with Siegmund Warburg, who also ranted and raved. I was sent to Arnold House (where I first met Nigel Althaus, who was also at Eton with me and then in the City, where he ended up as Government Broker) and then I went to Summer Fields, where I first encountered anti-Semitism. I got a scholarship to Eton, where at one stage I got ten marks out of two hundred in the two maths papers; I was good at humanities but my maths and science were always weak. I succeeded in getting a minor scholarship to King's, Cambridge, and the day after my nineteenth birthday I was called up and joined the Green Jackets, where I learned a lot of important things, including elementary man management. I went up to Cambridge in 1950 to read Classics and found it very difficult to adjust after life in the army and didn't get a very good degree.

Jack Spall (b. 1930)

I was born in Edmonton, into a working-class family. My paternal grandfather worked for the railways. My mother was one of eight daughters – her father had his own wholesale fruit and vegetable business and they were rather better off than my paternal grandparents. In 1936 we moved to a semi-detached house on a new estate in Enfield, three bedrooms, a sitting-room, a dining-room, a kitchen and a small garden. My father was a bus conductor and – it's probably after-knowledge of the event and I didn't realize it then – but things were fairly tight in the money sense because of the 1937 Transport and General Workers Union strike. I think my mother went out charring during the strike. My father was always a very keen member of the Union – he was not a socialist, but he was a Labour Party man, whereas my paternal grandfather was staunchly Conservative because he worked on the basis that they knew how to govern and the ordinary people didn't, which is a rather charming thought.

I got a scholarship to Enfield Grammar School and the form I was in was very swot-like and used to run from one classroom to another in order to sit in the front, so it was very competitive. I got carried along and I was quite good at school. The working class in those days, the ones that I knew, had enormous ambition for the children to get on. The horizons were smaller. People like my parents – I'm certainly not denigrating them – didn't know anything really of the outside world. The greatest thing a girl could do was be a secretary, shorthand-typing, that was *the* thing. My oldest sister became a secretary. My father wanted me to be a policeman because the police got pensions and in those days London Passenger Transport didn't pay pensions – so to him the thought of a pension was the most important thing. He only lived two years after retirement.

Sir Kenneth Kleinwort (b. 1935)

I was born in a nursing home in Harley Street. My grandfather on my father's side died ten days later but I remember going to have tea with my grandmother as a child; she was French and her knowledge of English was pretty sparse and I certainly didn't speak much French at that age, so conversation wasn't exactly that lively. On my mother's side, I never knew her father because he had already died before I was born but I was extremely fond of her mother and fairly close to her. She was called Joan Nightingale and her great-great-aunt was Florence Nightingale.

My father, Ernest, and his brother, Cyril, had been brought up in Sussex, the last of seven children, and they were educated at home entirely until they both went to university. My father grew up in an extremely large house with ten or fifteen living-in staff and substantial gardens, lots of horses and coaches. As children, my sister and I were very close to Cyril's children – all girls – who lived in what had been my grandfather's house, and we all used to get together frequently for tea and games and tennis and swimming. The house I grew up in had been built by my father and was only a mile up the road. There was a drawing-room and a library on the ground floor, a very large central hall, a dining-room, and then the kitchen quarters and all you'd expect out the back. Up on the first floor there was my parents' suite and three spare rooms and then there was, through the green baize door, a children's area where I eventually had what was originally called 'the night nursery' with my own bathroom, and my sister had what was the day nursery with her own bathroom. On the top floor were the staff quarters. The garden houses what is now the National Knap Hill collection of azaleas. There was a hard tennis court and a grass tennis court and there was an outdoor swimming-pool as well.

In those days, life was pretty formal. Once you came through the green baize door, so to speak, to the parents' end of the house, you were on your best behaviour; you were all dressed up in your best clothes and you were going to have tea in the drawing-room so you had to make sure that no crumbs were dropped on the carpet and all that sort of jazz. The butler held the strings of power in that he was able to say, 'Yes', or 'No, you may not go through', or 'It's been signalled that they don't want any interruptions for the time being'. So he really ruled the roost. And you did whatever nanny said at any minute of the day or night. I'm not trying to make out that nanny was a tyrant or anything but she was strict; that was her job to bring you up to be obedient.

I went to prep school at just over eight, initially to Cot Hill, but I didn't stay there for terribly long because I didn't like them and they didn't like me all that much. I didn't see eye to eye with the headmaster and I felt I was being victimized. I was taken away to Summer Field at St Leonards, where I was completely happy and never looked back from then on.

I went to Eton in 1948. I continued to do pretty well in maths and I loved languages. I left Eton in my last year – I had an emergency appendix and whilst I was in the London Clinic they discovered I had acute sinusitis and then tuberculosis in one of my lungs. I was sent to a sanatorium in Switzerland and I spent six months out there. It was a pretty nerve-racking experience and not one I can recommend. I was brought back to London and underwent surgery. It affected my life for many years afterwards because I failed the medical to get into the army. I was cut off from my contemporaries because they had all gone into the army or National Service and then to university. One was separated for four, five, six years by dint of those particular circumstances.

I was not able to go to Cambridge, which I had sort of set my heart on. I went to do a special course at the University of Grenoble, which is at sea level and therefore the air should have been good for me, but it was only a nine-month course.

Lord Rothschild (b. 1936)

My father, later Lord Rothschild, was a scientist at Cambridge, and he hadn't enjoyed N. M. Rothschild & Sons. He was an agnostic. My grandfather, Charles Rothschild, was first and foremost a nature man. He was an interesting man who, just before the First World War, drew up a list of some two hundred and fifty sites in England which he thought should be conserved and which were at risk. Now eighty per cent of them, I think, are at risk, have lost their bio-diversity, their point. So he was perspicacious. He saw these things coming. But he had a sad life. He was rather depressed, at all times. Didn't particularly enjoy the bank, although he was quite good at it. No, I never knew him.

My great-uncle, Lord Rothschild, *was* a zoologist, who started the Tring Museum. And also, in flashes, a Zionist: it was to him that the Balfour Declaration was addressed. And he never enjoyed the bank. His one passion was zoology, mounting expeditions and collecting species. And he formed this marvellous museum at Tring, which is now part of the Natural History Museum. Then after a bit, he left the bank and faded out. So that the bank, really, went away from my branch of the family, into the hands of Anthony de Rothschild, who was my cousin Evelyn's father. And that was really why we lost position, if you like, in the bank, because both my great-uncle, and my grandfather, and my father, were not central figures at any time in the bank. So it came to be controlled by the junior branch of my family, through my cousin Evelyn's father, Tony.

I went to Eton, and then on to Oxford.

Sir John Craven (b. 1940)

I was born in England in 1940 and my family was not well off at all. I was taken by my parents at the age of about seven to live in South Africa. My father was a consulting engineer. I had a brother who, sadly, was killed in a motor accident thirty years ago, and a sister, who is now married to Michael Meacher. I'm rather right-wing so, although Michael and I are friends, we don't talk about politics much.

I went first to a little school, Gayhurst, in Buckinghamshire and then to prep school in Johannesburg and then won a scholarship to Michaelhouse, which is near Pietermaritzburg, and where I was very happy. Since I left South Africa at the age of seventeen in 1957, I've only been back twice but I'm now a governor of Michaelhouse. I was offered a place at Cambridge to read Modern Languages but soon changed to studying Law. I graduated in 1960.

John Wolff (b. 1940)

I was born in Bushey, Hertfordshire, the second of five children. My father worked in the family company, Rudolf Wolff, which was started by my great-grandfather in 1866. My great-grandfather, Rudolf, came from Königsburg, which was then in East Prussia. His father and grandfather had been merchants in Königsburg, which is a Baltic port, and he came over to London in his early twenties. I suppose London was *the* place to come because it was very much the centre of world trade in the middle of the last century and the Industrial Revolution made England the great supplier of the rest of the world. We know that his early trading was supplying railway lines to Russia and that he was a founder member of the London Metal Exchange in 1877. He had five sons who fought on the English side in the First World War, one of whom, Phillip, was my grandfather. My grandfather went first to Antwerp to work in a shipping company and then was posted to Hong Kong where he eventually became manager of the Kowloon Wharf and Godown Comany. He married a Belgian lady in 1908 and they lived in Hong Kong (where my father, Frederick, was born) until 1920 when they came back to London and my grandfather joined the family firm.

My maternal great-grandfather was of Irish extraction and was a jeweller in Liverpool and his son, my grandfather, practised dentistry and went to Harvard as part of his training, where he met my grandmother, who was from a Scots American family. My mother was born in India, where my grandfather was the first dentist in the English army in India. He died of pneumonia in the 1930s, leaving my grandmother to bring up six children. My mother, the eldest, was eighteen when her father died, so she had to get cracking and work. She worked in Fleet Street for a big magazine group and stopped when she married my father in 1937.

I grew up in a large Edwardian house, not particularly attractive but very practical for bringing up five children. My mother always had charwomen and occasionally we had living-in help and we had a series of *au pair* girls at one stage. I went to a local prep school and then to the Oratory, a Jesuit boarding-school, where my father had been. I was brought up as a Catholic and I remain one, that's an important part of my life. I left school aged eighteen, with A levels in French and History.

Charles McVeigh III (b. 1942)

My mother's family came from Nashville, Tennessee, and her father was chairman of a large insurance company, which is now part of Willis Faber. My parents met at Martha's Vineyard. My father went into his father's law firm, where he became senior partner.

I grew up on Long Island and went to boarding-school, St Paul's, in New Hampshire and then to the University of Virginia to read English. My first job was at Morgan Guaranty in 1965 in New York and then I moved to Salomon Brothers at Number One, New York Plaza in 1971.

David King (b. 1945)

I was born in Ramsgate and then lived in London until I was eleven when we moved to Cheshire, where I lived to my early twenties. My father was a partner in the Warrington Electrical Company Limited and did sufficiently well to educate four children privately. My father left home on my fifteenth birthday and subsequently remarried, but my parents were still good friends.

I went to a state school in London and when I was eleven to an independent grammar school in Cheshire. Academically, I was average. As a teenager, I had long hair and would have worn fashionable clothes of the time – flares, large collars and wide lapels and large ties. Manchester was well known for clubs and I met the Beatles a few times because they used to play there – it was before they were famous. Everyone either was in a group or wanted to be in one. I worked my way through three guitars.

I left the school in Cheshire when I was fifteen and was sent to a boarding-school in London which it was thought would help me through my O levels but in fact I was put in a year above the one I'd been in in Cheshire and took my exams prematurely, with the result that I only passed two O levels: English and Chemistry. I spent the next ten years at night school and eventually qualified as a certified accountant – but it was a long struggle.

I spent two years at a technical college in Manchester, when my father supported me, and then I started work and always looked for a job which afforded me day release so I could continue studying. It was rather like serving a prison sentence; one knew there was light at the end of the tunnel. My reason for changing jobs was mainly money. As I've stumbled through life's pages, my career has been more driven by what the next salary level would be than what the industry has been. At the end of the day, you can satisfy your obligations to your family and your life-style if you have a reasonable income. If I hear somebody else say that, it sounds very vulgar, but it's not because I want a large bank balance, it's because money equates to a certain standard of living which equates to happiness.

Haruko Fukuda (b. 1946)
I was born in Tokyo and I have two younger sisters. My father was a senior official in the Ministry of Finance which is well known as the powerhouse of the Japanese financial community, very much the home of the élite. My father's father was the chief ship architect of the Mitsubishi shipyard in Nagasaki for all the ships built in Japan in the 1920s. The London Treaty of 1930 ended his career there and he became a professor at the University of Tokyo. My father's family was a Samurai family. My mother comes from a very wealthy family, whose family business is in mining and it is to this day the only private mining company in Japan. My mother's grandfather was one of the five founders of the Tokyo Stock Exchange in the Meiji period. He died with large debts and he left in his will a special message to his descendants that they shouldn't engage in any kind of speculation. I don't know quite what boom and bust he got involved in that led him to that demise, but he was also a big philanthropist.

My mother's parents lived in a very large estate right in the middle of Tokyo, in an enormous house with gardens with tea-houses and ponds with stone bridges. I visited them two or three times a week on the way back from school. Because there was a gravel drive they could hear I was coming and the maids would rush out and sit in front of the main entrance in the hall and would bow very deeply and say, 'Welcome to the house' and they would take off my shoes for me and so on. So it was very formal in the sense that a lot of attention was given to members of the family and we were expected to behave. Our life-style was modest and unostentatious.

The upper-class Japanese families lived a so-called sophisticated life which incorporated some Western influences – either they had a Western-style house, which my parents did, or they knew some of the leading foreigners in Tokyo and socialized with them. In those days the nuclear fall-out was still with us, so we weren't supposed to get wet in the rain for fear that we might get leukaemia or burns; ever since I was aware of my surroundings that was a part of my life, so it wasn't particularly shocking, it was just a fact of life. America was very much to the fore of my imagination and of the Japanese people in general because of the Occupation and of course the Americans had great muscle in Japan at that time, both financially and socially.

When I was three I was sent to a Catholic kindergarten and then to the Peers' School, the school for the children of the aristocracy. It was very regimented. We all sat absolutely still, nobody uttered a word, discipline was absolutely perfect. Girls had etiquette lessons and weren't expected necessarily to do well academically; so long as they didn't fail exams, academic achievements were relatively unimportant. I was there until I was fourteen when, in 1960, my father went to Washington as a diplomat and my family moved with him. It was quite a hard adjustment for me to make. It was a completely new world; girls at the school wore make-up and high heels and chewed gum, all of which were unthinkable in Japan. They had boyfriends! I was not critical of it: I just thought it was so incredibly different. Until I went to America I didn't have any kind of competitive spirit in me but when I went there, I desperately wanted to prove I was not stupid when I didn't understand the language. So I tried terribly hard to demonstrate that I wasn't so bad in various ways and when I suddenly became one of the best in the class at maths, that gave me a little bit of confidence.

I came to England with my family in 1962 when I was almost sixteen. My parents were very busy because of Princess Chichibu's visit, the first imperial visit to England since the war. We found a house with a garden in Hendon because my parents wanted us to be close to Channing School, where we had been given an introduction by a British diplomat in Washington. I had to work immensely hard to catch up with the other girls in my form, but I passed seven or eight O levels and English, History and French A levels and then I was offered a place at Cambridge to read History. When my grandparents came to stay with us soon afterwards, my grandmother kept saying, 'Please don't become a bluestocking. You're certainly never going to go out and get a job or anything like that when you graduate.' I burst into tears and said, 'I have just done this tremendous thing of getting into Cambridge and all you can say is "Don't work too hard!"' She was dismissive of the whole situation. Women in our society never worked.

The choice came when I was in my early twenties, as I was coming down from Cambridge. By then my father had been posted to the Philippines. I could stay here and marry my boyfriend but not be able to see my family very much and live a rather lonely life from that point of view; there weren't many Japanese here then. Or I could go back to Japan, live with my grandparents in this vast old-fashioned house with creaky floorboards and servants, and be married off to some other good family's son with whom I had nothing in common because I had spent too much time abroad and not done any of the Japanese bridal training. I could not be a very successful wife by Japanese standards. It was a choice between those two things.

David Verey (b. 1950)
I was born in London and I have an elder sister and brother. My maternal

grandfather was killed in the First World War but my mother's mother was a lively bird-like creature, who had brought up three children on her own. My paternal grandfather was a solicitor and there's a story that one of his clients was a Miss Rothschild and that she left him a string of pearls when she died and on the back of these pearls my father believed he and his brother and sister were educated.

I was brought up in a house called Little Bowden, just west of Pangbourne. We were sent to bed pretty early as children but if my father got home from the City early on a summer's evening it was very exciting. Otherwise we saw him mainly at weekends. My mother was very much a mother, she was always available and very cosy. We had a gardener and a cook and nannies and then a governess, who was pretty good hell. I first went to school when I was eight, to Sunningdale at Ascot, where my father had been and, after that, I went to Eton. I did A levels in English and History and I read English at Cambridge.

Davina Walter (b. 1954)
I was born in London and I am an only child. Mine was a typical fifties family; my father worked and my mother didn't work. I was looked after by a nanny and by my mother until I was about six and then my mother took over. We lived first in a house in Belgravia and then in a mansion flat in Chelsea. My father was a publisher so I didn't have much understanding of the City although I remember watching the Lord Mayor's Show when I was a child.

My mother's father was very much the reason for my going to work in the City. There was a sort of nepotistic link. He was called Frank Follett Holt and he was a senior partner at Cazenove. My recollections of him are very different from the man I understand worked in the City, where he was held in high regard but seen as a stern individual whom people found hard to talk to sometimes. I saw an entirely different character. He had a nice, comfortable house in Essex with wonderful gardens and I was allowed to bicycle like mad around the grounds. It never in a million years entered his head that I would end up employed at Cazenove although he was proud when I did. He had a son by his second marriage and always thought he would go into the firm but his son had absolutely no interest in the City.

I was sent to the French Lycée in South Kensington when I was five and stayed there until I was eleven, when I went to Queens Gate, mainly as a day girl. I definitely had a mathematical mind and that held me in good stead. I got eight O levels and two A levels. I didn't want to go to university. My mother insisted I did a secretarial course, which I did at Queens Secretarial College, a place where desperate parents send their daughters as part of their overall finishing. The thinking was that girls might spend a few years amusing themselves cooking or secretarying and then would marry and spend their lives looking after their children.

Valerie Thompson (b. 1956)
I was born at home in Dagenham, Essex. My maternal grandfather was in the navy and my grandmother was an office cleaner. My mother met my father, who ran a greengrocer's shop, in the Royal Oak pub in Dagenham and he swept her off her feet. He was the youngest of thirteen children that grew up in the same council house that I grew up in. My father always had a chip on his shoulder because he was the youngest and because he was very small physically. If he had the slightest hint that there could be trouble, he made it clear from the outset that he was going to fight to the death if need be. So that's his character. But he also loved the limelight. He used to sing in pubs at weekends and enjoyed a sort of celebrity's life – he was out there on the stage and had all these women after him and thoroughly enjoyed it. He's got charisma but he would leave my mother on her own with the three of us – my brother and sister and myself. She's always been extremely anxious and nervous. I used to think I took all my cues from my dad – and I learned a lot from him because I spent a big chunk of my life following him around and working for him – but I realize that my integrity and my values come from within. It is because of this, I think, that I ended up the strongest, most resourceful one in the entire family. I still enjoy my father as a character but I think he's just a tiny kid himself who could not face responsibility in his younger days. He's got a new wife now, who's younger than me, and four children who are younger than my children.

We had a school at the bottom of our road. There were a few nice teachers but we came from such a screwed-up background we didn't know how to behave and interact and I never felt comfortable. I felt I was completely abnormal, a foreign thing. Then I went to secondary school and I left when I could possibly get out. I left without any exams. The one thing I can remember doing at school was project work where no one was watching over you, I quite enjoyed that. And I came top of the class in maths because we worked in my father's shop and on stalls, and even at ten or eleven years old we were a match for the most experienced salesmen there – we could add up everything in our heads.

My father respects me and takes credit for my success. He says it was down to him teaching me. I was a good worker for him. I would be up at four o'clock even when I was tiny and we'd go to Billingsgate Market or the fruit market. Trading apples and oranges is not too dissimilar from trading securities; the principles are the same as in the City – if you're trading fruit and veg, they're perishable goods and if you don't sell them today you've lost everything – that's how I learned to assess risk. Sadly, there are some traders in the City who are barrow-boys made good but they lack gratitude and they don't really have any deep curiosity about life. They just get to a point where they get the Rolex and fast car and flash around doing things like Henley and Ascot and Wimbledon and drink champagne. They stop there, which is a shame. Some people are just not very bright or dedicated to inner development.

Philippa Rose (b. 1958)
I was born in Ceylon, where my father was a diplomat, and I was the second of five children. We were all brought up as Catholics (my mother having converted in her early twenties), which was rather odd, really, as my father was the youngest son of the Bishop of Dover. My maternal grandfather was killed during the war and so my mother had a very simple childhood, living with guardians during the war while her mother stayed in London earning their bread and butter as a secretary by day and working on the ambulances at night. My mother had no choice but to leave school after her school certificate at sixteen and go out to work. I know she was a tip-top secretary.

After a posting in Paris, my father left the Foreign Office and joined first Fielding Newson-Smith, the stockbrokers. He later joined and ran White Weld, and subsequently Paine Webber. In 1981 he set up his own firm, Stephen Rose & Partners. When I was a child I loved coming to his office in the City. It was full of men in smart suits and I dreamed of being married to one of them. I loved the intensity, the fact that everybody walked fast and looked important. Occasionally Dad used to have his whole team down to our house in the summer and I would be in my element, running round chatting with all these bankers.

All five children in my family went to boarding-school. I went to New Hall convent. I loved my studies, particularly maths, and I also loved all the extra-curricular activities – riding, ballet, choir, piano and tennis in particular. I was a rather over-zealous house captain in the upper sixth and as a result did rather worse in my A levels than I and my teachers had expected.

Ms A (b. 1959)
I was born in Surrey. My mother was a teacher and my father worked in the Bank of England. He hated the commuting. As children, my sister and I used to visit my father's office, which was great fun because we were taken to see the gold. It was a fantastic spectacle, thousands of gold bars, gleaming yellow. The other exciting thing was the Warden of the Watch.

The gold had to be guarded and soldiers from various regiments would be there in rotation every night. I remember walking into the Bank and how cool it was (I think it's marble-floored) and the enormous pillars, a rich red carpet and polished wood. I've never been back inside although I used to walk past it every day at work. By the time I was in the City, I was living a completely different life from my father and my perceptions of it became my own rather than second-hand through him.

I went to a private day school which had strong City connections. Consequently, some of us were invited to watch the Lord Mayor's Show and I've got a wonderful memory of being dressed in my school uniform in the middle of November in the pouring rain going round the City. I remember the Grocers dressed in the most extraordinary clothes. The height of the buildings crowded in on me – I still get that feeling now when I walk around the City.

I was firmly literary in the sixth form and I never thought I would end up in the City. I had a year off before university and worked in Harvey Nichols's Christmas sale. Then my mother said, 'You must learn to type', so I went and did that. At the secretarial school we were taught on manual typewriters with finger-cards and we would just copy type from pages on our left. (I remember working in the Civil Service on a manual typewriter in the early 1980s – mind you, they had a 1977 calendar on the wall as well!)

Eventually I went to university and read Philosophy and Modern Languages.

Ross Jones (b. 1959)
I was born in Huddersfield in 1959. I have two older sisters and a younger brother, and we were brought up as Catholics. We lived in a semi-detached house in the suburbs of Huddersfield. My father was managing director of a textile mill in Huddersfield but he died in 1972 when he was in his early forties and I remember the impact of being told that I was now head of the family and had responsibilities and should look after my mother. My mother sold up and we moved to London to a tiny two-up, two-down cottage at Harrow-on-the-Hill and she got a job working at the Land Registry. I'm grateful that she moved us to London because I don't think I would have taken the step from school to coming to live here on my own.

I first saw the City when my stepfather brought me to have lunch with his brother-in-law, a stockbroker, when I was about sixteen. I've always liked the idea of odds and gambling (not that I ever did any) and I followed the newspapers and used to watch share prices and indexes by the time I was thirteen or fourteen. I used to watch the Dow Jones even though I didn't know what it was – I probably hoped it was a relative! I knew it was something to do with the American Stock Market, probably a company. It seemed to go up every day and I used to think it must be good fun.

My mother was frightfully competitive for us and at school we were always given a target – mine was a chap called Wilford and when my reports came it would be, 'If you came second, where was Wilford?' I'm not clever, but I'm very competitive. I was at a private prep school in Huddersfield and then went to Ampleforth, which I didn't enjoy at first because I felt the boys were very snobbish. My school fees were mostly paid by the Grocers' Livery Company and I was very conscious of that; I once got a report that said I was lazy and I remember my mother got very upset because she thought it might put the help of the Grocers' Company at risk. I got ten or eleven O levels and did Latin, Maths and History at A level, learning parrot-fashion.

Entry into the City

Gwilym Lewis (b. 1897)

At the end of the First World War I was demobilized roughly a year before most of the rabble, which was a terrific help to me. Coming back into civilian life was quite a job; I had been leading flights over the lines and chaps' lives had depended on me and I was accustomed to handling people of some calibre. I thought about staying in the Air Force but my father's advice was to get out. I wanted to get on with something. My father suggested I go into the City. I knew a bit about the City from having lunches with him but it was like going into a big fog. My father said, 'You can come into my firm if you like. We'll pay you two hundred and forty pounds a year' – which was a good deal less than I was earning as a flying boy – 'Or else there's a firm at Lloyd's but they only pay two hundred a year.' I decided in favour of two hundred a year because I knew what my father was. He would probably have been tougher on a son in the business than anyone else in the firm. I didn't want to get into that position, so I went to Sedgwick Collins, one of the big firms at Lloyd's.

Lord O'Brien of Lothbury (b. 1908)

One's aspirations were really very modest, it was a case of getting a good job. My father and I were devoted cricketers and he used to play at the Roehampton Club. There were two men at the Club who were in the Bank of England. They weren't very grand people in the Bank but they said to my father, 'It's a very good place to work and if your son is interested in Economics and related subjects, if he's not going to university and has got to start earning his living, he can hardly do better than start there.'

First of all you had to find a director of the Bank of England who was willing to nominate you because you could only get into the Bank staff if you were personally nominated by a director. My father had been close to a Baring in the Guards, with whom he had played a lot of cricket. Pegging it on that association, he wrote to Lord Revelstoke, John Baring II, and asked him whether he'd be prepared to nominate his son to a clerkship in the Bank? I went up to see Lord Revelstoke and I hadn't taken my inter-

BSC at the time and he said, 'Well, come back when you've taken it.' I did, having succeeded, and he agreed to nominate me. Then I had to pass a Bank of England examination as well. English, French, Mathematics, it wasn't particularly tough. And then I started.

Lord Benson (b. 1909)

I became an accountant purely by chance. In 1923, when I was fourteen, one of my mother's sisters here in England was very ill and my mother came over from South Africa to see her. On the last day of the sojourn here we had nothing to do and my mother said, 'Let's go down and see the office.' 'The office' was the office of her family firm, Cooper Brothers, where her brother had been a partner. So we got in a taxi and went to the Mansion House and were shown in to see the partners. It was a pretty difficult interview because they hadn't seen her for fifteen or twenty years and they'd never seen me before. We arrived without an appointment and conversation was a bit stilted. I felt the tension in the air when everybody was groping for something to say. But in the course of, and because of, the difficult conversation with the partners, a cousin of my mother's, Stuart Cooper, said, 'Well, if you want this lad to be articled when he's finished school you can send him over here.' My mother didn't say anything until we actually left the office. As we crossed the threshold she looked at me and said, 'Well, that's settled. You'll come here when you've finished school in two years' time.' And that was never questioned by me, by my father or by the firm. It was accepted from that moment forward. So two years later I found myself in London, articled to Cooper Brothers. And that's how my life began. That single sentence.

Michael Verey (b. 1912)

I was anxious to go somewhere where, if I worked hard and it was a good firm, I would make some money. I was pretty sure that meant something in the City. I talked to my father and he said, 'I will speak to my friend, Alfred Wagg.' He and Alfred had been friends since they were little boys at the same private school together and were very close friends at Eton and Cambridge and thereafter. There was a, for me, ghastly, agonizing dinner party which was held in Alfred's very grand flat in Berkeley Square with a butler and footmen (not things we had), which my father and mother and I went to. My father and I wore dinner jackets and I said to my father, 'I'll just stay doggo so that he can't take against me. You do the talking.' So my father was frightfully good and swept Alfred along. I got a letter a week later saying Helbert, Wagg would take me on, to start on 3 September 1934 at the standard salary of eighty-six pounds a year.

Dundas Hamilton (b. 1919)

I had to wait until June 1946 before I was demobilized. I had the alternative of going back to Cambridge after nearly seven years and picking up where I left off, spending another two years there and then a year on research, or forgetting about being a scientist and going into commerce. I wanted to get a job, so I went into my father's stockbroking firm in June 1946, where I was the lowest-paid clerk in the business.

Leonard Toomey (b. 1924)

I was working as a page-boy at the Overseas League in St James's and I met a chap who was a member of the Club and who said did I intend staying there for the rest of my life? I said, 'No, actually, I'm looking for work.' And he said, 'Well, I work at Lloyd's and I know a firm at Lloyd's who are looking for an office boy.' I'd never heard of Lloyd's, it meant nothing to me. The only time I'd actually been in the City was when a friend and I went for a walk when I was about seven and the walk must have lasted for some miles because eventually a policeman grabbed us on Blackfriars Bridge and we were taken to Blackfriars Police Station. That was my only contact with the City until 1938 when I went for an interview and saw Mr A. B. Dick-Cleland, who was a Scotsman who started our syndicate at Lloyd's. About five or six boys applied but I got the job as an office boy at sixty pounds a year and started work in the second week in February 1939.

Sir Brian Corby (b. 1929)

I made an approach to the Prudential rather than them approaching me although they were in Cambridge interviewing potential candidates the same day in 1952 as I was up in London asking for a job. It was quite easy to get a job, it was just after the war and firms were anxious to strengthen their capabilities. My reasons for wanting to join the Prudential were rational and irrational. They offered me more money, which was a highly rational reason, not least because I was thinking of getting married. Also, they had a sports ground close to where I thought I was going to live. The other significant reasons were that they had an overseas operation, which most UK life companies did not have, and I wanted the opportunity to go overseas. Also, I felt it was better to get your training in a big company rather than a small one. I liked the attitude of the people I saw there.

Sir Martin Jacomb (b. 1929)

I was on holiday with Cyril Kleinwort and his family in 1966 or '67 and Cyril asked me if I'd consider joining his firm? Several thoughts started to surface, one that I liked business and finance and that this was a way of getting directly close to it. Secondly, there were two people whom I much admired who had already done the same thing – stopped being barristers and gone on to be merchant bankers. I don't compare myself to them, but I admire them; one was Gordon Richardson, who later became the Governor of the Bank of England, and the other was Philip Shelbourne, who went on to make a terrific success as a merchant banker. The third factor was a character trait. I knew if I said 'No', I would never know if the decision was right or wrong.

George Nissen (b. 1930)
I left Cambridge in 1953. I didn't know what I was going to do. There was a lot of nationalization going on at the time. The Stock Exchange was politically out of favour and was rather beleaguered and not looked on as a place of much excitement; there was talk of nationalizing it, which was a crazy idea. Most young men in the early fifties thought that Lloyd's was the exciting place to go to – invisible earnings were the thing.

I stumbled into my life in the City in the way in which I suppose a number of people did. I thought I might become a solicitor, but on my twenty-first birthday my mother took me to Claridges and across the room was the noble figure of Fred Althaus, wearing as always a red carnation in his buttonhole. He knew me because I was at school with his son, Nigel. He came across and discovered it was my birthday and gave me a white fiver and said, 'If ever you think of coming into the City, you should come to Pember & Boyle. It's not like other firms. Just think about it.'

Hugh Peppiatt (b. 1930)
In 1954, when I came back after my year in America, I had got a little bit behind my contemporaries. I had the idea that I might teach. I lived at home, this louche young man, mooning about the house, not getting up in the morning and drinking the gin and all these other things that my children do now! In the end my father said, 'Your mother and I think you really ought to settle down to something, you know. While you're making up your mind, why don't you come to Freshfields and spend a few days? You can lick stamps, that sort of thing.' So I did.

Peter Spira (b. 1930)
My career was shaped by accident. When I first came down from Cambridge, Lord Drogheda, a friend of my parents, said, 'Why don't you talk to a friend of mine, Siegmund Warburg?' I went to see Siegmund and said, 'What does somebody like you want from somebody like me?' He wasn't in the slightest interested in my academic career. He was more

interested in what I was reading or what plays I was interested in or what I did in my spare time.

He said, 'Without doubt, you ought to qualify as a chartered accountant. That will give you three years to see what the world is like. You will go round auditing different institutions and get a better idea of what opportunities there are. If you like, I will give you an introduction to the senior partner of Cooper Brothers, which is one of the top firms.' So I went off to Cooper Brothers and became articled to them. I hated it passionately and found it boring. Looking back, it was the right thing to do, although it was hell.

Jack Spall (b. 1930)
When I left Enfield Grammar School I really did know nothing about the outside world. My maths master at school knew somebody who was working at an East Indian merchants in Crosby Square in the City, so in 1947, at seventeen, I went there as the 'gofer'.

Sir Kenneth Kleinwort (b. 1935)
After university in Grenoble I came back to the UK and then within a very short space of time I started work for the family firm. I'd set my heart on going into the diplomatic corps because I thought this was going to be a wonderful way of being able to use my languages by being posted to various different parts of the world, but it was quite clear that without a university degree I would have no chance of passing the diplomatic exam and therefore I just had to accept that it was a non-starter. I didn't really want all that much to go into the family business, for one reason or another. But my father just said, 'Well, give it a go for six months and if you can then, at the end of six months, come and tell me with your hand on your heart that you absolutely hate it and you think the whole thing is so boring and ghastly, then we can sit down and talk about trying to find another avenue for you to seek a career.' I said 'OK, on the basis of six months, I'll give it a go.'

Lord Rothschild (b. 1936)
I can't remember when I first went to the bank. I think I may have been once before I actually joined it. But it was more a question of whether I would stay at Oxford. And then pressure was brought to bear on me: a lot of letters from my cousins at the bank, saying, 'Please, please do come and join the bank.' And I wasn't really clear what I wanted to do. So that's how I became involved.

Sir John Craven (b. 1940)

When I graduated in 1960 I knew only that I wanted to do something commercial. I felt it in my fingers. I decided to do chartered accountancy because I thought it would be a good combination with a law degree for a business career. I trooped off to a number of accountancy firms in London and found you practically had to pay them for the privilege of being articled and as I had no money at all, I enrolled as an articled clerk with a Canadian firm and, with my new wife, went to live in Canada, where I emerged at the end with a gold medal for the top marks in the country.

I stayed in Canada for three years, by which time my marriage was on the rocks and my wife wanted to bring our two children to England. I didn't want to lose contact with my children so I came back to London and, through a friend in Canada, had the good fortune of an introduction to Siegmund Warburg. I was about twenty-six when I joined Warburgs.

John Wolff (b. 1940)

There was a family business and I had decided early on that it would be rather silly not to at least try it. I didn't feel strongly about going to university because there wasn't anything I could study which would have helped in the trading and broking business we were in. In 1958 I came into the business for a year and a half and then went abroad to work for a year.

Charles McVeigh III (b. 1942)

When I joined Salomon Brothers in New York in 1971 they had just moved to Number One, New York Plaza, where they had built the legendary trading floor which was double-height and which served as the model for future trading halls established all over the world. The advertising for the firm for a couple of years focused on 'The Room' and what took place inside it. The makers of the movie, *Wall Street*, and Tom Wolfe, the author of *Bonfire of the Vanities*, both spent a significant amount of time in the Salomon Brothers trading room, studying the activity, the yelling and screaming and the tempo. One of my best friends at Salomon was the figure who became the protagonist of Tom Wolfe's book.

Salomon's London office, which they opened in 1971 with two people, was a total contrast. I started visiting London for Salomon in 1973, by which time they had moved to 1, Moorgate, right opposite the Bank of England, and there were about twenty staff. I moved to London in 1975.

In August 1975 we bought a beautiful house in Cheyne Walk from the Kleinwort family (which then became John Craven's home after we left it). The Kleinwort family were always very keen on the Americans because during the war, Cyril and Ernest had been shifted to the States to live with friends. Cyril and his wife took a liking to my wife and I and invited us to their country house and to dinner parties in London. If when you first arrive here you have introductions of that quality and get to know a few people who take a genuine interest in you, it makes an enormous difference to the speed with which you are integrated into society.

David King (b. 1945)

Within six weeks of qualifying as an accountant (I was twenty-seven and married with one child), I went to Iran, purely because of the money. I'd read an advertisement in the papers for a job overseas and filled in a form to apply. Somebody phoned my wife when I was at work and said, 'Would your husband work in one of the worst places in the world for a very high salary?' and she said 'yes', so we went. I worked for an American company in the oil business. We lived in Iran for two years and Saudi Arabia for three-and-a-half, where I took a job as financial controller for Combustion Engineering. The house I lived in before I went to Iran I paid seven thousand pounds for and when we came back I bought another house for eighty thousand pounds, so my property value had increased tenfold.

When I came back to the UK in January 1982, I was still working for the US multi-national I was with in Saudi and I decided I had the resources to take an MBA [Master of Business Administration]. I did a deal with the company and said I would give up all my holidays for the next two years and work overtime to make up the shortfall if they would allow me to take the course. I paid for the entire course myself (about four thousand pounds a year). Apart from giving me more confidence, the MBA formalized a lot of what I already knew about how a company should be run and I obtained high marks throughout the course.

The company I was working for was based in Northampton, where we went to live, but I felt it was sinking and did a small mailshot – wrote a c.v. and sent it to about a hundred companies with a covering letter. One of the criteria I wanted had to be money, and I wanted to work in London because I felt it offered more opportunities jobwise. I had a number of interviews and ended up working in Mayfair for a private Arab family from '84 to '87. Then in 1987 I did another mailshot to appropriate companies and also to recruitment agencies and head-hunters and I was shortlisted for two jobs. One was for a strategic consultant and the other was for my present job and it was a toss-up as to which I would take. I opted for the London Metal Exchange.

Haruko Fukuda (b. 1946)

When I came down from Cambridge in 1968 I wasn't intending to have a long-term career. Through a friend of my father's I was offered a job at the Atlantic Trade Study (later the Trade Policy Research Centre). I stayed for longer than I had expected and had a very interesting two years, editing and rewriting scholarly papers on Britain's policies towards the Common Market. I became a bit of an expert through this job on the effects on the developing countries of Britain joining the Common Market, the subject on which I wrote my first book a few years later.

The person who I was getting married to wanted to go to business school in America. So I wanted to go to America too. I was introduced to the Director of Economics at the World Bank in Washington in November 1970: he was looking for an assistant and I went to work there. I stayed only about a year. I was twenty-three, the youngest professional they had ever had at that time and one of only three women professionals in the bank. People were very kind but the World Bank was a huge bureaucratic organization with some three-and-a-half thousand people and the job I had was not terribly interesting – administrative work. I came back to England partly because I had fallen in love with somebody here (whom I later married) just before I went to America and partly because I got a letter from Macmillans saying they would like to publish a manuscript I had written while I was at the Overseas Development Institute in London. I went back to Cambridge as a graduate student and finished the book. Then I was commissioned to write a second book, about Japan's trade relations with the rest of the world. I knew nothing about Japan at that time because I had worked entirely on European affairs, but the philosophical issues were the same.

I came to London to look for a part-time job while I was writing the second book and a friend suggested that I should see John Drysdale at Robert Fleming, who said they didn't have a job for me but sent me to see John Clay at Vickers da Costa, which was a firm of stockbrokers. At that time, in 1972, Vickers were the only people who dealt in Japan. John Clay shrugged his shoulders and said, 'Oh yes. Why don't you come? Yes, why not?'

David Verey (b. 1950)
I distinctly remember having a conversation with my father at the beginning of my last year at Cambridge when he said, 'I think you should do accountancy because it's a jolly good grounding.' I said, 'There's absolutely no way I'm going to do accountancy. I've had it with exams. I'm not going to do any more.' Some time later I announced I was going to teach. He looked at me rather seriously and said, 'That's fine, that's a good idea.' Then he said, 'Have you looked at the Burnham Scale? I suggest you do, because the pay is pretty lousy even if you're at the top

end of the Scale. You're going to find it pretty difficult.' I thought about it and decided not to become a teacher.

My father said, 'Would you like to meet some of my friends?' I said 'OK', slightly reluctantly because I didn't have a conviction about what I wanted to do. He set up a series of meetings either in their homes or in offices and I travelled backwards and forwards to Cambridge to see these people. One of them was Oliver Poole, who was Chairman of Lazards. We sat in his room at 11, Old Broad Street for about an hour and didn't talk about business at all. We talked about T. S. Eliot (I had done my thesis on Eliot), and what I had been reading recently. Then he looked at his watch and said, 'Well, dear boy, if you want to come and be bored for a couple of years, do.' I got back on the train to Cambridge and just giggled and thought it was a wonderful way to offer somebody a job. I penned a letter back and said, 'If you meant it, I'll come.'

Davina Walter (b. 1954)

I got a secretarial job through Queens College and realized it was not at all what I wanted to do. I handed in my resignation after two days. I then worked as a temporary secretary for an agency in Beauchamp Place. It was a carefree time and I could have drifted along but I knew I wanted something more. I didn't think, 'I'm going to be a career girl', but I always wanted to be self-sufficient.

At the end of 1973 I got in touch with my grandfather, who had retired to Scotland, and said, 'I know nothing about the City. It's a mystery place, a financial centre. Do you think I might be able to do something?' He went to one of his fellow partners at Cazenove and said, 'Davina's desperate to do something in the City', or words to that effect. 'Please try and see her and give her some encouragement as to what she might be able to do.'

His partner very kindly got in touch with me and said, 'Come and have lunch at the Great Eastern Hotel.' I told him I didn't know anything about stockbroking and he said, 'I know a few women have just been admitted to the floor of the Stock Exchange and I think there will be more women around the City. Maybe I can get in touch with a small firm of brokers and see if they would have you to work for them.' We went back to Cazenove and the office manager came into the room and said, 'I knew your grandfather', and talked to me. Then he said, 'Would you like to spend three months here as a trainee?' He gave me a health warning about their not having had women there before – I don't know what he thought the back office were going to do to me!

Valerie Thompson (b. 1956)

I left school in 1971 when I was fifteen without any qualifications. I went for an interview in Ilford Town Hall where a toffee-nosed guy dictated to me what he expected me to do, general filing and stuff like that. He annoyed me and I got up and said I didn't want the job. I went to one of the recruitment agencies in Liverpool Street and got a job working for a firm of stockbrokers, Hitchens Harrison, as a filing clerk. I had a desire for money and the need for it would have acted like a magnet but it was pure chance that I went into the City.

Philippa Rose (b. 1958)

How I ended up running a head-hunting company in the City is a rather tortuous saga. My mediocre A level results and a professional singing diploma weren't top-university entrance, so rather than come to terms with the second tier, I decided to go to Bristol Polytechnic to do a more 'practical' degree – Business Studies. But after a three-month 'work experience' session in my second year, which I did in Paris, I found it very difficult to settle back into the course and so I left without telling my parents and went to live in Oxford for a while. Eventually I accepted to start a new degree at City University in Banking and Finance. To kill six months before the course started, I took a temporary job at Kleinwort Benson, and then begged them to let me stay on at the end of it – not that I was enjoying my job, it was just that I couldn't bear the thought of being a student again. They agreed and I became a degree-less member of the graduate intake of '79. I stuck it out for one-and-a-half years.

Bored out of my mind in fixed interest fund management, fiddling around with yield curves and exchange rates, I capitulated one morning, found an ad in *The Times*, attended an interview over lunch, accepted an offer by two-thirty and resigned by three o'clock. I was to become a recruitment consultant in a secretarial firm called Crone Corkill. I had been struck by the vitality, drive and personality of the two women who ran it, and if they had been making ink-wells I would have joined them.

I thrived and they thrived. I realized it was possible to enjoy work. We both did well out of the relationship. And I learned an enormous amount about business from them. However, after a year, I was once again frustrated. I wanted more. I thought about starting up on my own and asked them to back me. At first they didn't take me seriously, but it didn't take long to convince them, and soon after, 'Philippa Rose & Partners' was launched – an executive search firm that was to specialize in middle management investment bankers. A year later I bought them out, paid back all my debts and flew solo.

Ms A (b. 1959)

I had been to the Careers Office and discovered that forty per cent of the graduates who had done Philosophy were still unemployed four years after leaving university. When I graduated, we were four years into the first of Thatcher's electoral periods and there was a pervading feeling that you should be out there working. I considered a vast array of different things – journalism, law, interpreting – but nothing stuck out. I did the Civil Service exams but was three marks short of getting in. In the end, I applied to merchant banks – because their bumf said languages were an advantage – and to advertising companies. You had to go to London for the interviews for advertising whereas the merchant banks all came to the universities. You got more creative questions from the bankers than the advertisers.

I applied to American, British and Japanese merchant banks. There was an interview with an American bank with one person being Mr Nice and another being Mr Nasty, everything being done by the book. There were stupid questions, for example, 'Why do you think there's been such tremendous growth in the capital markets in the last three years?' I'd want to say, 'You tell me. I've been doing a degree.' It implied that you'd spent since the year dot reading the *Financial Times*.

Ross Jones (b. 1959)

From an early age, one had absorbed that you went from public school into the City. When I was coming up to leaving school, I was talking to the deputy head of Ampleforth, Father Edmund, and he said he thought I ought to work for a discount house in the City and he set me up with some interviews. I'd come for a lot of interviews with insurance companies and I thought their interviewing techniques were pathetic – totally impersonal, very much facts and figures. Then I came to see a contact of Father Edmund's, Alan Tritton, a director at Barclays Bank, and I was with him for about three minutes while he asked me my qualifications and my interests.

Through Alan Tritton, I came to see Roger Gibbs, who was chairman of Gerrard & National, and I thought he was the most charming man I'd ever met in my life. He sat me down and we talked about cricket for a while and then he said, 'Well, would you like a job? If you did come, when would you like to start?' I was taken round the office and then I went home. He phoned my mother that night to say he'd offered me a job and hoped very much that I would take it and that if she had anything she wanted to ask, not to hesitate to call. That sums up Gerrard & National under Roger. He looked after his whole staff like that. You couldn't have come to a more paternalistic company in the City than Gerrard & National.

I was very excited but I don't think I appreciated how lucky I was. I remember going back to school with this job offer of two thousand pounds a year and people couldn't believe it. In those days, three A levels was considered over-qualified.

Career

Gwilym Lewis (b. 1897)

I joined Sedgwick Collins in 1919, when I was twenty-one. It was a brand new office at 7, Gracechurch Street. The directors were in an area which you could call 'glasshouses', all in a line down the middle in offices with glass walls so that you could see into everybody else. People were very polite, very nice. My father was in a position of influence in the insurance world and he could support the firm I was in with business. There was no underhand side to it – Sedgwick Collins was one of the top three or four firms in Lloyd's – but it did give me some standing in the firm. I was noticed by the Chairman and it so happened that he liked me and that made all the difference all the way along. He was a 'Good morning, officer', type, an old Etonian, quietly capable, who couldn't be pushed about. He was called Harry Sedgwick. I used to stay weekends with him and play golf, that sort of thing. Later on, I was given a seat in one of the directors' rooms, which was a great privilege, but that was partly due to being my father's son. That irked me very much. I didn't care to be Hugh Lewis's son. I preferred to be Gwilym Lewis.

We dealt with the P. & O. fleet, an enormous fleet with strange names, and I set about learning those, which was quite a job. But I was on the learn all the time. I was taking evening classes and whatever I could. I gave a lecture to the Insurance Institute called 'Aviation and Insurance' – obviously my father had pushed me there – and I lectured all the big chaps in the City on the company insurance side and used lantern slides to show the aircraft. In the 1920s there was no insurance of aviation worth talking about. Looking back, it was all a big piece of nonsense, but it was pushing me and that's what I cared about. I was beginning to be myself.

I worked in various sections of the office until I became a chap who went up to the market at Lloyd's as what they call a broker. Business would come into the firm and a broker would take it up to the market. Lloyd's was at the top of the Royal Exchange in those days. The underwriters still sit in what are called 'Boxes', which come from the shape of where people used to have their meals in Lloyd's Coffee House. There's nothing like Lloyd's in the world. There are underwriters sitting at Boxes and brokers running around with their business, hoping the underwriters will take it. To broke a piece of business, you have brief details on a 'slip' – a slip of paper, really – and you go to an underwriter and say what you've got and would he be interested? If he's interested, he'll write part of it but usually not the whole thing. He'll write ten or twenty per cent and then others write the rest until you do a hundred per cent.

It was all men in the market. (I believe they've got women running around now, but not in my time.) Even when I started I was not a schoolboy – I'd been through five years of war – and I was accustomed to talking to chaps on very level terms. I didn't shake all over just because I was talking to somebody, I was too much used to people by that time. I was seeing some of the old characters in Lloyd's who are known in the history books now. There was Cuthbert Heath, a very senior Lloyd's man who was head of C. E. Heath and Co., which is still in existence. He was very much the father of Lloyd's and invented some of the special covers that Lloyd's specialized in. That's where Lloyd's really became of interest because they were prepared to sit down and work things out – everybody does it now, companies in America followed on. Cuthbert Heath was very good to me as a youngster. 'Inside' him was a chap called Monty Evans and 'outside' him was Matthew Drysdale, who later married my sister. You wanted to keep in with the underwriters but you always did better with some than others, that's just life. Later on they made me senior broker of my firm.

I was on the non-marine side. I got promotion and bringing in clients became very much part of my job – I was always on the look-out. You met a chap drinking a cocktail and you said, 'How about your insurance?' It's good to be liked. If there's a businessman like the head of Selfridges – who has an enormous account – he probably knows a number of brokers and, although I would never have admitted it at the time, the others are probably as good as you. But he then does business with somebody he likes and you get the order. It's a highly specialized side of life, very much the same with a stockbroker.

I was fortunate because Harry Sedgwick formed a new non-marine syndicate, and he asked me if I would like to join. I hadn't got any money and Sedgwick lent me the money and didn't charge me any interest on it, which was a pretty damn nice thing to do. By that means, I became a Member of Lloyd's, and then I paid him back. There are all sorts of brokers in England who are not Lloyd's brokers and so they can't reach the Lloyd's market.

In 1923 I went to America for the firm. My heart was in my mouth. I wasn't an ambitious man in the sense that everybody today seems to be, but if I was doing a job, I wanted to be successful. To go to America was the greatest excitement because that hadn't ever been in my realm. The Americans are a breed of cat on their own. I went to see the people we were doing a bit of business with, dotted around the country. I would go out there with a bowler hat and an umbrella and people would know I was British. I wasn't going to change for anybody. I was from Lloyd's! (These days, a chap from Lloyd's is just another chap.) I remember one good joke. I was outside a subway and there was a cop and I walked up to him and said, 'I want to go to Jersey City.' He had a look at me and said, 'Well, go to it then.' That taught me how to handle Americans, quite a lesson in itself. Bit too British!

America was very much developing at the time I'm talking about, '23–29, and I went all over the country. My father's company, the Liverpool London Globe, had big business there and I met his representatives and was picking up everything as fast as I could. With the British brokers I met, we'd quite happily have a drink together downtown in the evening and then the next day be ready to cut each other's throats and have a really good round over business. In those days, a stuffy, conservative, public-school type of chap from London didn't like to talk business at the wrong time, whereas Americans will talk business any time – playing golf, anywhere. Quite an important spot is the locker room where you change your shoes and one thing and another. They'll sit down there as often as not and start on some subject. That's where you might make a friend. After all, you want to get the feel of them, that they're decent sort of chaps.

When I got back from that first trip, I said I'd like to form an American Non-Marine Department and this upset the old boys quite a lot. There was a lot of argument about 'this young man rushing around and we don't know what he's doing'. Eventually they agreed and I started the department with three chaps. When the Crash came in 1929, I sailed through and had only one loss, whereas other Lloyd's brokers had some very nasty losses. Like everyone, our firm was affected by the Crash and business dropped off. We had to reduce salaries. Nobody ever thinks of reducing their salaries today; no matter whether the firm is going bust or not, they seem to ask for more. We had to go to the heads of departments and say, 'I'm afraid you're going to be reduced.' That's something I've never seen at any other time. If you think people came up and said, 'Thank you for reducing me', they didn't, but they didn't resign because they'd got nothing to resign to, had they?

By the Second World War, I'd built the American Non-Marine Department into the biggest department in the office. During the war I was part of the Cabinet War Room team at Storey's Gate. (Churchill's bedroom was just next door to us and the King and Queen came to visit sometimes.)

Some people at Lloyd's blamed me for going away and were rather annoyed about it. The underwriting room at Lloyd's was still functioning and my department had its own way of handling business with America, in codes and things of that sort. Having been leader of my department, I wanted to be in touch and I always kept a contact going with Lloyd's and had copies of all the cables going in and out. I don't say I interfered, but I visited the City from time to time.

After five years, when I was demobilized before the end of the war, everything was different. I found my department had done well and that any more pressure on the boys would be unwelcome. Things had changed. There was a new chairman, someone I hadn't been close to, although I'd known him because I'd been with the firm twenty-five years by then and was a pretty senior director. To my surprise, they thought they could get on quite well without me. That was a complete shock to me. You can't stop these young chaps who are pretty good being ambitious, but it took me a long time to understand what had happened. I had been away too long. Finally, I parted company with Sedgwicks in '47. They gave me a very fair deal.

I tried to get myself going by myself but I wasn't successful. I kept a bit of insurance going. I was busy as the dickens – got a secretary coming in and all that, but I wasn't making headway. I suppose I haven't got the ability to do it. Eventually someone said, 'Why don't you join so-and-so? He seems to be needing a bit of backing up. Go and have a chat.' I was waiting for an opening, of course, but I didn't get the right one. I made a deal with a chap, Henry Brooker, who was running a small firm. I joined on a 50–50 basis and we were joint chairmen. In the event, a sad thing happened – he died. Heart failure. So I became chairman pretty automatically. The firm was called Arbon Langrish & Co., a pretty old, established firm. I put my brother, John, on the board, which was very useful. (John was a Lloyd's man on the underwriting side and his son is very much a Lloyd's man now.)

When I joined Arbon Langrish, it needed bucking up and I pitched in on the American side and built that up. We were a small firm of maybe a hundred and fifty people. When I joined Sedgwicks from the Services, I very deliberately became a Sedgwicks' man and waved the Sedgwicks' flag but I didn't have quite that feeling with Arbon Langrish. I felt I'd had a rough time, the Almighty had given me a good kick in the backside. I concentrated more on my family and wasn't ambitious like I was originally. It was a different attitude. I wasn't building for life any more. In the end I sold the firm to Clarksons around 1965 for a lot of money. The firm's offices are now in Bishopsgate, opposite Lloyds.

I kept up my relationships, lunching at Lloyds, that sort of thing, but I ceased to be active day to day. I'm ninety-three now, just an old fossil. I'm the oldest Member of Lloyd's at the moment.

Lord O'Brien of Lothbury (b. 1908)

I was told that I had passed the Bank of England examination and all of those who had passed in that particular election were received into the Bank by one of the senior officials of the Secretary's department and instructed as to our initial responsibilities. Then we started our three-year probation.

After the First World War, the Bank of England found itself with greatly increased responsibilities and the need to recruit staff very quickly; for at least five or six years it recruited up to twenty new staff every month, a vast increase. I came at the very end of that period. They were looking for honest, faithful workers who harmonized with the general ethos of the Bank, which was a very gentlemanly institution. We all took pride in the fact that we were known as the 'Gentlemen of the Bank of England'. My social status was rather lower than that of my companions in the Bank, the predominance was still the public-school ethos, which I found very agreeable. I was fortunate, having started from a modest background, to get into a working environment which was of a superior grade.

I was allocated to the Private Drawing Office, that's to say, the banking office for private customers. In those days the Bank had a separate Public Drawing Office which was for government accounts and government business which, naturally enough in the Central Bank, bulks very large.

The principal figure in our office was Roland Grahame, a very aristocratic figure with a long moustache (and the brother of Kenneth, former Secretary to the Bank, who wrote *The Wind in the Willows*). In front of the office were the cash desks with the cashiers. If you go into the Bank now, you find girls on the counter, but then there were only stately old men. We, behind, dealt with all the work they pushed to us, credits to our private customers' accounts, debits, making sure that the ledgers balanced each night. The work as a whole was done in pen and ink. I enjoyed it but as time went on I imagined myself continuing to do this sort of routine work for the rest of my working life and I found that quite intolerable, lucky though one may feel one was to have had a job to start with in those years of the early thirties.

Excellence in the performance of your duties draws you to the attention of those senior to you and your name then goes forward for a try at something more difficult. There were offices in the Bank called special offices, where the demands of the work was far greater. The most important of those was the Chief Cashier's office. If one showed any kind of promise, one got a stint in there. It happened to me. To begin with one goes in as a probationer, very modest, and you're known as a runner, at the beck and call of the more senior people. You're observed in your deportment, how you perform the menial tasks. The general style in the Bank is very important, people who don't fit in are not very welcome – those whose manners are unpleasing, whose desire to shine is excessive, the sort of people in everyday life one doesn't like living with. But they are very well observed before selection, so that didn't happen very often.

I also spent a period in what was called the Central Banks, a new office created by Montagu Norman to give closer attention to economic and financial conditions in the many countries with which the Bank was connected. In about 1932 he had also set up a committee, the chairman of which was Austen Chamberlain, to look after the interest of the bond-holders of the League Loans. The loans had been issued after the First World War on the international capital markets to provide stabilization to countries in Eastern Europe, and by the time of the 1929 Crash all the plans had been thrown into disarray and the countries couldn't meet the service of the loans. I was made assistant to A. S. G. Hoar, the Secretary of this committee. There I was dealing with governments, with bond-holders, with the prestigious committee. Of course, I loved it.

I did that for a couple of years and then I was taken into the Overseas Department, to sit on the desk which dealt with the Balkans. I was just about to go to Warsaw when war broke out, after which I had a small team which had to start running exchange control. That in itself was a revelation because there was an increase in the background of legislation and regulation which we had to administer. I wasn't an ignoramus as far as exchange control was concerned, but developing it in a far more complex manner was very demanding. Work was something which went on all day long and far into the night (I slept at the Bank of England in the vaults, as many others did, male and female) and one had no complaint about that; one's brothers had gone into the fighting services and one was sitting in a reserved job, safe and well and well looked after.

One met enormous numbers of people. One characteristic of the pre-war Bank was that one met relatively few of the outside public but then the whole of the public came before us, mostly highly agitated as to what was going to happen. Amongst many commercial and financial people, we used to see strange characters like George Arliss and Gracie Fields and Noel Coward, all worried about their foreign exchange assets and so forth. It was good for the Bank in the end. The Bank undertook the job for the Treasury with some misgiving, feeling that this day-to-day contact with the general public in a regulatory capacity would damage the image of the Bank. It didn't do anything of the kind. It enhanced the reputation of the Bank, not the reverse.

At the end of 1942 I became Private Secretary to Montagu Norman and Lord Catto, who took his place as Governor after he left the Bank. Montagu Norman was the most magnetic personality that I've ever met in my life. His personality was so compelling that I often felt he persuaded people to do things they didn't really want to do and perhaps shouldn't have done. But he was a remarkable human being and inspired awe, and indeed fear, amongst many people in the City. He was Governor of the Bank for twenty-three years, longer than anyone else has ever been. He built up the modern Bank and made it a very efficient institution, sort of pulled it out of the nineteenth century; that's his legacy.

The Bank has always been in the political world with a small 'p', inevitably with the Governor being the confidential adviser to the Chancellor of the Exchequer and the government generally, but of course the political world has changed so enormously. In the nineteenth century, the part the politicians played in the bankers' world was so much smaller than it is nowadays. Contrary to a lot of people's opinions, Montagu Norman was extremely punctilious in his relations with the government, in his recognition that he was a confidential adviser and that in the end the decisions lay with the government. You had to make sure the government was kept in touch with what was going on and helped to make the right decisions rather than the wrong ones; he was very good at that.

I left Lord Catto in '46 and went back to Exchange Control until '48 when I went across to be immediately responsible for the administration of the Overseas Sub-Department. Then, in 1951, I became Deputy Chief Cashier. Although I was Deputy, I was immensely surprised when I was made Chief Cashier, absolutely delighted. The Chief Cashier was the senior official of the Bank, he was *primus inter pares* and he chaired the Head of Departments' Committee and was the man who had most association with the Governor. His department was responsible for the note issue, for all securities of the Bank and of the Bank's customers. In addition, he was responsible for managing the gilt-edged market with the help of the Government Broker. (This was a very wide area and it led, in the end, to the Chief Cashier's role being reduced. He is still head of the Banking Department and responsible for the note issue but he doesn't have the wider responsibilities for managing the gilt-edged market. All the things associated with the market are done now by a director of the Bank with a separate staff.)

I became an Executive Director of the Bank and I had been an Executive Director for two years when I was made Deputy Governor; to have it happen in two years was an agreeable surprise. The Deputy Governor traditionally (although traditions are altering now) was the man who was concerned with the Bank as an organization and made sure it was an efficient instrument behind the Governor. That has changed with changing Governors. When Kit McMahon was made Deputy, he came into the Bank as an economist, he was a Deputy Governor who was concerned with external policy as well as the internal running of the Bank. The Deputy Governor, generally speaking, is appointed on the recommendation of the Governor and with the assent of the Court of Directors. The Governor, naturally enough, will mention to the Chancellor of the Exchequer what he proposes to do. I would say the appointment of the Governors, including the Deputy Governor, has become more political than it was. The Directors of the Bank are supposed to be consulted about who the Governor and Deputy Governor should be. I'm not sure in recent years that's been done as punctiliously as it used to be done in the past.

I succeeded Lord Cromer as Governor of the Bank of England in 1966. I don't know from whom the initiative came; I would suspect that it came from the Chancellor and the Prime Minister in the first instance, but that it was discussed with the Court or with the Governor of the day and that the acceptance of the Court was obtained before I was appointed. I know I was paraded with my wife at dinner by a senior director of the Bank and I can only assume that it was in order to make sure that would be all right. Without being immodest, I think I had established, *vis à vis* the Labour government then in office, on my contacts with them and with the Chancellor in particular, that I knew what I was doing and had pretty clear views on what should and should not be done. Whether I was appointed because I was very much the local boy made good, I don't know. They might well have said, 'Well, look, here's one of us. A chap who's come up the line all the way.' You could ask Jim Callaghan if you want to. It isn't the case that there's tension between the Labour Party and the Bank, apart from Rowley Cromer (particularly *vis à vis* George Brown, who, brilliant though he was, was hardly a rational person anyway). In general, I think the Bank got on pretty well with the Labour Party and Cobbold certainly got on with Wilson and Co. I got on well with them myself, too, even though I don't share their politics.

We're there to do a job and we do it honestly whatever the government in power. We might have great trouble if we had a really wild government in power, but it hasn't happened so far. Of course, political wishes may well run against what one thinks is sensible in the monetary field but you have to give your advice and accept what the politicians on behalf of the people want to do. Of course, the Bank has a very strong influence. It's in favour of rational, sensible, wise control of monetary conditions. All central banks if they are worth their salt follow the same line. They spend their lifetimes looking at monetary conditions, assessing them, comparing methods of controlling them and what their effects are and so forth. So they have a high degree of professional skill and naturally enough their advice carries all the weight in consequence. And you might say politicians disagree with them almost at their peril.

For the Governor of the Bank of England, each day would be different from the one before and the one after. On several days in a week the Chief Cashier would bring the Governor the books of the Bank. That would lead to general discussions of policy and it might go on for half an hour. Then the Governor would always have a lot of appointments with people either in the City or industrialists. The Governor's calendar tends to be overfilled with so many people eager to see him. He'll be going at least once a week to see the Chancellor, unless there is a crisis on and he'll see him much more and even the Prime Minister. He'll keep in close contact with the Permanent Secretary of the Treasury and also in less close contact with the Foreign Office and, indeed, with other Ministers from time to time. He used to see the President of the Board of Trade and so forth. So he never sat in idleness.

I might say, 'I must see the chairmen of all the clearing banks because we've got to consider credit constraint.' I would give them advice or directions as to what I wanted done. Then the chairmen of the Accepting Houses Committee would come in one by one to discuss their balance sheets or I would see them collectively at a monthly meeting. One would lunch the chairmen of the clearing banks once a quarter and the chairmen of all the Accepting Houses also once a year. Then there are discussions with your lieutenants on matters of international moment, relations with other central banks, international problems with currency and discussions with your domestic helpers on the future of the markets, the need to govern finance, the effects of government financing on general liquidity and so forth.

I retired when I was sixty-five, in 1973. I put on my hat and left the building. Full-time Governor one day, nothing the next day. My whole life had been built round the Bank, most of my friendships after entering the Bank were Bank of England people. I'd spent forty-six-and-a-half years in the Bank and, although seven years as Governor had been the happiest in my life, I left without looking back. What I didn't appreciate was that once you leave an organization like the Bank, you're just on your own.

I didn't become involved in a lot of other organizations while I was active in the Bank. I was interested in many things but I really took them up after I left. I took up a number of directorships. I went on the board of the National Theatre; I became Honorary Treasurer of the development appeal at the Royal Opera House when I went on to the Council of the Royal College of Music; I became a Glyndebourne trustee; those things, too many really, but there we are. Busyness becomes a mania; unless you're busy you don't feel you're alive. I was living in a suburb where nothing much in particular interests one. From my point of view, I didn't think it was too much, but I think it was too much for my wife. I don't think it was fair to absent myself from home as I did because of these jobs. I was still travelling about twenty times a year. It's no good having regrets, regrets always come too late.

Lord Benson (b. 1909)

Cooper Brothers had started in 1854 and had been in the same offices just by the Mansion House from then until the time I became articled there in 1925. The senior partner then was Stuart Cooper and there was a strong family influence. There were four or five partners and the total staff was maybe a hundred and fifty, but most of them were out of the office on audits – we couldn't have housed them if they hadn't been. To become an articled clerk with a firm like Cooper's, you had to pay a premium of five hundred guineas before they would accept you but I'm happy to say it was remitted in my case because I was family – I don't think we would have been able to find the money anyway. At the end of my first year I got a cheque for ten pounds, which I sent home, and altogether in the five years I received about two hundred and fifty pounds.

Articles then were quite different. We worked all day in the office, learning the principles of accountancy and bookkeeping but we had to work for our examinations at home alone, with correspondence courses. I came fourth out of 1100 candidates in the final. I'm well suited to our profession because vague philosophy means nothing to me. It's something concrete, pragmatic, that interests me. I qualified in January 1932 and was made a partner at the age of twenty-five, which was extraordinarily young for a well-known firm. It was partly family influence and partly that they wanted young blood because some of the partners were getting pretty old. I was in the right place at the right time.

We had a great many contacts with people of wealth and position through the taxation work which we did on their behalf and, as a junior partner, one of my earliest clients asked me whether I would make an investigation into the financial affairs of his fiancée. He wished to become engaged and to announce this in *The Times* but he wasn't prepared for that to take place until he had firm knowledge as to the total liabilities his fiancée had incurred. I didn't think it was a very suitable basis for a future happy married life but I went to see the girl and found her completely enchanting and could well understand his desire to become engaged. I eventually collected a schedule of what appeared to be her outstanding debts and reported to my client. He presented the bill to the girl's parents, who paid off her debts, and in due course the engagement was announced in *The Times*. (Not surprisingly, the marriage didn't last very long and it became a society subject in the papers for two or three days when it broke up.) Even now, the firm has an enormous portfolio of private clients.

An important experience during my years as junior partner, 1934–9, was being sent to make an investigation for one of our clients, a company which was building a railway in the middle of Africa. That was the first big investigation which I undertook and it was a difficult assignment because all the staff out there spoke Portuguese and we had quite a problem understanding each other. I learned a great deal by doing it. In the main though, up to the war, I was just an ordinary audit partner in a firm of chartered accountants.

One of my colleagues in the firm was John Pears, who was nine years my senior. His father had been one of the original staff of the four Cooper brothers who started the firm and had eventually been one of the few staff members to become a partner. John had been to Rugby and then came straight into the firm as an articled clerk and had qualified and been made a partner aged twenty-six. We found we had a great deal in common – tennis, squash, golf – and an enormous interest in the firm. We were young and full of enthusiasm when we returned to the City after the war and we wanted to reorganize the firm and make it international like some of our competitors. The difficulty was that Stuart Cooper hadn't the enthusiasm to do what we thought was required and didn't think it necessary. The remaining partners left it to John and me to sort the matter out and after a fairly short time Stuart resigned and John was made senior partner.

John made a gesture to me which made a profound change in my life. He said he and I would work together as a partnership, and that was a considerable thing. It was one of the happiest events of my life. He loyally adhered to his gesture and never exercised his rights as senior partner without consultation with me. It had a dramatic effect on the fortunes of the firm for the succeeding twenty-five years. Working with somebody you totally trust and who trusts you and whose mind is working on the same objective is a really satisfying experience.

John and I wanted to get the technical side of our work up to date – I don't think anybody was up to date in the United Kingdom because of the ravages of five years of war. We agreed that I should write a manual which covered auditing and general administration. In the years thereafter, it was expanded and improved over and over again, but it was the basis of our practice. We required the manual to be observed by everybody in the office, administrative or professional, and by every office we established elsewhere in the world. Subject to minor variations for local conditions, the manual was a condition of partnership and if it was not observed we reserved the right to terminate the partnership; and very occasionally we did so.

The big client-getting job began after the war. Getting clients is the most extraordinary feature of one's life. The first thing is, you've got to get known. I used to look in my diary every week and if I had a free lunch date then I would see whom I could ask for lunch. I wanted either to get something from him or to tell him something. As soon as people realize you will give service, they pass it on to their friends and it quickly gets round the City. It's an astonishing thing and it grows of itself. Auditing was our main growth and taxation increased enormously but there were two other areas. A great many people wanted advice on what we now call management consultancy and we slogged away until, in 1962, we set up a subsidiary company to deal with that work. Secondly, there was a great demand for investigations; for example, companies wanting to expand or governments lending to Third World countries.

Unilever was a client I was particularly interested in and had a long history with the firm. William Hesketh Lever, the first Viscount Lever-hulme, didn't want his affairs to be examined by local accountants in Liverpool and came to the City in 1887 and went to the manager of the District Bank in Cornhill and said he wanted a London accountant. The bank manager recommended Ernest Cooper (I don't know whether he ever told Lever that Ernest Cooper was his brother-in-law) and from that time forward there was a very close association between Unilever and the firm, which lasts to this day. (In 1923 my uncle, D'Arcy Cooper, left Cooper Brothers and joined Unilever, becoming chairman in 1925 when Leverhulme died.) I've been closely connected with the Leverhulme family, the children and grandchildren and great-grandchildren of William Hesketh Lever.

On the retirement of one of the senior partners I also took on the firm's Pilkington work and formed a close friendship with Harry Pilkington, later Lord Pilkington. John Browns were another client, as were British Oxygen and Babcock and Wilcox. Later I took control of the firm's work with the Post Office and also our work with the steel industry, for which we became auditors. When steel was nationalized I was asked by the Minister of Fuel and Power in the Labour government if I could recommend anybody to take the chair of the British Steel Corporation and I gave Lord Melchett's name because I had formed a close relationship with him as a result of work when he became a partner of M. Samuel & Co. and I knew he wanted to get out of merchant banking and had a great interest in industry.

The work John Pears and I did immediately after the war meant we were building up a considerable network in what used to be called the British Commonwealth but the one area we were not strong on was America. We had a small office there but it was only for local clients. In about 1956 I received an overseas phone call and an American voice said, 'Say, would you like forty thousand dollars' worth of business?' So I said, 'Yes, please.' It turned out this was the senior partner of a well-established and reputable firm called Lybrand, Ross Brothers and Montgommery and they wanted us to take control of their London and Paris offices so they could concentrate on their American business. In 1957 John Pears and I saw them in New York and found they were anxious to follow our suggestion that we form an international grouping in conformity with our general philosophy. This was an enormous amalgamation because Lybrands had a very big business and that really was the foundation of the great international firm of Coopers & Lybrand that is now existing.

Michael Verey (b. 1912)

The Wagg family came over with the Rothschilds, three sisters having married three young men in Germany. One girl married a young man at the Sign of the Weighing Machine; one married a man at the Sign of the Red Shield; the third sister married a young man from Helberstadt. In Germany, Jews weren't allowed surnames, but if they came to England by law they had to have a second name. When the father of one of the boys said, 'I want you to go to England and set up a bank', he had to choose a name and so he called himself Rothschild. He suggested to his two brothers-in-law that they come too and the one who worked at the Sign of the Weighing Machine (*die Waage* in German) called himself Wagg and the one who came from Helberstadt called himself Helbert. So Helbert and Wagg came to London, brothers-in-law of Rothschild, set up shop as brokers and were exclusive brokers to N. M. Rothschild until 1912.

Alfred Wagg joined the family firm of stockbrokers in 1900 and then found in 1912 that there were to be considerable changes and among them that the Stock Exchange commissions were to be fixed, which he objected to most strongly. He said, 'A good Jew is never in a business where somebody else fixes the rates', so the firm decided under Alfred's propulsion to leave the Stock Exchange and set up shop as merchant bankers. It caused a tremendous stir. They were the leading brokers in the City and there were articles in all the newspapers. Of course, Alfred couldn't foresee that within two years war was going to break out, so it was only in 1919–20 that he really got going. He chose the partners, a remarkable collection of people, and the firm went from strength to strength and became one of the leading merchant bankers.

When I started at Helbert, Wagg in 1934 I got on all right with what in those days were called clerks and mucked in with them. They were the most splendid people for integrity and hard work and devotion to duty. Not probably madly ambitious, as I was, they were content to have a good steady job with a patron like Alfred Wagg. They were better paid and looked after than their equivalent in any merchant bank. One or two of the clerks were literally found on doorsteps in the East End. The firm never had to advertise for staff. If somebody retired or died – they practically never resigned – the head of department already had a list of people who had applied for jobs. The grand total of the firm would have been about eighty people, of which about eight would have been partners. There would have been about fifteen girl secretaries.

It was quite likely that the clerks would stay doing the same work all their lives. 'Upstairs', where I went after about two years, was marginally more interesting. It wasn't a question of taking any decisions, you just did what you were told, keeping the accounts of all the customers. There were quite a lot of family customers at that stage, among our more distinguished list, Monty Norman, the Governor of the Bank of England, and his wife, and a very classy collection of gentry. (There is something about a duke which is always more fun than a dustman.) And we managed five investment trusts, which was also a good source of income. We were the Prudential's agent for Europe. The contact with the Pru dated from the 1920s. Until Alfred set up the firm's group life pension scheme – I think the first in the City – you were dependent on the goodwill of the owners or managers if you got a pension or not.

Among the people at my level of the firm, we were all trying to score points, make no mistake about it. Not necessarily showing how clever we were but how sound and reliable. We were all quite competitive. I was put to work in the trading department, which was more fun because you rang the stockbroker and said, 'I want to buy one hundred and fifty thousand ICI' or whatever it might be. You had to know the prices and let the partners know them and write short notes of any excitements going on – like the Bank Rate going up – which were distributed round the partners. About six months before the war, the chap who bottle-washed for Lionel Fraser got rheumatic fever and Lionel chose me to come and bottle-wash for him. So for six months I did that for the man who was to become chairman after the war.

Until the last year before the war we were very busy but we began closing down all possible commitments. We had got interests in different companies and we wanted to sell the shares and turn everything into cash. No new people were taken on, the staff were encouraged to join the Territorials, which I had already done some years before with the Warwickshire Yeomanry. Helbert, Wagg made up my salary on top of my army pay and it was only when my army pay exceeded my office pay that they stopped doing that. They did that with everybody. During the war, the firm went down to a staff of ten and it was all 'care and maintenance', doing as little as possible. The furniture had been stored to save rates and the firm ticked on on one floor with just one partner. After the war everyone was offered a post again although some were not encouraged very much. Everyone was brought back on their pre-war salary; the firm had an uncertain future and couldn't promise what they couldn't perform.

Quite quickly all the profits went up. I started to learn about investments as opposed to just booking them or buying and selling under orders. If you were clever you learned something every day. There were about six in the department. We were getting business pouring in and for the next ten years we scarcely had a fortnight without a new piece of business. To a great extent it was pension funds. We were not looking to foreign affairs virtually at all on the investment side, and we were trying to get rid of the dukes and duchesses and aim for companies. We were very much the most modern of the merchant banks at the time.

I was made a partner in 1948. You then got a fixed salary and a share of the profits and a tiny expense account. My salary went up from eight hundred pounds to one thousand one hundred pounds and the share of the profits was worth about two thousand. Either at lunch or dinner one saw a lot of people from Eton or Cambridge who had come into the City. At nearly all the leading firms there was someone, more or less a contemporary, that I knew and liked. As they grew up in their firms and I grew up in mine we remained friends, so it was a good relationship later on.

Competitors didn't spot the pension fund business for about six years and by that time we had got a tremendous lead. Our policy was to choose the highest-class, best-run ordinary shares. We either knew the people on the boards or could find out about them easily because we had immensely widespread contacts. We were looking to the United Kingdom and up to a point the Empire; a certain amount from Australia, South Africa, Canada. And of course, America. We were aiming for caution and care, not to hit the high spots and certainly not going with the latest whiz-kid. We were sticking to the old and tried. Nowadays there are three or four hundred people in the investment department of Schroder Wagg (which is partly because the number of clients has grown) and they are managing hundreds of millions. The back of an envelope is not popular now. It must all be annotated and approved and all the rest of it, but that doesn't mean the pension fund or the pensioners will do any better.

The take-over by Schroders of Helbert, Wagg in the 1960s started with the friendship between Lionel Fraser and Schroders' chairman, Gordon Richardson. Lionel thought that, in a changing world, we ought to get bigger. Richardson wanted to modernize Schroders, which was a good steady banking business but had scarcely got a corporate finance division and was pretty old-fashioned on investment. Through the merger Richardson got, at one move, ten partners who were all professionals in a thriving business. We, of course, were much smaller and didn't do any banking: didn't want to and didn't need to.

I didn't regard there as being the slightest necessity for us to merge with anybody and I was dead against it. I was the awkward squad, the only one who really opposed it, but once it had been decided I got down to it and did my best for it. One of the oddities of life is that within a relatively short space of time after the merger Lionel resigned and several of the other Helbert, Wagg people left and in due course I became chairman of Schroder Wagg and of Schroders Limited.

Dundas Hamilton (b. 1919)

My father's firm, Carroll & Co., was tiny; it had three rooms in Copthall Avenue. It was a nice life in 1946. I used to drive up every morning in my father's car – there was no question of the traffic being held up – and park it outside the office. I never locked the doors and every now and then the police would leave a note saying, 'There have been some robberies, people have been stealing rugs out of cars. We think you ought to keep yours locked.' I used to wear a short black coat and striped trousers, my school Sunday uniform. In the City one had to wear a bowler hat and carry an umbrella. I wore stiff, white collars and, on Fridays, an old school tie. If I had worn anything else to the Stock Exchange, I'd have been howled out.

When I joined the firm, my father was the senior partner and there were three other partners. I did everything in the general office. I typed my own letters, I did my own so-called research into statistics. The office consisted of a girl who worked with a comptometer (a sort of machine where you got your fingers in a certain formation and banged away at the keys), a man who kept the books, an office boy and a girl typist. We all sat in the outer office. There were gas fires, the lift went by hydraulics and not electricity, so when you got in you pulled a string and when you got to wherever you wanted to stop you had to grab the string and try and make sure the bottom of the lift hit the right point for opening the doors.

I wanted to revolutionize the office because it appalled me that they had handwritten ledgers. It seemed to me absolute nonsense to rewrite the whole thing in longhand, so I photographed the sheets but nobody particularly wanted them. The older partners thought my photography system too modern. I wanted to have envelopes with windows in them and that wasn't considered to be the kind of business we had – we had the kind of clients that expected sealed white envelopes. So there was a lot of resistance to change. And we were making very little money indeed.

In 1948 I became a Member of the Stock Exchange and a partner of the firm. (I had been a Blue Button for two years during my apprenticeship, running messages on the floor of the Exchange and not allowed to deal.) My father was marvellous and said, 'Now you're a partner you can't have fathers and sons working together. You will believe you know better than everything I as your father say and I will think I know better from my experience than everything you do – so I will retire.' And he did. He thought the younger generation should be given the chance of making something new of the post-war Stock Exchange. He stayed in Surrey, gradually disintegrating because he had no interests. The one thing I learned from him is that once you're out of the Stock Exchange that part of your life ends and you have got to have other interests.

Becoming a partner didn't really change my life. My earnings went down and down, going through another bad period, so from 1948–51 one's reward became very slim indeed. In 1951 my total earnings for the year were a hundred and fifteen pounds plus a hundred pounds tax-free allowance for expenses – on that I was keeping a flat in Chelsea, running a Mark Five Jaguar and having one or two girlfriends. Life was difficult on two hundred a year all in. I managed to modernize the firm a little but I gradually realized I was never going to. The main problem was Claude O'Carroll, one of the partners. He was enormously generous in some ways and astonishingly stingy in others; if I'd made a mistake, crumpled up a piece of headed writing paper and thrown it into the wastepaper basket, it was taken out, smoothed out and I was told to finish it off properly.

In 1951, on the Stock Exchange floor, I bumped into a man called Frank Douglas, whom I'd met during the war and who was senior partner in a much bigger firm called Fielding, Son & Macleod. When he heard I was in my father's firm, he said, 'You're never going to survive. The tendency is for the big firms to get the business. You really ought to be thinking of joining us.' That coincided with my own views and, reluctantly, I resigned from my partnership with Carroll & Co. and joined Fielding, Son & Macleod. In 1958, Frank Douglas led the merger with another firm, Newson-Smith & Co. and we became Fielding, Newson-Smith.

Pension funds were a neglected operation and I realized that nobody else (apart from Phillips & Drew) had really looked into it. In 1954 we started a Pension Fund Department and when we sold the firm in 1985 we were managing two thousand million pounds' worth of money. The 1961 Trustee Investments Act opened our Pension Fund Department to Local Authority funds, which were very large indeed and that took up most of my time in the early 1960s.

In 1960 I also had a brainwave that Japan looked a very exciting economy and might well become the country of the future. We brought two Japanese over for a lecture tour of the institutions in London and Scotland and I went out in 1961 and we specialized in Japanese securities. We were the first firm to do any sort of statistical survey on Japanese companies. Unfortunately it was the Local Authorities versus Japan, so one couldn't spend too much time on the more difficult one and we didn't do as well in Japan as we might. What we ought to have done was spend more money in hiring another person to specialize in Japan but we were a terribly tightly controlled firm and unless there was a very obvious pay-back, we didn't hire anybody.

In 1970 I published a book, *Stockbroking Today*, and that led me to be put on the Stock Exchange Examination Committee, and in 1972 I was asked to join the Stock Exchange Council. A year later Martin Wilkinson, who'd been chairman of the Stock Exchange for twelve years, announced his retirement. George Loveday, his deputy chairman, said he would do two years as chairman and I was put in as deputy, which I think ruffled a few feathers because I'd only been there a year.

1972–5 was the biggest slump in the Stock Exchange, much worse than the 1929–32 slump. The Index went from five hundred and seventy down to about a hundred and sixty, a third of its value. Sixty out of three hundred and sixty Stock Exchange firms went out of business. It was a real financial catastrophe. There was no support for the Stock Exchange as there was for the banks which went bust at the same time. We tried to arrange mergers for those firms that could be merged and the Stock Exchange Members individually contributed to the Compensation Fund that paid out the clients of the firms that went bust. Every Stock Exchange Member put about three hundred pounds extra into the Compensation Fund and that, together with the assets of all the partners in the firms that went bust – and I mean *all* their assets, their houses, their cars, everything – when liquidated paid off the firms' debts. Fortunately in February 1975 the Prudential Insurance Company took the lead and decided to buy up as much of the equity market as they could afford. When they saw the Pru going in, everybody else poured in and the crisis was over.

Big Bang became inevitable when the Competition Act came into force and we found we were up against the Department of Trade because the Stock Exchange rules were a restriction of trade and if we didn't change our rules (and that meant our membership), we were in trouble. Originally we were going to have a court case and we put about a million and a half into solicitors' fees. Ultimately, Nicholas Goodison (who was by this time the chairman of the Stock Exchange) made a bargain with the government that we would relax our rules in respect of allowing in foreigners, allowing non-members on to the Council and abolishing fixed commission. That was really when Big Bang happened. Nicholas was able to postpone Big Bang from '83 to '86, so we had three years to move into it.

All the banks were scrambling to buy up brokers and jobbers and in 1983 one of my jobs as a senior partner of Fielding, Newson-Smith was to decide where we were going. At one time we had six different suitors, all of whom wanted to take us over – they were American firms, a European bank and a London clearing bank. Fielding, Newson-Smith had by then become the number nine firm and in my seven years in senior partnership we grew at forty per cent per annum compound, so that was a pretty big growth and it was a very profitable company. We thought we were quite a snip to be taken over. Ultimately we went to the National Westminster Bank and it turned out to be rather a tragedy.

The National Westminster did not understand the management of that kind of securities operation. They took it on under County Bank, the merchant bank side of NatWest and I think they lost about forty million pounds. A banker and not a securities man ran it. It was a disaster. When we were taken over in 1986 we were just about two hundred and fifteen people. They built it up by 1988 by another three hundred people, I think. Some time that year they sacked three hundred and sixty of them – all the best people went, a lot of my partners disappeared. The firm literally disintegrated. Our firm was one hundred and thirty years old and we had never, in my knowledge, had a loss in any year, not even the terrible slump year. We never had a redundancy. Every year we paid a bonus to our staff and made profits for our partnership but the new owners managed to lose money and staff after two years. It was a real tragedy.

The take-over suited me, personally, marvellously well. I was then sixty-six. I should have retired from my firm aged sixty-five, which would have been in 1985, but they kindly kept me on for a year longer than I should have done in order that I should take my share of the sale proceeds without tax problems.

Leonard Toomey (b. 1924)

When I joined Lloyd's, in 1939, it was in Leadenhall Street and everyone knew their place. It was a magnificent building, awe-inspiring to a kid, not like the ghastly Richard Rogers thing today. Protocol was rigid. The heat in the room was dreadful and you were never allowed to take your coat off, however hot it was, but you'd have no more thought of taking off your jacket than trying to jump over the rostrum. The underwriters were God, they had all the power, particularly the Mariners. Prior to the war and between the wars they had incomes of staggering sums of money. They were arrogant, but by and large they were decent, honest people. They're all dead now.

The active underwriter of our syndicate was Mr Dick-Cleland. He lived six hundred miles away in Scotland and never came near the firm. I never found my background, which was totally different from the rest of the people in my firm, any handicap whatsoever. (Of the other members of the firm, the Dick-Clelands were at Harrow; the Sharmans at Sherborne; Fred Williams went to Wellington.) I've never mentioned it to the man who sits in the next Box to me at Lloyd's, but I discovered his grandfather was the man Holloway Brothers – the firm my father worked for as a stonemason – was named after. I found out by accident when I stagged an issue called Holloway Properties, which was the same family.

I was a grafter, I worked. The fear of poverty was the only drive I've ever had – the abject poverty of my youth and the terror of ever reverting back to it, nothing else. They wanted to make me a partner when I was still in my twenties but we realized that if one of the partners died – two of whom had enormous incomes and no capital – I would become liable for their taxes, so I refused. If I hadn't turned it down, I'd have been the first non-public-schoolboy to be a partner.

We formed a sole proprietorship in the late forties with Mr Dick-Cleland as sole proprietor and, when he died, his son John became sole proprietor and I worked very hard for him in the fifties. John was a nice guy but he never did a day's work in his life – used to go off for six weeks skiing, that sort of thing – and he was an alcoholic. He would have eight or nine salary cheques to sign and he'd do about four of them and then decide he needed to go over to Shorts for a drink, where all the boys that drank at Lloyd's used to hang out. He'd go home afterwards and it was just tough luck on the people whose cheques hadn't been signed because you wouldn't get paid. It was hopeless.

Becoming a Member of Lloyd's was the greatest moment in my life. I wanted to become a Member from the day I walked in there. I sponsored myself with my own money, which was why we had no children for many, many years after we got married and why we used to live with my mother.

We had one room in her house and my wife and I just worked and saved. To go on one syndicate you needed seven thousand pounds and five hundred pounds entrance fee. Most people who work at Lloyd's are sponsored Members which means their firm puts up the money for them. Only one person in the history of my firm had been sponsored and that was out of the pocket of Mr Dick-Cleland himself. Fred Williams offered to help me but I turned him down flat. I wanted to do my own thing and not be beholden to anybody. One minute I'd got enough money together and the next minute the shares dropped and I hadn't got it.

One day, I was sitting at the Box and I wrote all the figures down from the board on a scrap of paper and thought, 'I've got it!' I ran upstairs to see Sid Nicholls, the Registrar of Lloyd's who'd known me since I was a little boy when I joined my firm. I said, 'Mr Nicholls, I've got the money to become a Member.' He said, 'You sure, boy?' I gave him my piece of paper and he put the Corporation of Lloyd's stamp on it – he'd get shot if he did that today. 'You'll get that properly typed up and the accountant to agree those figures, won't you?' he said, and it was agreed. He trusted me. We all trusted each other. It was an enormous amount of trust. I was very proud.

The thing that affected my working life most during the sixties was that Fred Williams, who was senior to me and worked with me in the Box at Lloyd's, went mad. We were on holiday with the kids in Swanage when John Dick-Cleland came down and said, 'You've got to come back. Fred's gone completely round the twist.' I found out that he was suffering from persecution mania. I was very fond of him and didn't know how to handle it. John and I went to see the chairman of Lloyd's and he sent us to the deputy chairman, but we were unable to get a lot of help from the Committee. In the final analysis, I ordered Fred away although I was junior to him. He would ring me at night when I got home from work and I'd have to drive over to Bourne End because he'd say all the food was being poisoned by 'the gang'. Within three months, every window was barred and the only way through the front door was by a combination lock. My wife and I had two safes put in his bedroom where we used to store the food because he thought people were coming in through the roof with poison. I'd drive him off to get bread and we'd go as much as twenty-six miles and visit about twenty bakers because when we got there he'd say one of the gang's cars was outside the shop waiting for him. At the same time I was trying to run the Box, which was an enormous responsibility. Looking back, I was on the verge of a nervous breakdown because I couldn't sleep at all. It was a terrible burden on my wife and family (I had three kids under five) because the firm came first for me. I couldn't be ill because if I'd stayed away the firm would have collapsed. Eventually the police rang me one morning to say that Fred had committed suicide.

At the same time, John Dick-Cleland was ill with cancer of the throat and I wondered if the firm would survive. While John was in the London Clinic having treatment I formed a company in 1963, A. B. Dick-Cleland Underwriting Agencies Limited, of which John and I were the sole shareholders. John died in 1965, leaving me in control of the firm. I was chairman and the Active Underwriter. There was one other Dick-Cleland in the firm, Michael, who was a lovely man. I had a man there, John Kearsey, who's there to this day, who's like the Rock of Gibraltar. Without him, I couldn't have survived.

I started our Members' Agency in 1967–8 and that's turned out to be the greatest thing since sliced bread. In the finish our Members' Agency had about thirty-odd syndicates. I also used to lead a lot of the jewellers' block and diamond dealers' business in America and we did very well out of that for about sixteen years. By the late sixties and early seventies I had a very large income relatively speaking. I can tell you to the penny about my earnings because I've noted everything down since I've started work. In 1947 when I came out of the army and went back into the firm, as a married man I earned four hundred and seventy-eight pounds gross. Ten years later I had an income of about sixteen thousand pounds. Twenty odd years ago I was on syndicates like Dickie Porter's marine syndicate and I'd get a cheque for ten thousand pounds from just that one syndicate. Taxes were high though, eighty-three per cent and ninety-eight per cent on unearned income. With inflation, looking back, I was better off then than I am now.

I've always saved. When I earned a pound a week, I'd save half a crown. There's a lot of people who are very land rich in Lloyds but have no money; they haven't always got the cash, as I have. I could realize all my assets, other than my house, today because I've only got to lift the phone and get hold of my stockbroker and sell everything. But if you've got land, you can't get rid of it – or you won't get rid of it because it's like parting with an arm or a leg for people who've been landed for generations. The only other interests I've had apart from Lloyd's is the stock markets. My wife and I both saved our money and I'd buy a share. The first money we invested was two hundred pounds we'd saved – our life savings – and we lost the lot. I was told to buy that by Mr A. B. Dick-Cleland. After that I've never taken advice from anyone. I used to sit in bed reading balance sheets; it's not been very pleasant for my wife. Except that she's quite wealthy now.

You can lose a lot of money at Lloyd's. But you're told that. I've sponsored many Names at Lloyd's and unfailingly when you go to the

Rota for the Committee at Lloyd's, they always impress upon every Name the unlimited liability aspect of Lloyd's; they are most particular about it. So for Names, after the event, to say they didn't know is a load of cobblers. They're told in no uncertain terms. A lot of the Members lost their nerve following the Stock Market crash of '87 and got out and Lloyd's has never really recovered from it. Suddenly, if you're a Member, you needed a quarter of a million in net assets instead of a hundred thousand pounds.

A lot of the losses that are coming in now were written as far back as the forties. The record for pollution is a loss that goes back to 1897, which was one of the American railroads where they were dipping the railway ties in great pits of creosote and over the hundred years the creosote has spread and polluted everything. There have only been three underwriters in our Box since 1919 – four now that my son has joined a fortnight ago – and if the previous two underwriters were alive now and I said, 'I've just been advised today of a loss which you wrote forty years ago', they wouldn't believe it was happening. Our firm is running out of space for our records – we've had a vault at the Midland Bank in Leadenhall Street for the last sixty years and we can't get another thing in there. We've had to destroy a lot of old records, which I bitterly regret with the losses coming up today on slips that are forty years old.

After 1965 I could see this worsening going on on the back years – it wasn't over asbestosis or pollution at this stage, they were unheard of – it was just general casualty risks and workmen's compensation and malpractice business. I started cutting back on this type of business in America and by the end of 1968 I'd come off every casualty treaty that had ever been written in the States. At the time, people thought I was a nutcase and I was referred to as 'Gloomy Toomey'. People said, 'He's lost his bottle.' For instance, I came off before the worst treaty in Lloyd's for asbestosis, the Travellers Treaty. But even though I wouldn't write under my own syndicate, I've been a fairly big punter and many of the marine syndicates I'm on have written the risks anyway. I've already picked up three run-offs on other syndicates; one in particular hits me and my wife – who is also a Member – and every year it costs me around ten thousand pounds. This isn't very pleasant, it soon eats into your profits. I've left the syndicates now, but I've got the run-offs. I'm not wingeing. It's a fact of life.

The massive increase in capacity at Lloyd's occurred in the sixties and seventies. When I became a Member there were only about six thousand of us and there are now thirty thousand odd. First of all they let foreigners in. You had to be British to be a Member of Lloyd's when I became a Member, it was a written rule, and that's changed in the last ten years or so. In the last ten years, when Lloyd's got so large, a lot of people have become Members who should never have been elected; they're not proper people to be Members of Lloyd's; they get into trouble; they take profits but they don't want to pay. In the old days everyone was far more honourable and people paid up. In the last twenty years it's the brokers who have become the ones with the power in Lloyd's. They all became very rich when they went public. I was a shareholder from day one and I thought it was money for old rope, which it was.

Lloyd's is going to be for big players in the future and the smaller or medium-sized family firms will not survive. Since we moved into the new building the costs there and the staff and the regulatory bodies are so enormous that expenses have gone sky-high and you can't survive if you're smaller. I'm very sad because some of the mega-people in Lloyd's today started off in a small way. You won't be able to start a small firm like ours. We merged with Chesters, Bruce & Wright in January 1989. We had to get bigger or go under.

It's more soulless at Lloyd's now than when everyone knew one another and we were all on one floor of the old building. Now lots of the firms are public companies and they're bringing in underwriters from outside who *can't* have the feeling that I've got for Lloyd's. When I joined, the Corporation of Lloyd's, which runs us, used to be relatively small and there was an immense amount of trust between the old clerks and the people that worked here. Now the Corporation of Lloyd's has an enormous staff and people come and go so fast we don't even know who we're dealing with – you never see the same man twice. I've been in Lloyd's fifty-one years and I sit in the room nine hours a day, five days a week and I've never met the current chief executive of the Corporation.

We've had two years to change three hundred years of Lloyd's and we've been swamped with legislation. It's impossible to do it in that timescale and it's costing the earth. You couldn't put a figure on the computerization of Lloyd's. When we moved into the Rogers building we were told we were going into a paperless society – I reckon they must be chopping down five forests a week to deal with the paper the hierarchy in the Corporation is churning out by the ton. We can't cope with it and as a consequence the whole of our time is spent in meetings – you can look in any of the conference rooms and they're packed all day – so we're doing that instead of underwriting which is what we should be doing.

Lloyds was a marvellous place. Even for people with my grotty back-ground, no barriers were put in your way. It would be foolish for someone of my background to aspire to be chairman of Lloyd's and that's why I never stood for the Committee. There hasn't been a chairman who wasn't a public-schoolboy; I'm not railing against it, but it's why I sent my children to public school. I've been a very lucky person to stumble in there; to have walked into that place when I knew nothing about it and to have had the standard of living I've had and met the wide variety of people I've met. I'd never have made the money I've made elsewhere. I've had a ball in Lloyd's. It's turned a bit sour on me recently but, other than that, I've loved it. About two months ago we put up my lad to take over from me as the Active Underwriter.

Sir Brian Corby (b. 1929)
I joined the Prudential in August 1952. Actuarial examinations then, and substantially now, are taken by people working full-time, studying by correspondence course through the Institute of Actuaries. The exams had a bad name because they took so long – the average time in those days was eight years to qualify. I'd decided I would work hard enough to get through quickly without any failures, which I did. It was an element of self-discipline and encouragement from my wife. I put in twenty hours a week; if I didn't get home until midnight, I still put in my stint. I qualified in 1955.

When I joined the Prudential many of the people I was working with were graduates, all training to become actuaries. By the standards of today it was a leisurely way of working and we gave a great deal of consideration to most issues. Our attitude to customers was not the same as the one we have at the moment; they became almost an interruption in the smooth flow of business, which certainly wouldn't be regarded as an appropriate attitude now. We regarded enquiries as being addressed to us as qualified people who would give a detached professional view as opposed to people who ought to have been trying to further the business of the company. It was more a debating society than a business.

The Prudential has been around since 1848 and has had periods of rapid development and periods of consolidation like any major institution. Really significant developments had taken place in the twenties and, to some extent, the thirties, with some expansion overseas, initially providing services to customers who had emigrated to the British Empire, the bits painted pink on the map when I was at school. The war made us more inward looking and the late forties and early fifties were harking back to the thirties rather than looking forward to the eighties. Virtually all the major institutions had that period of consolidation when you weren't competing with people and by and large you were concerned only to make sure that what you were doing worked well rather than to investigate new departures.

We still have to some extent – it's slightly watered down now – the concept of the Prudential family. The concept was developed more in this century than the last, a strong feeling of rapport between Prudential people, that they all belonged to an entity which was itself caring and would look after them in a positive way. Like all concepts, it can be overdone and, if so, your performance suffers, your customers suffer. We've always been a good employer and we did take it slightly too far and become too paternalistic. The times have changed and the fifties style of management would not be appropriate to the problems of the eighties and nineties. We're in a harsher, competitive, deregulated world.

Around '71 I got involved in a variety of operations in the United Kingdom in connection with the organization of our agencies. That was the beginning of a period of change that was taking place in response to the changing external environment. We began a series of experiments which would alter the way we operate in this country but the timing wasn't right. People were uneasy because they don't like uncertainty and we didn't have the will to push them through it. But what those experiments did was create a climate of opinion within the company that change had to occur. So, in the last two or three years, we've actually made very positive movements to implement ideas not very different from the experiments in the seventies.

The seventies very much set the scene for the eighties in the financial services sector, for example the higher rates of inflation led to concern about one's expenses. Also, the development of technology made things possible which hadn't previously been and the equation between installing computers or employing more staff had a rather difficult solution. (The Prudential had actually been in the forefront of introducing mechanization in the mid-fifties but we saw it as a way of administering our business more cheaply rather than using computers as an integral part of our business to give our customers better service, so a big shift has occurred there.) In addition, we had the beginnings of deregulation, which has blossomed in the eighties and brought the pressure of more competition. It led many of us to reconsider the way we ran our business.

I became Chief Executive of the Prudential Corporation in 1982. In 1985 we went quite heavily into unit trusts, which hadn't been there before and clearly were becoming a more popular investment medium. That was the first diversification. It was a fairly massive entry into a savings market that was not associated with life assurance cover. The second diversification in this country was the estate agency development and we're now approaching eight hundred estate agency branches, which is a rapid move since we only started three years ago. We've also been looking at overseas development. For many years we've been conscious that we were not present in the very large United States market and at the end of '86 we acquired a fairly substantial and rapidly growing company in their life assurance industry. Those are our three major diversifications over the last two or three years.

The Prudential's reliability is absolutely crucial to us. We're in the securities business and that requires the utmost confidence. We have to be very careful as we move from being slightly responsive to being much more proactive (ghastly American word) in the way we run our business. You have to ride two horses but the need for security does not detract in any way from the need to run the business as efficiently and aggressively as we can.

When I started work you very much grew your own timber. We've had to go against that because we were developing specialisms, even in things like personnel management, where if you did try to grow your own timber you lost out. There are dangers of going too far the other way because you might not identify the talent in your own ranks. The concept of lifetime employment that we used to have is no longer with us and we've lost something by that. An interesting remark was made to me a couple of years ago by somebody who was retiring. He said that the most significant change he could think of in the organization in a cultural sense was that if you went back long enough, when you got promoted it meant you could arrive later and leave earlier. Now it meant that you had a particular job to do and the chances are you'd be arriving earlier and leaving later. We have moved from people having ranks in a hierarchy to people having jobs to do. It may sound silly and simplistic but there's something significant in that.

Sir Martin Jacomb (b. 1929)

I was recruited as a director of Kleinwort Benson in 1968. I didn't realize it at the time but Cyril Kleinwort wanted someone who was neither a Kleinwort nor a Benson to come in and neutralize antipathies as there had been difficulty in combining the two cultures after the Kleinwort and Benson firms merged in the early 1960s. I think that's why I was asked, because I certainly didn't know anything about the business.

Initially, I was totally lost. Two or three experienced corporate finance directors explained to me what they were doing and how they worked with their clients and they used to take me along to meetings and show me how they dealt with the problems raised. Gradually you get the hang of it. I wouldn't say I understood how to do the technicalities quickly, but the general principles I understood very quickly.

Whilst I was working at Kleinwort Benson they won the mandate from the Government to privatize British Telecom, at that time by far the biggest equity issue – over three-and-a-half billion pounds – ever undertaken anywhere in the world. I was lucky to be working with two ace colleagues, James (Lord) Rockley and David Clementi.

Mrs Thatcher wanted it to be a stunning success. At first, the concept of wider share ownership was secondary to the primary objectives of raising the money and getting Telecom out of the private sector and properly run. The fact that we had to go to 'Sid' – that is, to persuade the general public to subscribe for massive amounts of shares – became a political objective only after it was identified as a financial necessity. We had regular meetings with Mrs Thatcher and her ministers. She was like a cat with a mouse (her ministers she saw as mice) on issues that were likely to have a political impact. A crucial part of the exercise was making sure that there was a prevailing trend of falling interest rates when the issue came to pass, so the flotation had to be fitted in with overall government monetary policy.

Nothing like the Telecom privatization had ever been done before so I couldn't be confident. It took a year out of my life. The whole thing was a gigantic management job, a juggling act to keep this great juggernaut moving forward and everybody involved under control. We had to make sure there was demand for the shares abroad and in Britain – which led to the development of a completely new type of demand among the wider public here. Overwhelmingly, we had to make sure that there was going to be more demand than shares available. We had to ensure that a management was in place which would mean BT was a well-run concern able to bring growth in terms of increased profits. We had also to see that there was a system of regulation that would allow the profit growth coming from increased efficiency and better management to come through to the shareholders.

For months prior to D-Day, we had a crescendo of activity in our War Room at Kleinwort Benson. The planning was exactly like a military campaign, with levels of people thinking of all the things that could go wrong. Shortly prior to D-Day, the thing started to go massively public. There had been a long PR campaign run by Dewe Rogerson (who came up with the idea of 'Sid'), fed appropriately by us. We then held a press conference for about four hundred journalists, designed to explain enough about the terms of the sale for them to recommend it to their readers – or not – a completely crucial part of the campaign. Such was the interest that the tabloids – the *Sun* and the *Mirror* and their Sunday equivalents – had City comment for the first time in their existence. We wanted them to advise Sids to buy. The crucial press conference was in the Connaught Rooms where we announced that the price was going to be attractive (i.e. low) enough to achieve a certain dividend yield. It was very important not to get a single word wrong. We'd then started out, the bridges were burned and there could be no turning back.

The final negotiation on price took place on D-Day Minus One. It was conducted with Nigel Lawson, who was then Chancellor and whom I'd known as a friend for many years, but that didn't stop it from being a tough meeting. We had then to give instructions to the printer – a massive printing operation which had to be confidential because you couldn't have it in the papers overnight. We went to bed calm but on tenterhooks because you never know what is going to happen in the markets – you can wake up in the morning and find people have taken fright over the whole market. I did sleep, although I was in touch with Tokyo by about five-thirty, but that's a habit of mine anyway. All seemed smooth.

Then all the buttons were pressed. We had a great banner on the Kleinwort building at 20, Fenchurch Street with the price on it. The actual selling was by then out of my hands but I followed it very closely and was also doing press and radio interviews. The result was still uncertain because there was an interval between D-Day and the time when people had to send in their cheques and applications – a no man's land of several days where you didn't know if the flotation had been a success or not.

The scene of action switched to a warehouse in the suburbs where there were hundreds of clerks hired for the occasion to receive the thousands of envelopes and cheques. You can then begin to see a pattern building up but you don't know for sure that it's worked until the last minute before the final time for applications because everybody who knows the markets withholds their application until the last safe minute they can in case the market as a whole goes down, in which case the price for the shares would have been set too high. It was exciting. The flotation turned into a huge success. We were several times oversubscribed. We then had to decide on allocation – marrying what was possible mathematically and convenient on the one hand with what was politically acceptable. David Clementi and I were involved on the one side and there were civil servants who knew Nigel Lawson's wishes on the other. The allocation we devised kept institutional shareholders quite short of stock so they had to buy more to make up their holding to their full allocation or be in danger of being left behind on a share that was going to rise rapidly.

The price was quite steady to begin with, a healthy but not exaggerated premium over the issue price, but then it rose higher than anybody on my side would have liked. Nigel Lawson was slightly attacked for that in the Commons, for selling off the family silver too cheap, but he was robust in answering. (He had a withering scorn for people who didn't understand financial markets.) The price was much debated in select committee meetings afterwards. I don't think it could have been set any higher. Floating an issue is a bit like a see-saw. If you are on the wrong side of the fulcrum you have a massive failure on your hands and if you are on the right side of the fulcrum by definition there are more people wanting to buy than to sell and people will scramble for the shares. Given all the facts I know now, I would have chosen exactly the same price, and more remote events have shown that to be right.

The immediate effect was tremendous public interest in the whole process of privatization and the concept of capitalism, which had a very beneficial effect on the whole country's approach to business and enterprise. It was one element in the whole changed approach to the trade union stranglehold. The work-force of Telecom started by opposing the sale and were won round by the prospect of being shareholders. People had seen the work-force resistance collapse and that Sid certainly wanted to be a shareholder. It made a great swathe of the population feel more involved in the wider productive economy. That was all positive. But it was a disappointment that masses of Sids sold out and didn't remain shareholders. It hasn't gone on to make us yet a population dedicated to productive enterprise as the Japanese or Americans are. It's a not unpopular thing in America for a politician to say, 'I believe in General Motors. General Motors must be successful and profitable.' Our English politicians wouldn't think of saying that business success comes before the health service or the Welfare State. The population doesn't really accept that yet and that's a pity.

George Nissen (b. 1930)
I started work at Pember & Boyle (which had been founded by a man called Pember in about 1870) in 1953. It was pretty obvious that starting to do a routine job would be pretty boring after the amazing indulgence of the marvellous life at Cambridge; it was just an inevitability really. Certainly the lack of holidays was a horrific thing. In most City firms you got two weeks and that seemed very little.

The firm's predominance in the gilt-edged market dated from the 1930s and, by the time I joined, the gilt-edged market was the biggest section of the Stock Exchange turnover in terms of value. I knew the Pember & Boyle office because I had worked there during the long vac for a few weeks. Our premises were excellent – the office was in Prince's Street, right beside the Bank of England. We used to walk through the Bank to get to the Stock Exchange, which was not actually permitted. I spent a year in the office, perhaps eighteen months, and then I spent a year down in the Box as a Blue Button in the Stock Exchange, ending up with a short period as an authorized clerk (that is authorized to deal).

There were certainly plenty of old public-schoolboys on the floor of the Stock Exchange but there were plenty who were not. It was a very equal kind of community, the floor community, which was quite different from the actual offices. The qualifications for a good dealer in the Stock Exchange were in a way the qualifications of a really good barrow-boy. You had to be very quick, you had to have a good personality – not necessarily a very pleasant personality, but you had to have the ability to get on with people. There was always a way into the partnership at Pember & Boyle through the dealing side. It would have been realized that the senior dealer needed to have a great deal of clout in the market and needed to be seen to have the backing of the partners and, indeed, would be a partner. The classic in Pember & Boyle was the senior dealer much of the time I was a partner, an extraordinary and very difficult man who was not much liked. He wasn't on anybody's visiting list, certainly not on the partners', and he wouldn't have made any effort to cultivate the other partners socially. But he made quite a lot of money. He probably regarded us as rather pathetic amateurs. He felt that he was our superior in that he knew the trade much better than we did but we knew that he had his shortcomings, too.

Space near the Stock Exchange floor was very much at a premium because it was important to have your dealing Box as close to the centre of action as possible. The Pember & Boyle Box (a tiny office) was presided over by Miss England, the order clerk, who was a great character and on very jolly terms with everyone. There was a lot of stress, the telephones were always ringing and she presided over the affairs of the Box with a lot of skill.

The gilt-edged market resided at the Bank of England end of the old Stock Exchange building with bits and pieces that went with it, other types of foreign loans, bank shares, and to some extent shipping shares. Then you moved into the centre where the main body of equities were traded. There were one or two special corners where, for instance, breweries were traded. At the eastern end there was a great area devoted to the South African gold mining shares, which was universally known as the 'kaffir market' because the kaffirs were the black chaps who worked in gold-mines in South Africa. That part of the market also attracted things like tea plantations and mining shares and other things. It was always thought that the people who inhabited the kaffir market were pretty sharp practitioners and the price of mining shares was always subject to rumours in a way that probably the market in ICI was not.

There was a strong feeling coming from the gilt-edged area that the kaffir end of the market was an esoteric and strange place. The stock trade of some of the jobbers at that end was taking bets on horses; they were bookmakers. It was accepted that that was what they did and they had a marginal business in securities. There was quite an active business in betting on things and that actually got reflected in the rules at one time – a rule was written prohibiting people from making prices in majorities in an election. But there were plenty of people who would make you a price in the total number of runs in a test match, things like that were very common. The people on the floor were all lively and accustomed to make money out of dealing in things and it was a bit of light relief.

Speculation and making money was the name of the game. Most firms were duly sensible about the kind of business they were trying to do as brokers. But the idea of dealing PA (by which I mean for yourself) was totally accepted and there was very little control over what you did for yourself. Most people did very little but some did enhance their income quite a bit and they ran risks. Increasingly, firms began to have house rules about their staff because there was obviously a danger that if you got things disastrously wrong you could be a financial liability; the firms knew that they would ultimately have to stand behind the bargains for their staff. The whole ethos has changed immensely in this area. Nobody thought that it was a disgraceful thing if you got a tip from somebody who really knew something about what was going on in a company; there was nothing disgraceful about helping yourself to a few shares if you possibly could. At the time of denationalization of the steel companies, we were all very much aware of what was going on and followed it extremely carefully and generally assumed that there were going to be good profits to be made from it. Indeed there were. Most of us dealt in steel shares and applied for denationalization issues and made money out of it. No one thought there was anything bad about that. It was simply that we were tuned in to what was likely to happen and what the general perception was about what would happen to these steel companies.

In those days there was no public gallery at the Stock Exchange so the place was extremely private, its own little world. There were all sorts of jokes and pranks. Occasionally there was a small amount of rough-housing, but not much. There was an enormous amount of flicking of paper darts, quite childish in a way. There were some established characters – there was one man who used to come in with a straw hat on May Day and there was a ceremonial where he was ragged and the hat was stamped on the floor. On Fridays, there was one old boy who used to come in after lunch and a great sort of shouting went up and everybody started singing this song. It was a lot of fun and subsisted until the public gallery opened and people started to behave better.

It was a very curious scene. The waiters used to go round watering the floor. It was very dusty and efforts had been made to try and seal it to keep down the dust but they weren't very successful. There were wonderful watering cans which did a fine sprinkling job. There was a huge amount of wastepaper, really masses cleared up at the end of every day. By the time I got there, the house closed at 3.30. At 3.15 a rattle sounded and smoking was permitted and everybody lit up.

On Thursdays we used to look out of the window of our Box because at 11.45 the Government Broker used to walk across from the Bank of England with his top hat on, accompanied by a messenger, to announce what the Bank Rate was going to be. He walked up Capel Court and went into the Stock Exchange and made an announcement. Usually it didn't change and as he walked down the Court he would make a gesture with his hand and we would all be looking out of the window and would then ring our clients and say, 'No change in the Bank Rate.' If he didn't make the gesture then everyone dashed in to hear what the announcement was; that was a moment of great excitement.

As a Blue Button I was the lowest of the low. You were expected to pick everything up and the idea of being taught was not accepted. You were supposed to know which jobbers dealt in which shares. I don't know how many firms of jobbers there were in 1954 but there were well over a hundred of them and there was no way of telling who they were or where they sat. There would usually be a board on which the names of stocks were written but not all of the stocks that they dealt in or the prices, and there was no name of the firm there at all and no name badges. You had to try and persuade your seniors in the dealing Box to tell you which jobbers dealt in which shares and then you tried to remember who worked for Akroyd & Smithers or Bone Oldham or whoever so that you didn't make a fool of yourself going to ask the wrong person. It didn't help the competitive process at all. It was a sort of convention – 'I made it to the top and I did it through my own efforts and there's no reason why I should give you a leg up' – a slight tradition of that. The people who felt they would probably spend their life on the floor accepted these conventions and probably never really questioned them. I was all right because I was on a social track in a way. Gradually it changed. There was a wonderful thing called 'The Squirts' Diary', which was a book which was kept by one of the firms of jobbers in a shelf and had written in there against every stock the names of the jobbers who dealt. In due course that book was institutionalized and made available to young dealers but when I was first on the floor it was not available.

1956 was a great turning point in my life because I got married and I became a partner in Pember & Boyle. Jumping from doing the job of a clerk to becoming a partner – which in my case was a simultaneous move – was the critical move forward. The shares in the firm always changed hands at a nominal value, a thousand pounds each, and I got one share. You couldn't be a partner without becoming a Member of the Stock Exchange, quite a complicated process, and you had to get at least two people as sureties, who undertook to meet any obligations there might be, but Pember & Boyle found those for me. It was all very formal. You had to appear before either the full Council or the Membership Committee, I can't remember which. You marched in to this large room and there were a great many people sitting round a table. It wasn't nerve-racking really. One felt, as it were, that the Establishment was behind one and would see you through. In our case, Fred Althaus was already senior partner of Pember & Boyle and was a prominent member of the Stock Exchange Council. He knew everybody and the firm had a great reputation.

When you rise to partner, you move into the partners' room – ours had a wonderful coal fire – and you are expected to start developing ideas about things. There were hardly any private clients so it was a business of dealing with the major banks and, increasingly, pension funds and a number of trusts and other institutions. In 1973 I joined the Council of the Stock Exchange and that opened things out in a very big way and it all became more interesting. I became Deputy Chairman of the Stock Exchange in 1978, I was rewarded with a significantly bigger share of the partnership of Pember & Boyle and became senior partner after that.

I became a partner before the 'cult of the equity', a term which described the gradual realization that inflation (which, remember, was a post-war problem) was actually diminishing the real value of gilt-edged stocks and other fixed interest securities all the time, and that the only way that you could cope with inflation was to have a share of the real value of things – like companies – by holding ordinary shares. The cult of the equity was promoted by a lot of interesting people, including a wonderful man called George Ross Goobey, who I think was the pension fund manager for either British American Tobacco or Unilever. He believed it was perfectly reasonable for long-term funds like pension funds to be almost entirely invested in equity. That was an idea that had never been heard of, and pension funds were only permitted to be invested in certain types of fixed interest security, which were gilt-edged and some types of local authority fixed interest stock. The passage of the Trustee Investment Act, which must have been in the early sixties, really did transform investment in these various types of securities.

During the sixties and seventies the volume of gilt-edged issues went up and up and stocks increased enormously. Although some pension funds were pursuing a policy of increasing their proportion of equity, they all had some gilt-edged and they regarded them as a kind of base. It's curious to look back on the extraordinary importance of the Annual Budget Statement; so often a significant change was made in the taxation arrangements which affected the gilt-edged market and the equity market. On Budget Day we all used to sit listening to the radio and ringing up our clients to tell them what the latest thing was. It had a huge bearing on the amount of stocks which were going to be issued. Now Budgets seldom contain anything of great importance in that way. Most of the extremely complicated structure of tax concessions and the imposition of different types of tax have been swept away and the whole thing has been simplified enormously.

As the years went on, the income we made from gilt-edged switching was regarded by the institutions who were our clients as very comfortable and they were always seeking ways to reduce it. They felt it was money out of their pockets, which indeed it was. Some of them were much more critical of the rates of commission charged in the gilt-edged market than others although much more commission was earned in the equity market. Rates were centrally fixed by the Stock Exchange Council. People like the Prudential were always going on about it. It was a kind of formal quadrille. Everybody knew that from time to time the Stock Exchange Council considered the levels of commission and they were reduced in all manner of different ways gradually over the years. I suppose the clients appreciated that and looked for new concessions. I very much admired the position of people like Fred Althaus, who conducted a brilliant rearguard campaign against the commission cutters.

In the summer of 1983 the Stock Exchange Chairman, Nicholas Goodison, made a deal with Cecil Parkinson that the Stock Exchange would eliminate fixed commission scales altogether. Parkinson paid lip service to keeping the distinction between jobbers and brokers, but that only lasted six months.

There was conflict between the jobbing and broking system which operated in the UK and the unrestricted system which operated in the rest of the world. There was a growing unease and real tensions. Many of us felt there was a beauty and a quality about the separation between brokers and jobbers which was very worthwhile. Some of the people on the Stock Exchange Council only voted for the deal with Parkinson on the basis that a real effort could be made to preserve single capacity. Looking back, I'm sure it was an unreal hope but I certainly hoped it could be done and a lot of people clung to the old system and believed the new world would be pretty disastrous.

The people who voted in the great Council debate about the Parkinson proposal realized it was a momentous decision. The fact that London was committing itself to a three-year process involving total change in almost everything was understood to be a challenge. Goodison had asked for five years and I think five years would have been the best time, but it was all done in three. The concentration on restructuring firms was obsessive; you hardly had time to think. If firms hadn't been so busy trying to reorganize their businesses for Big Bang, maybe there would have been better argument from the City about the hugely complicated structure of the Financial Services Act.

With Big Bang, the whole structure of the Stock Exchange was different. There was a very strong feeling that the whole world that we knew was crumbling away very quickly. It was very exciting from the point of view of firms because everyone was madly scrambling to make an arrangement which they thought would be suitable for the future. In our case, Pember & Boyle ended up by getting ourselves taken over by Morgan Grenfell. It was a wonderful deal at the time; Morgan Grenfell offered us a good price, they had the right connections, they had plenty of capital, which is what we needed to run as a market maker in the gilt-edged market, and they were very clever people and could develop the business. The philosophy looked exactly right, although in the event it didn't turn out like that.

We recognized that it was the end of an era. The firm had been around for over a hundred years and people had regarded it as a way of life. They knew perfectly well that nothing was going to be the same again. But all the partners had suddenly become rich in a way that we had never expected to. In April of 1986 Morgan Grenfell became one hundred per cent owners of Pember & Boyle and we moved into 20, Finsbury Circus, the new securities building which they had fitted out, in time for Big Bang.

We took all the staff to a great dinner at Madame Tussauds and I remember telling them that it wasn't the end of the world, it was simply that everything was going to change and it was all very exciting – which I thought potentially it could be. But it became pretty obvious quickly that it wasn't right.

My feeling now is that we maybe expected too much. It was difficult for Morgan Grenfell to analyse the requirements for a securities business and plug in suitable resources. In the end they closed down the whole of their securities business. Fortunately that happened fairly early, so that the people who were good found it reasonably easy to find other niches. If it happened now, it would be more difficult.

I don't think it's any good thinking that something which was basically inevitable was a tragedy. Probably the task was a much more difficult one than any of us thought and very few people have really made a success of it. There were twenty-six or twenty-seven market makers in the gilt-edged market at one time and we're now down to eighteen. Of those there are about five or six who are doing a worthwhile amount of business.

Hugh Peppiatt (b. 1930)

I had had a relationship with Freshfields since I was five when my father joined the firm, and I knew the partners because they would come to our house. It was a small firm – during the war when two had gone into the services, that left about four active partners. The building in Old Jewry was utterly demolished by a flying bomb – I remember the telephone ringing in the night and my father walking off at five in the morning to get a train to London. After that, the firm moved into the Bank of England, where it was when I joined in 1953, in an undeveloped part of Bank Buildings with unpainted breeze blocks and all the telephones and electricity lines ran outside on the walls.

I was articled with my father in about 1954 and I certainly wouldn't have had anything like an interview. There must have been about six or seven articled clerks at the time. We followed the first articled clerks who did not actually pay to do articles. I didn't pay, but equally I got paid nothing, except at the end of the first year we got twenty-five pounds at Christmas as a gift. The majority of articled clerks would have come from upper-middle-class backgrounds that could afford to finance a boy (no girls) through two or three years' articles. About four years later someone – who is now a partner – said he couldn't afford to come to Freshfields and some sort of pay for articled clerks was then instituted.

The articled clerks went round the firm's departments. There was a substantial private client department; now, sadly, closed. We acted for a lot of household names and that's what I cut my teeth on, the buying and selling of ordinary residential houses. At that time, a lot of what I did could have been done in any firm in the country, which worked while Freshfields was quite small beer. We probably got a better grounding in the general principles of law than many students get at big law firms today – including Freshfields – simply because there was more routine work. We were probably not paid much more than provincial firms whereas later

there was a significant rise in the salaries in the City. Today you cannot
deal with the conveyancing of a residential house when the lawyer costs
per hour are 'n' pounds in the City whereas in Wrexham they are 'n'
pounds over eight per hour. This is a bad development but it's econom-
ically unavoidable.

1958, the year I qualified, was the year that things started to change.
The Reynolds TI case [British Aluminium Battle] was absolutely central
to the start of more business activity, and also American business was
starting to come to England, which my father was very influential in
bringing to Freshfields.

In 1960, I and four other articled clerks were made partners in addition
to the seven existing Freshfields partners. We were on the ladder in a
system which you could regard as pretty well assuring yourself of a
lifetime's job. For three of us in the group, that's exactly what did happen;
we stayed our whole lives at Freshfields. It was never said that you were
making a lifetime's commitment but we'd all have thought it slightly bad
form to go off and do something else. In the era of which I speak, it turned
into something you could call a one-way option; it would never have been
in our minds to suggest a partner should go because he was somewhat
weaker than the others. In the harsher economic climate of today, it's a
matter of common knowledge that that is no longer the case. Economics
simply drives it.

Freshfields had generally been considered to be the leading firm but it
had in some respects slipped over fifty years. One reason often cited was
that we acted for the Bank of England which meant, when banking and
financing started to be important, that we did not get as much of the local
banking business as we might otherwise have done. A senior American
lawyer said that Freshfields would never take off until it ceased to have
the millstone of the Bank of England round its neck. Others said
Freshfields would be dead without the Bank. Neither is a correct statement, but it brought inhibitions about the clients for whom we act in that
we would never act for a client in the direct financial field without
consulting the Bank of England. On a number of occasions, I would speak
to someone senior at the Bank about some seemingly respectable bank
and he would say, 'Let me put it this way; I wouldn't if I were you.' That's
all I needed to know. It would not surprise me to find, three weeks later,
some fearful revelation about that institution. So we were saved from
some situations by the Bank, but equally some work did not come to us
specifically because of our connection there. While we could be loyal to
the client, we clearly couldn't do something that was wholly contrary to
any line the Bank had laid down.

My father had been the Bank of England solicitor and I was designated to do the Bank of England work. The Bank never had a legal department of its own, so when the Bank was advising the Treasury, in a real sense we might be said to be advising the Government. We also did all the housing loans for the Bank's staff and there was work in relation to foreign governments. Then there was the bank-note reproduction business; for example, if you produced an enormous poster of a bank-note to advertise something, we would come down on you like a ton of bricks and you'd have to withdraw the poster. Everyone took it seriously. I took it very seriously. I sometimes wonder why, looking back. Of course, in the end we were laughed out of court by many magistrates.

In the late sixties, Freshfields did not have a strong position in the lucrative Euromarkets. We were strapped for resources and didn't have the large teams required to build up positions. Compared to our main competitors – Slaughter and May, Linklaters & Paines and Allen & Overy – Freshfields had fallen behind in size. (There was talk of removing the limit of twenty partners in solicitors' firms and it wasn't an important issue to us, whereas it was to the others.) Not only were we not large enough, we were not getting enough people of good quality. Freshfields had relied on the traditional methods of someone at the club or the school knocking on the door saying, 'Could you take my boy?' and it was soon found that was an extremely inadequate way. Early in the 1970s my role somewhat changed, when I got into recruiting. My overriding priority was to ensure we had a good intake of articled clerks.

I systematically devised a scheme that was pretty novel for the City. I went out to universities in the spring of the year and met dons and teachers, predominantly Oxford and Cambridge, but also Durham, Birmingham, Exeter, Southampton and Warwick, the whole idea being that when we came to recruiting in the autumn they should say to the young men, 'You should think about Freshfields because there's this highly personable fellow called Peppiatt.' We were the first to give little lunch parties for the dons in our building; then I would go to the universities and meet the young men – at the beginning, it was young men but by the end of five years it was men and women and now it's a steady progression where it's fifty per cent women, but it was from a starting point of zero. We had a big blue chauffeur-driven Mercedes (we don't have cars now) and we'd interview at Warwick one day and Cambridge the next, and I thought this had got to be the best job in the world. I loved it.

Then the competition started to heat up and more than once I would handwrite an offer letter without any second interview; I'd just take a view. Richard Ballard, now a partner at Freshfields, had a handwritten letter which I remember taking to his college at eleven o'clock at night. None of us were specialists in recruitment, whereas now we do have such specialists. What has changed today is the numbers. I was dealing in manageable numbers – twenty or thirty people a year, not the seventy or eighty that a big firm takes on now. Socially, the law is massively more open than it was. The recruiting I was doing was a sort of microcosm of what was happening at Freshfields.

In 1977 I moved with my family to the United States and, with another colleague, set up our office there. I was in New York until 1981. It was very stimulating, but I recognized that it was quite a long time to be away from the centre, our London office. That probably said something about my age – I was about fifty – and I'd been a generalist, as most of my generation were. I always knew that re-entry in London would be painful. I came back in September 1981 and I was very glad to be back – my closest friends were here – but I was doubtful about what there was for me to do. If what happened next hadn't happened, it's quite possible that I might have left and gone to do something different.

The senior partner of Freshfields was due to retire and there was the matter of the selection of his successor. I got elected and took over in April 1982. Before long, I was spending substantially all my time on the firm's affairs and that became the pattern of my life for the succeeding six or seven years. It was a big job, being 'Mr Freshfields'. I would try to be routinely in pretty early in the morning and I would work long hours. Work would come home in my mind and people would come at weekends to talk things over. I don't look back on that period as one of great fulfilment, but it was a worthwhile job.

The firm grew very fast during my time as senior partner and it was a very successful period, for which I take no credit. There was more change then than before or after. We tried hard and aimed to catch up with the other guys, with Linklaters and Slaughter and May. When I joined Freshfields there were eight partners and less than a hundred heads under the roof in our one office and it rose during my time with the firm so that there were seven offices (the main one in London and six abroad), eighty-seven partners and a total of nine hundred and twelve heads. With the growing pains, it was very important that the conscience of the firm was well looked after and that it remained stable and well-anchored. There was a lot of very high quality work and we were prosperous. Everyone was busy and there were serious problems of overwork and the attendant personal breakdown problems – family problems which go to the root of a partnership. So there were bad things, but nevertheless as a working, economic unit the firm went from strength to strength. It was certainly very good fun.

I retired in April 1990 after eight years as senior partner. I didn't look forward to retiring as I came up to it; I just had the most interesting job in the world, so I was sorry to give it up. There never have been anything in the nature of consultancies or continuing jobs at Freshfields. No sooner did you walk out that evening and you're no longer a partner. It was actually a very traumatic way of doing things.

Peter Spira (b. 1930)

After I qualified as a chartered accountant, I went back to Siegmund Warburg and, to my surprise, he said, 'Why don't you join us?' I started on 1 October 1957. I remember distinctly thinking on that day that I would never understand the business. I went home and said to my wife, 'I am going to be working very long hours. I don't think I'm going to be seeing much of you so you'd better have a baby to keep you occupied.' Nine months later to the day, our first child was born.

It was an exciting time in Warburgs' history and the British Aluminium Battle – where the City Establishment lined up against Warburgs – was in '58, the year after I joined. Warburgs had gone up in the world in 1956 because they had bought Seligman Brothers, which was a member of the Accepting Houses Committee. The Committee was the élite of the merchant banks. At that time there were fourteen accepting houses and the only way you could become a member of the club, if you weren't already an accepting house, was to buy one. That's why Warburgs bought Seligman's. They were still very much outsiders and not part of the Establishment, which was dominated by the Hambros, the Morgan Grenfells and the Lazards people. If one had been at a drinks party talking to someone from those banks and said one worked for Warburgs, I dare say they would have turned up their noses and said, 'Oh, you work for that shower, do you?' Warburgs was thought of as a Jewish house and there was still anti-Semitism in certain quarters of the City.

The offices were known for being spartan although they had good furniture and beautiful clocks. When I joined, Warburgs was at 9–13, King William Street. There were a large number of Chinese paintings and the significance of these was that there was not a single idle man in any picture. The 'uncles' – Henry Grunfeld, Eric Korner and Ernest Thalmann, the original trio who started Warburgs with Siegmund – all wore black felt hats, not hard homburgs like Anthony Eden's, but bankers' hats. Henry Grunfeld is still at Warburgs, aged eighty-six, and has the finest mind in the City – and part of the great success of Warburgs after Big Bang I attribute to the fact that he was there to guide and advise. He's shy and never sought the limelight so Siegmund got all the publicity but Henry deserved half the credit. It never took him long to come up with solutions and he would laugh to himself and say, 'Well, that's clearly the answer but now we'd better make it look more complicated.' He was quite happy to blind people with science. He and Siegmund were a fabulous team.

I've always regretted that I never learned the alphabet of banking. I never did the sort of training of going round the different departments of the bank. I was thrust straight into the Corporate Finance Department and did no investment management at all. I felt that, as a merchant banker, I ought to know all the answers and disliked having to call in an expert from another department. It shows you how narrow the business was, relatively speaking, when I started that one could even think one ought to know all the answers; it's quite different now the world has become so specialized.

On my first day, I was put in a room with five people, one of whom was Frank Smith, an early director of Warburgs. He was a tremendous element in the success of the bank – one of the creators and craftsmen of the take-over scene – and he didn't suffer fools gladly. I remember being terrified of dictating to the secretary he and I shared because I could feel his eyes boring into the back of my head.

Frank was a kind man, for example, his behaviour to me when I worked on a public issue of Polycell with him. Individuals in the bank had an opportunity to take shares and Frank said, 'You've been working on the deal. Would you like two thousand shares at one and threepence [the placing price]?' I said, 'I'd love them but I haven't got a hundred and twenty-five pounds.' He picked up the telephone and asked the dealer to sell two thousand of his shares and wrote me a cheque for the difference between one and threepence and the market price of one and tenpence halfpenny, with which I bought the back half of the carpet I still have in my drawing-room. It was typical of the man – a way of saying, 'You've got your first foot on the ladder and now you're going up.'

At Warburgs there was an incredible system of communication, enforced with rigid discipline, which was possible because it began as a small group. You would write a note on a meeting and then copy that note to all the people working on the transaction – it was before the days of Chinese Walls when one department mustn't know what another is doing because of conflicts of interest. In my day there was a Yugoslav lady who spoke about eight languages and who would come in at eight o'clock and summarize the 'mail list' – the incoming management mail from that morning and the outgoing management mail from the night before, a carbon copy of which would have been sent to her. All the directors had a copy of the mail list, which got thicker and thicker as time went on. When I became a director in 1963, there were eight directors and we all met at 8.45 every morning and read the incoming mail of the day and copies of that of the previous day and all the inter-office memoranda. At 9.15 we had a directors' meeting and each director had to chair it in turn, which was wonderful experience. We used to have directors' dinners at the Connaught on Monday nights.

Siegmund was a wonderful teacher. We learned certain standards from him, what he used to call *'haute banque'*, a phrase you don't hear nowadays, which meant doing what is right and proper, all the obvious things like thoroughness and the client's interests coming first. There were negative sides. He was very political; you were either awful or wonderful. What was unfair was that people were put in the doghouse for months and left to bite their nails without knowing why. Once, when I was in trouble with Siegmund, as I frequently was, I remember Eric Korner called me into his office and said, 'Spira, you are still under a cloud. But it is no longer raining.' The fact that Siegmund fell out with his son and that George was not going to succeed him meant that he was always looking for a surrogate son and I became one of those for a time. When we were young he regarded us as seed-corn for the bank and would take four or six of us to Bach concerts or the theatre to get to know us and our wives. One used to have high tea at six o'clock because he didn't like late nights. He was exceptionally kind to me and lent me his house in Italy to take my four children on holiday when I got divorced. If you had a personal problem he was extremely good. He was a shy man in some ways, better in a small than a large gathering.

In the mid-sixties I was put in charge of the International Department, very much concentrating on the Eurobond business, which Warburgs had been crucial in developing. The Eurobond's origins go back in history. After the First World War the Americans raised various loans to provide funds for the reconstruction of Europe; these were examples of finance being raised in one market for use in another. Siegmund was very conscious of these and he was also very close to Jean Monnet, sometimes known as the Father of the European Community. One of the first institutions of the EEC was the European Coal and Steel Community and it raised its first international loan in the New York market through Kuhn Loeb, an American house which was a leader in the bond market at the time. Siegmund was a partner of Kuhn Loeb and he and a colleague, Gert Whitman, thought it was ridiculous that the loans should be done in New York when about seventy per cent of the money was being raised in Europe. They thought, 'Why not start a bond market in Europe?' There was the right atmosphere in London, which had always been strong on the entrepreneurial side and, although we had exchange control, the Bank of England was always extremely flexible and positive about trying to establish London as the financial centre of post-war Europe. The Eurodollar market grew quickly. In the early days the bonds were quoted on the Luxembourg Stock Exchange because the London Stock Exchange made complications; they were a pretty stick-in-the-mud organization with rigid rules and weren't particularly interested in innovation. Eventually the Stock Exchange saw the light – it was losing out on what was going to be a very big business – and we were able to quote the bonds in London.

The Eurobond business attracted publicity out of proportion because it was so new and had a mystique about it. It was an extremely useful calling card in developing other business, for example, Warburgs' business with the Japanese. In about 1962, a senior director at Schroders (Alexander Hood) organized the first post-war delegation of senior British bankers to go to Japan, and it included Edmund de Rothschild and Siegmund. Siegmund's enthusiasm was fired particularly by meeing Jiro Shirasu, a very feudal type of Japanese who had been educated internationally (he was proud of his Cambridge affiliations) and who played a crucial role in the reconstruction of Japanese industry. He became an unofficial adviser to Warburgs and would organize business dinners for us in Japan. I first went there in 1964 and from then on I probably went two or three times a year and would spend quite a bit of time with the Japanese when they came to London; certainly a senior Japanese would need to be greeted and entertained.

Warburgs has changed out of all recognition. When I joined, there were a hundred people and they now have five thousand and have become a power in the land. I left in 1974, when I was forty-four. Although Siegmund was living in Switzerland he would be on the phone for hours every day and his presence in the firm was as great as ever. I was tired of the fact that septuagenarians still ran the place and, although one was in a position of seniority, it was frustrating to be treated, to a certain extent, like a small boy. Quite a number of people couldn't stand that. They knew Siegmund wasn't going to change his spots, so they left. Some people will tell you that there was jealousy between David Scholey and me – we were both made vice-chairmen on the same day – but there was never any jealousy between us. What did come into it was that I had been in the City twenty years and the prospect of doing the same old thing for another twenty years horrified me. I was thinking, 'What else can I do?' when the opportunity to go to Sotheby's came up. The greatest compliment I was paid when I left Warburgs was a note from a young man I didn't know at all well, who wrote, 'Sorry to see you go. You're the only reasonably competent merchant banker I know who is not a total shit.' I thought if you could get that accolade and be only a partial shit, you were doing pretty well!

After eight years as Group Finance Director of Sotheby's, Peter Spira returned to the City, as vice-chairman of Goldman Sachs International (1982–87) and then as deputy chairman of County NatWest after the Blue Arrow affair (1988–1991).

Warburgs is an example of a successful house which tackled Big Bang in the most expensive way. They bought Rowe & Pitman, one of the top jobbers, plus Mullens, the Government Broker. They had an élite group of companies with a very good merchant bank management. Another crucial factor, not often mentioned, is that the executives in those firms have known each other for a very long time. They would have been at school and university together, done National Service together, worked on a lot of transactions together. Taking it to its ultimate, there were two brothers in the firm they bought, Brian Peppiatt, joint senior partner at Akroyd & Smithers, and Robin Peppiatt, a senior partner of Mullens. That's an example of a group of people who were '*sympathique*' to each other and made it easier to meld the cultures. There were houses like Lazards who said they were not going to have anything to do with Big Bang and decided to stay small and concentrate on merchant banking rather than trading and broking. They're the ones who've come out of it best. The ones who took the middle course, like Kleinwort Benson, didn't actually appear to shine.

When I joined County, I thought it was an up-and-coming merchant bank and my role was to help it into the first league. My contract was for just over three years and involved working four days a week (for health reasons). On 11 January 1988, my first day, I went to my first board meeting and the first thing that happened was that Brian Winterflood, whose team of jobbers County had bought as a part of their Big Bang strategy, stood up and read a statement saying he was resigning. I can't remember whether he said he was taking the twenty-eight people in his team with him or whether the departure of the most important part of County's trading team just followed. I remember turning to a neighbour and asking if this was normal form at weekly board meetings and him laughing and saying, 'Well, more or less.' It became apparent by the end of that day that morale was absolutely rock bottom. That was the day the challenge started.

Five weeks after I joined, the Chairman and Chief Executive left in the aftermath of Blue Arrow. Looking back, I had not done sufficient homework before I accepted the job at County, which was naïve of me. No one suggested that there were problems, but that's no excuse and I should have made it my business to see what the situation was on that front. (Had I discovered, I suspect my decision to join would have been the same; the fact that I'd joined after Blue Arrow and wasn't tarnished in any way was an important factor.) It was a period of not very high-pitched business activity, there was a lot of holding the place together, dealing with the people problem, keeping doors open with clients. The crescendo was in mid-December 1988 when the DTI announced they were launching a full-scale enquiry into Blue Arrow.

The campaign against us in the *Economist* kept morale low and we lost several mandates because of it. It was extremely difficult to keep people together as, quite understandably, the head-hunters were crawling all over us. Although we had a completely different senior management post-Blue Arrow, from the clients' point of view there was still uncertainty about what the outcome was going to be and so the business flow began to drop. We had one very important deal, acting for Nestlé when they acquired Rowntree, where Nestlé were totally loyal to us, but unfortunately it wasn't enough to hold the flood tides back. We had to keep our contacts up with clients and potential clients on the basis that Blue Arrow would blow over in due course, so we had a lot of depressing client cultivation in the knowledge that it was all for some way in the future. The clients, individually, were extremely understanding and said, 'We wish you luck, but you can understand we can't afford to take a risk in case something really unpleasant comes up.' Which, of course, eventually it did.

The fact that I had a retirement date fixed meant that psychologically I was under relatively little stress. My whole time at County was during the crisis and low level of business activity, so I didn't go from a peak of activity into retirement. I'm still a director of NatWest Investment Bank and I'm a consultant to County and visit Japan twice a year for them.

Jack Spall (b. 1930)

When I was seventeen I joined an East Indian merchants, Wallace Brothers' in the City as a 'gofer'. There was a big pile of used envelopes and a big pile of sticky labels and I'd wipe them with a sponge and stick them on, that was my job. Eventually I was allowed to touch the stamp book – there were no franking machines, of course – and to enter things in it, like 'To Messrs Smith & Jones – 2d.' The firm was an importer of teak and had a general merchanting business with India – coir matting and tea and things like that – and it exported bicycles and railway engines and things.

It was a family firm, the biggest shareholder was old Dandy Wallace, who lived up in his country estate in Scotland. Another of my jobs was taking letters to the directors' room for signature and standing there with one of those rocker blotters. That's when I thought I should like to be a director of a company because they had a very nice time – came in after lunch on Monday, went off to the country on Friday afternoons. And I thought, 'That's what I want to do.' That's when my ambition started to take hold.

In those days in the City a man used to come round and light the gas lamps. We had coal fires and the housekeeper, Charlie Elliot, a delightful Cockney who used rhyming slang, would come and fill up the coal scuttle. One of the directors – they all looked a hundred and five but were probably in their fifties – used to want me to go and get cigarettes for him, which was the worst possible job because you couldn't buy cigarettes after the war and I'd have to tour the City. It was the time when there was a House of Bewlay in Throgmorton Street, a big shop with different kinds of mixes of tobacco. There were plenty of tobacconists but all with their cigarettes under the counter – you had to wheedle away.

The whole aura of the Bank of England was really quite something in those days. I remember going in that enormous portico with the huge copper doors and walking through the tessellated pavement and turning left into the Cashier's office. All the notes were new, of course, and these very smooth men (who were so different to the people in the ordinary clearing banks) had this wonderful knack of getting hold of a hundred notes of one kind or another and fanning them into a very extended fan, and they'd just run their fingers through it and count that way. As a seventeen-year-old, I just stood and gazed in awe and amazement. When I got my little stack, I tried to do the same thing, but there weren't enough notes!

I went and did National Service in late '48 and came out in May '50 and came back to Wallace Brothers. Around '57, '58, the Coffee Futures Market opened in London and Wallace Brothers had bought an interest in an East African coffee outfit and started trading on the futures market under the name of Leslie and Anderson. The war had stopped all these things and there was rationing till '53, so it took a long time for these markets to get going again. Wallace Brothers had an older man and a young man to do the coffee trading. The older man left and I was put into his place and I went into the coffee trade. I then went to Hamburg for three weeks to learn how to taste coffee, my first trip abroad.

The first thing I was taught about the futures market, the most difficult thing for people to understand, is that you can sell something you haven't got. And sell short. It's paper trading, quite exciting and nerve-racking. The Coffee Exchange was in Plantation House in Fenchurch Street. It was a very large room with various rings around for trading, for example, rubber, shellac or coffee. (Shellac was used for paint but more importantly for 78 r.p.m. records and the shellac market didn't last very long because it was overtaken by plastic and chemical paints.) Cocoa was in a different room, sugar was in a different room.

We all stood round in a ring and shouted, about twenty or thirty people with their orders to buy and sell at various prices – I wasn't very good at it. The atmosphere could get quite intense and fist-fights sometimes happened. It was difficult but it was good because there were a lot of people about my age in the coffee market, they were a very nice bunch and so it was very enjoyable. It was an open outcry system and it worries me that the Stock Market people now sit in front of screens. Perhaps you get more mistakes when you have people meeting but it generates activity and excitement, even the noise. If in New York you get the silver market going like hell, that will bring up the noise level and affect the oil market and so on – the buzz is contagious and it's very difficult to believe that can happen in front of a terminal.

I was only in the coffee market for about two years because we lost money in coffee – I think it was twenty thousand pounds – and so Wallace Brothers decided to close the whole thing down in 1961. They offered me a job to stay but I'd had a taste of a more exciting world in the futures market. I'd worked for Wallace Brothers for fourteen years and I knew of no other existence. It was a leap in the dark. Merrill Lynch at that time was very small indeed in London, there were about thirty people for everything – the commodity side was two fellows and a girl – and I heard they wanted somebody else and went along. They gave me a psychological test, it didn't seem to be earth-shattering, Mensa stuff. I didn't hear anything and I rang and kept being fobbed off and then I rang and spoke to the manager, Sherman Gray, a delightful soft-spoken, grey-suited, tall, Gary Cooper style of American, and he said, 'Gee, Jack, what we figure is the company you're working for, it's a pretty easy life and we don't think you'll be able to take on the more onerous hours and things.' That made me absolutely furious and I went round there and banged the table and said, 'How ridiculous!' I have a temper and I can get cross and that swung the whole thing in my favour.

The transition to Merrill Lynch wasn't particularly easy, it was a complete culture shock. Its offices were just by Fenchurch Station and it was a whole new ball game to me. People earned a lot of money, there was a sudden display of wealth, which I was unused to. I wanted some of it, in the normal way. The offices were grotty. Rain used to come through the roof, they tried to tart it up a bit but it was unsatisfactory. Most of the dealers were Americans and because it was the early days of Merrill Lynch in London, there was a good spirit of camaraderie and help, no great rivalries. It's called 'Mother Merrill' in the States. It wasn't paternalistic in

the way that Wallace Brothers was, but we actually got paid money and
that was the difference. One of my colleagues was a woman, who was
absolutely spot-on and one thought, 'God, I'll never be as good as she is.'
I probably thought, 'My God, if I can't do better than a woman, then . . .'
But she's just a sweetie, a delightful girl. She left to have a baby.

In '64 I went to America for four months to the Merrill Lynch School in
New York to take exams to become a registered representative. Wall
Street was a lot of fun, different and exciting. In London at the time, 'My
word was my bond', but there it was always, 'Let the buyer beware'. After
America, I was what is known as an Account Executive. I'd left Wallace
Brothers on nine hundred a year and in five or six years I was earning five
or six thousand a year, which in those days wasn't bad money. Then, in
'67, I had a not particularly good clientele, so I thought, 'I'll try for silver,
I'll try for plywood, and I'll try for lumber.' I knew a little about plywood
(which was a new market coming in) and about lumber but nothing about
silver, and the silver turned out to be a bonanza and I got paid quite a lot
of money. It's really the most enormous poker game in the world and if
you get it right you're a world champion and you walk home and your feet
don't touch the pavement. If you get it wrong, that's something else again.
You have to shrug it off and say 'I'll get the buggers tomorrow'. I carried
on till 1970 when I left to go to Sharps Pixley.

I wasn't particularly looking for another job at the time but I'd been
working as an Account Executive for Merrill Lynch for nearly ten years
and I suppose I was getting dissatisfied with what I was doing. I was
making a lot of money but taxation was eighty-three per cent so there
wasn't a great percentage in earning a lot of money in those days. I always
figure that at forty a man either changes his job or finds a mistress or
something like that, so I changed my job. I was doing a lot of business with
Sharps Pixley and was chatting to one of the fellows there and must have
had a particularly bad day and said, 'If you get any more jobs in the vault,
let me know.' And it went from there. I was ready to move into an English
company. Merrill Lynch taught me a great deal but I never regretted
leaving.

There were really only five main people in the silver and gold market in
London in 1970 – Mocatta & Goldsmid, Rothschilds, Johnson Matthey,
Samuel Montagu and Sharps Pixley. Mocatta had been involved since
about 1600 and reckoned they pre-dated the Bank of England and there
was still a family member, Jock Mocatta, in the firm in 1970. Sharps Pixley
was founded quite late, about 1850, and the original Pixley was a Bank of
England official. In fact, Stuart Pixley was the MD when I joined although
the firm had been bought by Kleinwort Benson in 1966. Ernest Kleinwort
was semi-retired and Cyril Kleinwort was running the bank – he thought

gold was an anachronism and even when we made a lot of money in '73 I felt he wasn't all that happy about it; he would have preferred it to have been made in banking or investments. We were not terribly involved with Kleinwort's because we were an autonomous company, although personnel and the payroll were handled by Kleinwort's, but we had our own board and weren't even in the same building at that time, although we later joined them in 20, Fenchurch Street. I joined Sharps Pixley in September and became a board member in the New Year.

The bullion market is not a futures market, it's a physical market; I buy from you and you have to deliver it to me tomorrow and I pay you the money tomorrow. When we wanted to ship the gold or silver, a forklift truck would go to the vaults and load it. We had vaults in Tooley Street, old cheese vaults, and we were frightened of the floor giving way under the weight. One of the porters lost his bicycle because a pallet collapsed and a ton of silver descended on it! The porters used to tell me how in the past they took gold round on a top of a bus, wrapped in a bit of newspaper – they'd have to take five bars to one or other of the banks for collateral. In people's minds gold has a connotation, it means a very great deal emotionally. If you have a bunch of hardbitten journalists and you hand them a four-hundred-ounce bar of gold, the first question, whether it's them or a group of schoolboys, is 'How much is it worth?' And you say, 'A hundred thousand pounds', and they're all delighted to hold this shiny chunk of gold. A good gold bar looks really something.

I was with Sharps Pixley for eighteen years – there were about twenty-five people when I joined and at our peak we probably had eighty-five and by the time I left in 1988, about sixty. (Technology changed enormously but I'm never quite sure whether computers reduce costs or not.) I was running the dealing room for years and I went to Hong Kong for a year to deal when we decided to open a Hong Kong office – it was so-so successful. And then I came back, went into the dealing room again and then became Deputy MD, then MD and Deputy Chairman, which is what I did until I retired. The retirement age was sixty and I was fifty-eight-and-a-half when I left. Things were changing and I'm not altogether sure I would have been entirely happy if I'd stayed. I have always mistrusted older men who become 'Hail fellow, well met' with younger people, it's patronizing, it doesn't feel right. I don't really see how a sixty-year-old could be matey-matey with a twenty-year-old. I'm quite anti that.

The City has changed. When I started off, most companies were paternalistic and there was tremendous loyalty from the people to the employer and the employer to the employee. Also, because of the high taxation rate, it wasn't really worthwhile anybody moving from one company to another – if you got ten thousand pounds a year more, you got seventeen hundred pounds out of it and there wasn't much point in destroying your life for seventeen hundred pounds. So people stayed within their niches and this rather cosy situation built up. Then the tax rate came down to sixty per cent and people started becoming more mobile, and when it went down to forty per cent even more mobile. People became greedy. And the employers became less loyal to their employees because they were paying them vast sums of money and if they didn't perform they were out. So both sides round, it altered the situation. As much as anything it was the reduction in income tax that altered the whole situation in the City. People got paid too much in the end. You can't pay someone five hundred thousand pounds a year and expect to make money at the end of it. You have a twenty-five-year-old today and say, 'Here you are. Here's a telephone. Now deal.' They're bound to go crazy because they know they've got to make enough money to cover their five hundred thousand pounds a year or whatever. It never made any sense.

Sir Kenneth Kleinwort (b. 1935)

When I joined Kleinworts in 1954 it was a wonderful old building on the same site as the now twenty-two-storey tower at 20, Fenchurch Street. There was a wonderful high ceiling in the banking hall, going up the equivalent of two storeys.

As I was growing up, my father had described the general notions of the business; in those days the main part was the financing of the movement of goods internationally; the movement of wool, for instance, from Australia and New Zealand and Uruguay to the big wool-combing plants on the Continent and up in the north of England; the movement of cigars from Cuba to the various wholesalers on the continent of Europe and in the UK; the movement of meat from Argentina to Europe.

When I joined the firm, my father and uncle were in charge of the day-to-day workings of the bank. They complemented one another extremely well. My father was certainly one for detail whereas Cyril much more took on the overall general view of the underlying soundness of a transaction. When they first started in the business, they ('the boys') and my grand-father sat in the same room together and they learned quite a bit by listening to their father either talking on the phone or to managers who came in to consult him. My grandfather was an exceptionally successful businessman. He was invited by the Governor to go on the Court of the Bank of England whereupon the old boy turned to the Governor and said, 'You've got your Bank to run, I've got mine to run. I prefer to continue running mine rather than have anything to do with yours.' Running the family business with 'the boys' excited him so much that he just wanted to concentrate all his time and energy on that. When he died, my father and uncle were young men of about thirty-four and thirty and had been in the bank for about ten years, learning the business under the supervision of the grand old man.

I must have arrived behaving like an extremely nervous kitten. I did a five-year traineeship going through practically every department in the whole building. Most people coming in at a young age were taken on the payroll but they were taken on as, for example, a potential Collection Department Clerk and then sat down and learned the job, whereas I was being rattled around from department to department to have an overall appreciation of the entire business. I lunched with the partners quite frequently because it gave me an opportunity of hearing them talk business and therefore of learning from them. At the end of six months I was enthralled by the whole thing, so fascinated that I never looked back.

My early years at the bank, the middle and late fifties, were pretty stable. We as a house were not involved in the Aluminium War. It was one of the first major contested take-overs and it was thought that the tactics used by some of the firms involved were perhaps 'not quite what one does in the City, old boy'. It was when, if you like, Americanized methods started to be applied in the City and the whole atmosphere became less smooth, less gentlemanly than it had in been in the past; a wave of toughness hit the City. It was inevitable to a certain extent if it can be perceived that the methods being used on the other side of the Atlantic were bolstering the p. and l. account on the bottom line at the end of the day (maybe in the course of that process a few people got a bloody nose) and that those methods were going to come across and be applied in the City. It was a relatively slow process which then gained momentum as the years passed.

My father and Cyril saw the changes coming. Perhaps they tried to put off the evil moment for a time but the fact that we had a merger in 1961 between Kleinworts and Bensons is a sign that we saw the inevitability of the getting-together of two complementary businesses, one being basically a commercial banking operation, financing world trade, the other being basically an investment banking business with corporate finance activity as well.

The merger came, as so many things did in those days, through personal contacts, individuals in the two separate entities getting to know one another and then the thought process dawned and the seeds were sown and it just sort of germinated from there. The announcement had to be kept totally secret until the last minute because you couldn't possibly afford to let it leak out because there would have been gambling going on, people buying shares on the Stock Exchange on a whisper that something was going to happen.

It was all very exciting. Effectively you threw two teams of people of roughly equal size together, into a pot where everybody was fighting for their future. What we'd never seen before in a family-run business was that with the passage of time you'd get the development of political in-fighting, people jockeying for position, thinking about who was going to be the next chairman, et cetera and so forth. My father was the first chairman of the combined banks and he and the deputy chairman had their work cut out to try and and stop too much open rivalry.

So the scenario was really very different. You were responsible to the public because the public were shareholders in the combined enterprise, whereas before you were responsible to yourselves because you were the owners. By the time we merged, I had the very most junior managerial status that you could have. My perspective of the future was completely different. I didn't really think about it. I just concentrated on trying to do the job I had to the best of my ability and just hoping that if I did it well that would be recognized and I would reap the rewards in due course. I was extremely aware of the fact that I was only ever going to get promotion some time after I would have got it if my name had been Smith, because the powers that were there were going to make sure that nobody could possibly argue in any way that there was nepotism or whatever you like to call it.

My father retired in 1966; he went a year early so his younger brother could have an extra year as chairman. My uncle retired at sixty-five and went upstairs on to the holding company and was chairman of that, succeeding my father. Even when he was non-executive chairman of the holding company, he was still in the office every day and one could go and see him whenever you wanted. He was a sort of fatherly figure to be consulted, you could talk to him about absolutely everything. But when he finally closed up his desk and vacated his room, obviously the atmosphere changed. It was a pretty serious loss. There was a big blank area because he was no longer around.

In about 1971 I was promoted from senior manager to a director and I took over as director in charge of commercial banking in German-speaking Europe. I visited Germany virtually every other week. It could involve as many as forty customer visits in a week and you were moving from town to town after work in the evening. It was extremely exciting, very rewarding. I used to do a calculation on the flight back to London as to how much business I'd generated, what the potential profit might be, just to make darned sure that would pay for all my week's expenses.

Obviously, the absence from home was quite a strain but the adrenalin of the whole thing kept one going. But I do admit that you get home on Friday night and I tended to sleep right through until mid-morning on Saturday. From the point of view of seeing the children, it really didn't make any difference to them if I was commuting up and down from Sussex to the office in London on a Monday to Friday basis; I would leave in the morning before they woke up and I would be back in the evening after they had gone to bed, so they probably didn't see me (or very seldom indeed) between Monday and Friday evening. From time to time there were social activities either on a Saturday or a Sunday but it certainly wasn't a heavily involved social programme, I couldn't have taken it.

After I'd done the German part for many years, I then switched to the whole of Latin America, which meant not less than four trips a year, each of three weeks' duration, which was a killer because my Spanish was nothing like as good as my German, so I had all the language strain on top of everything else. And of course, the distances were absolutely vast. Life was just becoming too much of a strain and I could see disaster looming around the corner unless I let up very substantially.

In 1976 I left the board of the bank, which is the executive side of the group, and became a director of the holding company, Kleinwort Benson Lonsdale plc. I went to live in France in 1976. Tax played a not unimportant role because in those days a Labour government was in office in the UK and with the fairly substantial family I had in those days and the level of outgoings I was running, it was a question of changing life-style and changing scenery as well. I felt I'd had enough of the rat race by then and I wanted to be around for a few more decades to share the life with the rest of my family rather than end up in a wooden box prematurely. My working life changed very substantially because, being no longer resident in the UK, I could no longer be an executive director of the bank, so basically I had to give up all my executive functions.

I've lived in Swizerland since September 1985. I attend all the board meetings in London. I still try to feel part of the City. The person in the City who I've stayed closest to, who was at Eton with me (although he was a few years older) is Bruno Schroder. When my first son was born, he was the person I asked to be a godfather; we've been close friends from the very earliest days onwards and that really goes back to a relationship between his father and my grandfather and then his father and my father and uncle. They were very close in that they understood each other's business extremely well; they were always comparing notes and helping one another out.

Big Bang produced circumstances where everyone was in a sense moving in the dark, making very major decisions. It was quite different from the normal decisions that bankers have to take every day, which are important in their own right but not quite so vast in their long-term effect. This was probably the decision of the century. It's a completely different game and a completely different set of rules, unknown territory. All the various houses in the City made their preparations; some did it one way, some did it the other, there were always variations on the theme. Probably almost everybody would admit today that they hadn't foreseen how drastic the changes were going to be and that they hadn't done enough background spadework to prepare.

Some people took the route of buying an existing stockbroking firm and others took the route of becoming more of a niche player and hiring individuals and putting a team together. By the time we actually got round to taking the decision in the affirmative (if there had been a unanimous decision one would have moved much earlier) that we did wish to buy a firm, there were relatively few left that hadn't been acquired by other people. Grieveson Grant seemed to fit from the point of view of the customers they had and from the point of view of the size and what it was going to cost to buy them. They became housed at 20, Fenchurch Street. We've gone from a firm of a hundred-plus people, including everyone from the commissionaires and the tea-lady upwards, to a worldwide group of close to three thousand. I come into the office once a month on my trips over to London and quite often I will go down in the lift and I won't recognize a single face.

We've never had a hostile bid at KB so far. A fairish percentage of the ordinary shares are in what I would call family hands, that really means in the hands of the descendants of the two sons of the original founder of the firm, namely my grandfather and my great-uncle. All their descendants – which means thirty or fifty of them alive today – between them would have around a twenty per cent shareholding, so the chances of a take-over are minimal. It's not a worry.

Lord Rothschild (b. 1936)
I made a fairly quick decision to get out of the bank and learn, as soon as I joined it, because it was a very family atmosphere, and I think quite a difficult place to learn in. And therefore I went off to Cooper Brothers, the accountants, for a year, to do some investigation work. And then I went to Morgan Stanley in America. And then I joined two skilful financiers and worked with them for a year: Herman Robinow who had been one of the original colleagues of Siegmund Warburg, an investment

expert, and the other was Clifford Barclay, an accountant. Robinow was of the old German Jewish school, and a wonderful person to learn from. He had that kind of discipline and dedication, resolve, strength of character, which is very rare in England. And that, those virtues – his steeliness, discipline, powers – all those things, you know, impressed me very much. And therefore I learned a little bit of the rigours that I think are necessary if you're going to be a successful investment banker. Having an attention to detail, and being serious.

When I first arrived, the bank was very family-orientated, rather run-down, frankly. It had had problems during the war, and it had recovered from those problems, but its level of activity was pretty modest when I was there at first. It ticked along, but without much dynamism or real point, perhaps. They'd been slow in getting outsiders of any stature to come into the bank and perceived the bank as being a family business to be run by the family. And, of course, we were, even then, you know, thirty-five years ago, moving into a more competitive era. And they were slow to adapt to the new situation. I don't think they were particularly ambitious. They were sentimentally ambitious: I mean, they wanted the Rothschild flag to go on flying, but their first priority, I think, was that it should fly under a family mast, and didn't really want outsiders involved to any great extent.

They lost most of their capital at the beginning of the war. They had very little business, frankly, in the thirties. Those were dark ages for the Rothschilds, in particular in England, in the thirties and forties, and fifties. Up to the turn of the century, the bank was extremely important. But its decline in terms of power and influence and wealth really started shortly after the First World War, and continued for a long time. It's been quite successful in rebuilding its capital in the last decade. But it had a very difficult period after the war.

I was expected, I think, to animate the business, make it more lively, you know, to go out and get business, to do the things that were then becoming fashionable and profitable for merchant banks, like corporate finance. There was the important period after the taking away of the Interest Equalization Tax in 1963, which made it possible for what are now known as Eurobonds to be issued globally. Before that, that type of business was really done in the American market. So the traditional business of N. M. Rothschild, which was raising loans for foreign governments and foreign entities, became possible again. And we were very, very active indeed in that business. We won an incredibly important piece of business with the Transalpine Pipeline Company, which was a huge pipeline going through three countries in Europe, which was owned by the twelve leading oil companies. And that was a fiercely fought-over piece of business. Warburgs were part of our syndicate. We actually led it, and the prime responsibility fell on me. It was a very complicated thing to do, because we had twelve banks, I think, in our syndicate. There were twelve oil companies. Very prestigious. I can't remember how old I was, I think I was under thirty, but, you know, I had to orchestrate these giant meetings with all these characters present.

So we became, as a result of that, once again, an international investment bank. And I think that was important in terms of giving a new life to the bank.

I shared a room with the non-family brains of Rothschild's, a chap called Michael Bucks, who was the Chief General Manager. I think they allowed him to become a partner, at the end. But he was the chap who did all the work. And he and I got down to trying to develop the business. Because I was incredibly young, a product of nepotism, even though I'd done these two or three years outside. I found myself in a very dominating position, almost immediately, and probably when I was far too young.

I was in a bank which was controlled by cousins of mine who were many years older than me, and suddenly they had this incredibly active younger cousin pushing them the whole time to do more. And I'm sure they found it uncomfortable and brash and, at times, dangerous. Just the sheer pace of doing things. I don't think we were taking huge risks with our own money, but the pace became totally different.

We used to have regular partners' meetings every morning, and then it became a Limited Company. And then we would have meetings of the Executive Committee, which was democratized to some extent. There were non-Rothschilds on that Executive Committee fairly soon.

I stayed in the bank for seventeen years, I think it was. And then came the parting of the ways.

My father decided he wanted to come back to the bank, which he'd only spent a few months in during the rest of his life. All of us were a bit sceptical as to whether this would work. On the other hand, he wanted to come back and he was a distinguished, extremely clever man, with wonderful connections, and a tremendous intellect. So we all felt he might contribute greatly to the bank. However, the chemistry, the three – my cousin Evelyn, my father and myself – just simply didn't work. None of us, I think, would have ever guessed that it would have ended in a rather violent parting of the ways, which is what happened. So I departed from the bank rather swiftly, at the end of seventeen years, and sadly. No, no, my father then stayed. He stayed, yes. That was particularly difficult.

I think family relationships, in a very small environment, are particularly difficult. It so happens that both Evelyn and I have led happy, successful, interesting lives, so it may well be for the better that what happened, happened. But as I'm not radical about family relationships, I'm very sentimentally attached to the history of our family. I think what would have happened would have been that we would have found different niches within the Rothschild firmament that was growing all the time, and it should have been a large enough one to have accommodated us both. And that would have made, in the long run, for a stronger Rothschild presence. I would have liked to have had a go at keeping N. M. Rothschild in the global first eleven.

I took with me the Rothschild Investment Trust, which I'd stimulated and grown whilst I was there, which was controlled, in management terms, by my friends and myself. And I decided to grow that Investment Trust into a financial services company, over a period of time. My original intention was to create some tremendous all-singing-and-dancing financial services company, because I believed that that was the way forward for certain types of City institutions. I believed that either institutions should be small and specialized, or they should be large, well-capitalized and competitive across a range of skills. And I wanted to go the high road. We moved at a great pace, and we took over all sorts of firms. We bought a stockbroking firm. We bought a merchant bank. And then we tried to merge with an insurance company called Hambro Life, and we were a bit unlucky. The merger, really because the stock market fell out of bed at that time, didn't come off. So we made a hard and painful decision, which was a retreat from Moscow! All the things that we had laboriously put together, we then decided to get rid of. To become small again.

And here we are fifteen years later, a rather small, compact financial services business, with nothing like the ambitions that it had, but which has been a success for our stockholders, and has done some interesting things. We basically, now, do two things. First, we have a portfolio of stocks and shares, and we own a little property. Second, we give backing to new ventures in financial services like J. Rothschild Assurance and Global Asset Management.

Sir John Craven (b. 1940)

I joined Warburgs in 1967. There was a three-year training programme. My big break came when I was asked to join in meetings connected with an attempt to finance the Channel Tunnel and I later became involved in the Eurobond market. I remember Peter Spira, who was head of the international side of Warburgs, saying, 'What are you doing between Christmas and New Year?' I was separated and not yet remarried, so I said, 'Not very much', and he said, 'That's a good thing, because I'd like you to go to America.' I went with two shirts and two suits for what I thought would be four days and ended up staying six months. I found I was a rather good salesman and in the six months I grew five years because I was by myself, battling with the American investment bankers to win the business. When I came back in the middle of '69, to my utter amazement, Warburgs said, 'We'd like you to take responsibility, reporting to Peter Spira, for running our international bond business. We'd like to put you on the board.' That was quite an accelerated process – from mail room to the board room in two years. Other than Rupert Hambro, at Hambros, I was the youngest person ever to go on the board of a major UK merchant bank.

I spent the next three years very happily flogging round the world becoming a specialist in the Eurobond market. There were about twenty of us who made up the market – two or three in Hambros and so on – and we were always meeting. Every time you signed the documents for an issue you had a formal dinner and we were bringing each other into each other's syndicates, so I made some very long-standing friendships from those days. Today, when I look around, it surprises me how many people at the top of their organizations were with me in the Eurobond market thirty years ago. The days of friendly co-operation and friendship changed dramatically in the mid-seventies when it became an ugly business and one or two people were very keen to make a name for themselves. That's when unpleasant practices came in – in terms of paying investors under the table in order to take bonds and even a little bit of improper entertainment of guests in flats in London – and it undermined the whole spirit of the thing. It became big business and far more people got drawn in. The whole ethos changed.

In 1973, an American firm called White Weld, which was a key player in the Eurobond market, asked if I would be interested in joining them. White Weld was a very old-line and respectable – what we used to call a 'white shoe' – investment banking firm. They were the only American firm to keep their London office through the Second World War. The people there were friends of mine and I decided to join them, becoming a shareholder in the firm. I opened an office for them in Japan and then was asked to come back to London and run their operations here. We were the leading players in the bond market. It was fun owning a stake in your own business. In 1975 we sold part of the company and became Credit Suisse White Weld and in 1978 we accepted an offer from Merrill Lynch to buy the American part of the company – which later became Credit Suisse First Boston – for about twenty-six million dollars, soon after which I left the company.

When I left I didn't have any plans at all. I had a little money and I retired to my house in the country for three months to think and spent my time riding and taking the children to school, which was a very pleasant break. I came from a background of no money at all but by this time I had made enough not to worry too much about how the school fees were to be paid, but I wasn't wealthy enough never to work again. I wasn't sure I wanted to go back to the same line of work I had been in. I was open-minded. Then I got drawn into discussions with Siegmund Warburg, with whom I had remained on good personal terms even though I had left the firm. Out of that came a suggestion that I should go back to Warburgs, which I did in 1979.

I don't think anyone has ever gone back to Warburgs and I wouldn't recommend anyone to do it. That's not an *ad hominem* remark. I discovered that although I had many friends at Warburgs (and still have), organizations are dynamic and you can't leave and just parachute back in four years later. Also, I made it clear to Siegmund that I didn't want to do what I had been doing before and that I was interested in mergers and acquisitions work, which wasn't an enormously active field in those days. I think there was a lack of communication between Siegmund and myself and my future colleagues because, despite what I had said, I was asked to run the international bond issue activities and, lo and behold, found that I was a square peg chosen to fill a round hole.

Warburgs is a superbly political place. I used to come home nearly pulling my hair with frustration because of the way the human relationships worked. We all had channels of communication – you couldn't have drawn an organizational chart, it would have looked like a map of European air routes! Some people liked certain people, others had worked together and had a better understanding of each other. Some people hated each other. It's the sort of place that gets in your blood. Most people stay, if they can, all their lives. However, it was only a short time before I realized I should leave. The structure of Warburgs had moved on. I didn't fit back in and I didn't have anything to do which interested me. It was a hell of a difficult decision. I thought that in leaving Warburgs a second time, when I hadn't yet reached my fortieth birthday, I was probably writing the death knell of my own career.

I didn't actively go out and look for another job but one day I got a call from David Norman of Norman Broadbent, the head-hunters. I thought he was probably ringing me to ask me to go shooting but he asked if I would agree to meet his clients, who turned out to be Merrill Lynch who were seeking someone to become Chief Executive of Merrill Lynch International. They had approached a good friend of mine, Lord Swaythling, to be Chairman and it appealed to me to work with David. We joined together at the beginning of 1980 and it took me three days to realize I'd made the most awful mistake. I discovered rapidly that Merrill Lynch was very centralized and run from New York and although they were good at giving responsibility to non-New-York-based people, I felt I did not have the authority necessary to fulfil that responsibility. The ethos was one within which I found it impossible to work. In the end David and I gave up. After eleven months, we took the Concorde and were in the Merrill Lynch New York office by nine-thirty in the morning and by ten o'clock were back on the street, figuratively speaking, cheques in our hands for the unexpired terms of our three-year contracts. We took the twelve o'clock Concorde and were home for dinner.

Suddenly, there I was, just forty years old with a reasonably successful story behind me with White Weld, an unsuccessful tenure of seven months as Vice-Chairman of Warburgs and an unsuccessful tenure of eleven-and-a-half months as Chief Executive of Merrill Lynch International. It was a pretty dented career. I wasn't sure what the devil to do. I had two year's net salary from Merrill Lynch but I also had five children and a wife to support.

I knew I had to find another job. I was approached by a head-hunter for a job as finance director of an international gold-mining company and if they had offered it to me I would have accepted it because of the insecurity I was feeling and because I felt I had blown my career as far as merchant banking was concerned. I wouldn't have been any good because the finance director's job is essentially internal, receiving and being sold to and controlling, whereas my talents are external and selling and I love things that are moving the whole time.

When the gold-mining company didn't offer me the job I remember thinking, 'Oh my God, what am I going to do now?' and feeling let down. It was just one of the turning points in one's life. My wife now says, 'The best thing you ever did was join Merrill Lynch. If you hadn't, you wouldn't have been out on the street with no career and no money. You would never have started your own business.' It was the most extraordinary series of events.

The day the news hit the headlines that I had left Merrill Lynch, I got a call from a fellow running the Bank of America's international investment banking business saying, 'Our international investment business is in a bit of a mess. Would you be prepared to spend some time giving us some advice?' I think it was 1 January 1980. I hate consulting work but it gave me something to do. It took up about half my time and gave me a good excuse to get round the world and see a lot of people. Then on 15 February I had a call from the Finance Minister of Mexico, with whom I'd had business dealings before, asking if I would come and address some financing problems that Petroleos Mexicanos had got itself in to? Then in the middle of March I had a call from the Treasurer of the International Monetary Fund saying would I come and talk about an important assignment the IMF had? That was a six-month job and very interesting.

I worked out of my home in Chelsea. We were redecorating the house at the time and I can remember competing with the builder for time on my own telephone! He wanted to order some 4 × 4 and I wanted to ask the National Bank of Abu Dhabi if they'd take a two million dollar participation in some credits. That's the way it was. It was a wild time. I had a briefcase and an address book. I had the secretary who had worked for me at Merrill Lynch, who used to come and work for me in the evening. I spent my life in aeroplanes.

About the beginning of 1982 I realized there was the beginnings of a business and I invited a friend, Philip Sears, who had been at White Weld with me, to join me and he, fortunately, had the courage to do so and became my partner. We rented two rooms from the London office of a firm of American lawyers in Basinghall Street and we got a secretary and paid for our telephone and telex calls on an item by item basis. We had the use of the dining-room once a week. That's how we began.

In 1982 I sat down with my wife over a bottle of wine and said, 'I'm going to incorporate the company. What shall I call it?' She said, 'You can't call it Craven and Company because it will probably fail and that'll be another black mark. Isn't there something about a bird rising from the ashes in mythology? Why don't you call it Phoenix? Hopefully, you'll rise from the ashes of your disastrous career at Warburgs and Merrill Lynch.' And that was how it became Phoenix Securities.

One never knew where the next job was coming from. In the first year I operated, I made a net loss. My air fares alone came to sixty-three thousand pounds. Until halfway through 1982 we were running the business on a string but the Mexican operations became quite profitable and what was a modest sum to the Royal Bank of Canada was a significant sum to Mr Craven and Mr Sears. We quite quickly made a couple of million dollars. I loved it. I had no boss and for the first time I was answerable to nobody. Every penny I was earning, I was earning myself and that's quite a satisfactory feeling.

We got to the end of the Mexican business and had a little dabble on the Mexican Foreign Exchange Market because we thought the Mexican peso was going to be devalued, which it duly was. We made a bit of money and then closed our position and ended up losing six or seven hundred thousand dollars in two or three months. We were sitting in our office twiddling our thumbs when a most extraordinary thing happened. The telephone went and it was a friend of Philip's who said, 'Do you know anything about Canadian gold-mines?' We both said, 'Not a thing.' He then said, 'I have two friends who think they've found a very exciting gold ore deposit in Northern Ontario and they need another two million dollars to determine whether it's commercially feasible to support putting in the mining facilities. Do you think you could raise two million dollars?' We agreed it was worth spending the air fare for Philip to go out and see what was what.

We hired the best gold-mining consultant geologist in Canada, who came back with a report saying basically, 'This is the largest and richest gold-bearing ore deposit in north American mining history and definitely worth financing.' We underwrote two million dollars' worth of shares with our own money and had seven weeks to place the shares. We called on friends of ours on the fund management side at Rothschilds, at Credit Suisse, at Warburgs and managed to find buyers for all the shares we'd underwritten. In the meantime, share prices were spiralling. We underwrote at five dollars a share and then it was ten dollars. I went to a tennis match at the Albert Hall with my wife and Philip and his wife, and Philip kept coming in and saying, 'The share price has moved another three dollars ... another four dollars', and finally it hit twenty-four dollars. We found out it was because the prospectus had fallen into the hands of two or three of the major Canadian mining groups and all of them were excited at the prospect of getting control of this huge ore body. The trouble was they couldn't control it because we, together with the two people behind the two gold companies who had called us in, had something like forty per cent of the shares – the shares we had placed with European placees. Our investment had turned into about twenty-eight million dollars in eight weeks and we hadn't put up a cent. I'm pleased to say Philip and I allotted all the shares in full to our clients – so we made a nice fee and a lot of friends.

In 1984, through David Norman, we got another important job, with Wedd Durlacher & Mordaunt, who wanted advice on strategy following the agreement between the Stock Exchange and the Secretary of State for Trade and Industry which changed the terms under which the Stock Exchange could operate. We eventually advised them that the best broking firm for them to deal with was de Zoete & Bevan and the best institution for us to negotiate with on their behalf was Barclays Bank – and that gave rise to BZW, which is now a very well-known integrated securities house, and to the receipt by the Wedd partners of one hundred million pounds for the goodwill of their firm.

The word got round and after that we were inundated with firms saying, 'If you've done that for them, can you do something for us?' We spent two happy years doing nothing but that. Maybe out of thirty significant Stock Exchange marriages that were done at the time of Big Bang, we handled over twenty. There wasn't anyone else who was completely independent who could do it. It got to the point that people didn't want to be seen coming into Phoenix Securities because they were seen as advertising themselves as being for sale. That work took us to the end of 1985 by which time our scope had broadened. As one door closed, another opened. We moved to an office in Bishopsgate in the Hongkong Shanghai Building and we had four partners and two younger associates. The total staff was probably twelve people plus a chauffeur, a cook and a bottle-washer. The firm remained that size until I sold it two years later. I was reluctant to sell it but I did it for reasons I'll explain later.

In December 1986 it was announced that the Department of Trade and Industry had launched an enquiry into the conduct by Guinness and its advisers, Morgan Grenfell and Cazenove, over a bid in competition with Argyll for Distillers. It was quite apparent that Morgan Grenfell were going to have to appoint a new Chief Executive. Six or eight weeks later I got a call saying I was on the shortlist but I said I wasn't interested. A couple of weeks later I was approached again and gave the same answer. Then David Norman came into my life again and, since my encounters with him have always been rewarding, I went to see him. He said, 'I know you've been approached and I know you've said "No", but I've been asked to enquire whether you would change your mind if Morgan Grenfell were to buy Phoenix Securities?' I took a cold, hard financial view, given the fact that one had wives and children and commitments. I went to talk to my partners. After a certain amount of discussion, I went back to David Norman and said that at a price we were prepared to sell Phoenix and that I would go to be Chief Executive at Morgan Grenfell. I hired Warburgs to negotiate for me. Our instructions were that our price was fifteen million pounds and not a penny less. I have a certain nostalgia for the days at Phoenix but I have no regrets. What I have been doing for the last five years has been utterly different but very rewarding in its own way.

I joined Morgan Grenfell in 1987. They needed a new broom to take over. The Morgan Grenfell franchise was clearly badly damaged by the Guinness affair. It had the reputation as the firm you use if you really want to win or defend yourself, but it had also got the reputation with the authorities and with its competitors in the City as being just a little bit too buccaneering. Although I realized the Guinness affair might cost us a bit of money, I thought that, with the changes in personnel, it shouldn't be too difficult to get things back on the rails and that it would just be a matter of repairing relationships with the City generally, with the authorities and with some of the important customers and then we could go from strength to strength. The Guinness problem dogged the firm for five or six years but what I found was that Morgan Grenfell had some rather more deep-seated problems that were much more difficult to fix.

Of the deeper issues I found at Morgan Grenfell, one was that from about 1983–6, on the back of the extraordinary profitability of the corporate finance activity, the company had embarked on an expansion programme, both organic and through acquisition, which had taken the number of people employed from around one thousand in 1980 to around two thousand seven hundred by the time I arrived. You can't expand a company that's been relatively small for a long time at that speed without losing some of the control and quality of the organization, the *esprit de corps*. The overhead expenses of the company had expanded from something like fifty million pounds to two hundred million pounds a year in the space of three or four years. When the boom in the take-over business stopped we had a p. and l. problem of some magnitude. We reduced the head count – it reached a peak of three thousand five hundred in the middle of 1988 – and now have around two thousand people. In real terms, we cut about seventy million pounds a year expenses out of the business.

A more serious problem was the securities business. At the time of Big Bang, Morgan Grenfell espoused the view that you needed to have an integrated capability. But by the time they got round to making up their minds what to do, all the desirable blondes had gone! They ended up buying jobbers Pinchin Denny, a good firm but only number five or six in terms of size, and brokers Pember & Boyle, which was really a gilt broker and not an equity broker – and equity broking was what it was all about. Having bought these two small units, they compounded the error by putting in charge people from Morgan Grenfell who had no experience in the equity markets. The number of people employed in our securities business went from about a hundred and twenty in 1985–6 to approaching four hundred and fifty to five hundred by the middle of 1988. We had to take new space, spend money on computers and so on.

We had to build rapidly if we were to have a market share that would put us in the top ten firms. Shortly after I moved to Morgan Grenfell, I moved my offices into the securities side and sat in a glass-walled room right next to the dealers so I could see what the hell was going on. I spent a lot of time walking round every day trying to understand how the business was running. Everything went well for 1987 because there was a huge boom in Stock Exchange business and we were beginning to think, 'Gee, we might just make it.' Then in October 1987 came the big crash, which sorted out the men from the boys. From that moment on, our business share began to collapse. We watched the figures on a daily basis. It was losing about one million pounds a week.

•

Sometimes you see things more clearly from a distance. I went away to Spain and I'd been there about a week when the penny dropped: 'This business is not going to survive. If we stick with it, it's going to bleed us absolutely dry. And therefore we have to get out of the securities business altogether.' It was the most difficult management decision I ever had to make in my life. It involved about seven hundred and seventy jobs and about forty-five million pounds write-offs. It also involved going back on a statement we had made in the prospectus when we went public in 1986, on the back of which we'd raised a lot of money from the institutions.

You can't get up one day and close down. You have to get your personnel department to prepare the P11/Ds, or whatever they're called, for seven hundred and seventy people – you can't just put them on the street one day. You have to prepare the outplacement people so that, the day you tell people they're no longer going to be employed, you can say, 'However, there's a consultant waiting in the next room to help you with your problems.' We had to prepare what we were going to say to the press, what we were going to say to the institutions who had backed us, what we would say to our corporate customers to whom we'd been selling the idea of an integrated securities company for the last two years. It was an incredibly difficult process. The closer we got to D-Day, the greater the consensus there was in the group immediately surrounding me that this was the right thing to do. We had it all set up to do on a Friday – we were told that a Friday afternoon was the right time to do it, to give people the opportunity to go home and talk it over with their families over the weekend rather than putting them out on the street on a Tuesday morning.

Unfortunately, what happened was that someone – it was an inside job – talked to *The Daily Telegraph*. It was the Tuesday evening and at one o'clock in the morning I had a call to say that an early edition of *The Daily Telegraph* – which had been on the streets for an hour – carried the full story: 'Morgan Grenfell Closing Down Its Securities Operation. Seven Hundred and Seventy Redundancies.' I went into the office at seven and we had chaps and girls coming in, having read their newspapers on the commute up saying, 'It can't possibly be true!' We had a microphone system for the whole of the dealing area and I had to say, 'I'm sorry. You will have read in your newspapers that we're going out of the securities business. You will have heard me and everybody in a senior position saying for the last two years that we're totally committed to the business. It will sound a phoney thing to say, but when you've had a chance to think about it you'll realize that had to be said until we had taken the decision to go. The board meeting is at nine o'clock, so I can't tell you officially, but I can tell you unofficially – and this will be confirmed by a press release at one minute past nine – that we have, indeed, decided to withdraw from the securities business. This has a lot of human implications for all of you. We had hoped it wasn't going to come out the way it did. Somebody, unfortunately, has leaked the story. We were planning to do it this Friday, which means we've been caught on the hop. We had hoped there would be a package for each of you explaining exactly what your benefits and redundancy agreements were and to have consultants lined up to see each one of you. But now we are not ready. All I can tell you is that the business is over. I'm very sorry. I want to thank you for everything you've done for us. You don't want to listen to a great justification from me, but in short order, we just don't have the market share to survive. We're bleeding at a rate of a million pounds a week. Please stop dealing now. There are a few people that we would like to stay behind to help get through the day but otherwise I suggest you go home and you will receive a telephone call in the next two or three days and be invited back to hear what we propose in the way of severance arrangements and so on.' It was one of the most difficult days of my life.

We had one or two young chaps bashing down computer screens. We had one joker who, before he left, dialled the weather announcement in Sydney, Australia, and left the phone hanging and we found it twenty-four hours later. Nobody was unpleasant to me or my management colleagues. Perhaps the most difficult was the press, because they got on to it instantly. I left our securities office and had to beat a retreat with the press chasing behind. It was real news because we were the first ones. Strangely enough, it united the rest of the firm because the bit we got rid of was the bit that had been added on. If we'd have been getting rid of something we'd had for forty years it would have been a different story. Today, there is no one at Morgan Grenfell who would query for a second that it wasn't absolutely the right thing to do.

I was concerned about the redundancies. It's not just seven hundred people, it's two thousand eight hundred people because they've all got a wife and children – and you're cutting off their livelihood. We tried to bend over backwards, which is why we had such a big bill. Six months later I had a survey done by our personnel department and of all the people we could reach who had been in Morgan Grenfell Securities, only something like three per cent remained unemployed. Of the remaining ninety-seven per cent, something like fifteen per cent had decided they wanted to get out of the City altogether – they'd gone to run pubs or work in publishing or whatever – and every one of the others had got a job in the City. Some had better paid, more secure jobs than they had had with us. I bump into them from time to time and I've never had a rough word from any of them. I can't say they come and kiss me on the cheeks, but a number of them have said, 'It was bloody difficult for us, but it must have been bloody difficult for you, too. You did the right thing. The business was not going to suceeed.'

In 1989 the Deutsche Bank bought Morgan Grenfell for nine hundred and fifty million pounds. One of the conditions of the purchase was that I remained as Chairman for a reasonable period of time. I was taking responsibility for taking an organization with a one-hundred-and-seventy-year independent history, employing two thousand people, into the ownership of a foreign bank. I had an obligation to make sure it worked. I couldn't have walked away and left it rudderless. After the acquisition I became a member of the board of managing directors of the Deutsche Bank. I'm very privileged because the bank has been in existence one hundred and twenty years and I'm the first foreigner ever to have been on the board. There are just twelve of us running an organization of seventy thousand people operating in fifty countries. The managing board meets a full day every week and the meetings are in German. I had not a single word of German when I started so I just had to learn it. I'm fifty years old now and I consider myself hugely privileged to have had the opportunity to take a totally new direction in a new language in a new country with new colleagues. I'm still here in London and Chairman of Morgan Grenfell but I spend two or three days a week in Germany. Siegmund Warburg would smile in his grave if he knew I had become a director of the Deutsche Bank. If there was one bank he held in awe it was the Deutsche Bank and he even tried to sell Warburgs to them at one time. It's now the first of March and it's the first week I've been in England for a whole week this year. I shall be going to Geneva on Sunday. It's a terrible life-style and I certainly won't do it until normal retirement age if that means sixty or sixty-five.

John Wolff (b. 1940)
When I first came to work at Rudolf Wolff, my grandfather and great-uncle were still partners and used to come into the office twice a week but by then they were in their eighties and they didn't contribute much and they didn't take much out. They retired soon after I joined. My father, two of my uncles, a second cousin and a man married to a second cousin of mine were also in the company. It was envisaged that I'd take the baton on in due course and continue a certain ethos and atmosphere. I've been conscious all my working life of having to work that bit harder to be able to say, 'I've done this on my own merit, not because I'm a family member.'

There were rather more characters in the London Metal Exchange in those days. The overall volumes traded were smaller and you could be – as my father was – the senior partner, the senior dealer and the senior business getter of your firm in one. I went on to the Exchange in the most junior position on the Floor. It sounds strange when you first go; there is a special language for trading and certain expressions that get used. For example, the price may be one thousand two hundred and forty-eight dollars per ton of a given metal and the man bidding in the ring wouldn't say, 'I will buy at one thousand two hundred and forty-eight.' He'll shout, 'I will give eight.' And the seller might say, 'I'll sell at nine.' Everybody knows what the big figure is. If he uses the expression, 'How much?', it means he's prepared to deal in five hundred tons instead of the usual twenty-five tons. When I joined, the Exchange traded in copper, tin, lead and zinc. Aluminium and nickel didn't come in until '78–79. Trading was from twelve till one-thirty and three-forty until five o'clock. It was much more leisurely than now – people didn't arrive until nine-thirty, sometimes ten, and usually went home between five-thirty and six. The amount of work that had to be done was less because post-war restrictions on world trade were still very much in force and the industrial world was smaller. The trend towards longer hours has been very much a thing of the 1980s.

When I joined the LME, most of the companies were traditional City partnerships and now all of them have been taken over, including my own. We had a sort of Big Bang in the Metal Exchange a few years before the Stock Exchange one because of the growth in business. The amount of money required to fund the business and the risk became too large for private partners so there was a sort of natural evolution whereby the companies got taken over by bigger groups. My own company got taken over in 1971 by a Canadian mining group, Noranda, who had been a client. As a family member it was sad, but I don't think there was any option but to sell. I wasn't a partner in 1971 so I got the worst of it in the sense that the people who were selling were coming to the end of their working lives and they got the money and didn't have to work under the new regime, whereas I was not halfway through my career. Funnily enough, you feel it more for the next generation. There's no business for my children to come into. There's a company called Rudolf Wolff but it's certainly not a family business.

There was a clash of cultures because we were taken over by a company who were a big business and we were a small, entrepreneurial company with a much more seat-of-the-pants way of going on. We had to marry those cultures – it worked in the end but it was quite painful to start with because if you stifle an entrepreneur too much, he'll die. On the other hand, the entrepreneurial side needs some kind of control; getting the best of both worlds is a difficult thing. In the intervening twenty-five years occasionally there's been discussion about changing the firm's name to that of the parent company but it's felt to be a bad thing by the vast majority.

My main area of work with Rudolf Wolff is now the marketing side of the metals. As well as this, in 1990 I became Chairman of the London Metal Exchange. The LME board is involved with maintaining an orderly market and providing user-friendly contracts. There has been a lot of change in the last ten years and the workload at the top has been higher than most of the previous century.

The first major problem we had at the LME was the Tin Crisis in 1985, which left a trail of debt by twenty-two member states of about five hundred million pounds to bankers and brokers. That was a devastating time and we weren't sure if the LME would survive or not. Day-to-day normal business just didn't take place. There were a number of legal cases going on and certain members of the committees were sued for enormous amounts of money. I was being sued, personally, for a hundred million dollars (not that I had that much). It was an action brought by an American company that was trying to shoot everybody in town. The court case went on for nearly nine months. Being grilled in the box was very unpleasant. There were, I think, twenty thousand documents in the court and the prosecutor could say, 'Please now refer to document so and so', and you got it shoved in front of you and you had to answer questions on it. You're free to say if you can't remember and the judge has to judge whether you're lying. Your instinct is to speak a lot to try and explain what you did and why and to justify your actions, whereas you're advised to say as little as possible. If I had to do it again it wouldn't worry me so much, but it was my first time in court.

My legal fees were paid by the LME but the sums were so large that had the case gone on much longer the LME would have run out of money and I don't know what would have happened then. We won, lock, stock and barrel, and were vindicated by the judge and awarded expenses. Little by little, we got through and came out the other side. Like any major experience, it matures one. One of the other six involved in the court case had two strokes before the case came up. He was a bit older than me and had a medical condition that probably meant he was going to get a stroke at some time, so one can't prove that this brought it on, but I would have thought that it did. I certainly wouldn't want to be at the helm in another crisis like that because you're sticking your neck over the parapet for no reward and there's a lot of risk. I don't envisage anything like that happening again.

Charles McVeigh III (b. 1942)

I joined Salomon in London in 1975 as vice-president. There were twenty-five people in the London office then and it grew by about five to ten people a year at a measured pace during the late seventies (when we got involved in the Eurobond business). It then exploded in the early 1980s. At first it was very much a hands-on management, you could get your arms around virtually every aspect of the business and all the different personalities and get the maximum benefit out of everybody.

From the point of view of the Brits, the Americans were setting a frightening standard in the City in terms of the hours we were keeping. We would come into the office at seven, which was a good hour or two before most of our English counterparts. We were using London very much as the base of our European business and the Continent was always an hour ahead. If you wanted to be on the phone by eight-fifteen, you had to assimilate a lot of financial data that had come in from New York the night before and from the *Financial Times* to be able to be succinct and convincing. We would get on the telephone with clients using relative value financial data that we'd developed ourselves and start to build investment cases for selling one bond and buying another. Our method of valuation was considered pretty high-tech stuff in those days, even though most of it was manual. The office was buzzing from eight o'clock with people on the phone, in any number of different languages, to various parts of the Continent or the United Kingdom. We often went out to make client presentations, typically in the City, but a number of people from Salomon would also travel to Europe. The clients would be life insurance companies, pension funds, unit trusts, all the principal asset management categories.

There tended to be quite a long afternoon because in a firm like Salomon Brothers another part of your life begins when New York opens each day: you're in constant discussions with a variety of people about business opportunities which you think New York should be grasping or vice versa. The effective leverage that you get out of having a very important parent organization in the United States becomes immeasurably significant. My management style in London was based on being completely integrated with my colleagues in New York, and their trust in what we were doing was a by-product of the amount of co-ordination and sharing of information that we did. There was a period in my life when I went to New York literally every single week. If I was in London, I would tend to leave the office at about seven and go straight home or to dinner.

I was made a partner in 1977. In 1979 the business took off and by that time I'd developed a lot of close relationships in the City. The amount of fixed income business was exploding and the opportunities for expanding our European business were extraordinary. We were starting to build a larger investment banking capability and we started building our sales force dramatically. From the twenty-three staff here in London when I arrived, it's now grown to one thousand three hundred in Europe and we have in excess of a billion pounds' worth of capital here.

In 1977 there were fifty or sixty partners and by 1981 there were seventy-seven. Our senior people tended to be American but the decision to have Americans in most of the key positions started to wane in the early eighties when we recognized that we had to hire a lot more Europeans to be effective in Europe. We have a strong culture at Salomon and a unique way of doing business which has been more successful than most of our competitors; we didn't want to scrap that. We wanted to recruit first-class Europeans who would grow and replace the Americans. That's ultimately what happened. We have very few Americans today. There are over thirty nationalities in London alone.

We've had superb recruitment and superb training. We wanted to breed a very aggressive, meritocratic spirit in the people who were joining us. We wanted them to believe they should win and achieve every day, every week, every month. Most Europeans didn't start their careers with this sort of attitude. There are very few senior people left from the early days. Of the seventy-seven partners in 1981, only three of us are left among the one hundred and eighty-four managers we have today. Turnover within the employee base has been as great.

Part of the meritocratic behaviour of people had something to do with the fact that they were trying to prove something to themselves and to others and that was part of our success. Very few people who arrived at Salomon had any money and their partnership and subsequent capital creation was a function of their success in the business. People took enormous pride in being a partner. As a partner, you were paid a salary and then any share of the firm's profits went directly into your capital account at the firm, where it was untouchable.

Your capital continued to grow in profitable years, and you were paid interest on your capital, but your capital was always at risk in the business; if something went wrong in the marketplace and Salomon Brothers had large positions, it could affect your capital account. You didn't really think of it as yours; it was nominally yours, but I don't think people lay awake at night thinking of how they were going to spend it. If you left the partnership there was an onerous exit arrangement which was designed to prevent people from leaving and to maintain Salomon Brothers' capital position, the strength of which differentiated us from most of our competitors.

In 1981 Salomon Brothers merged with the world's leading commodity trading house, Philipp Brothers. The merger made an enormous difference to me, personally, because I and the other Salomon partners suddenly woke up on 1 October 1981 knowing that two hundred and fifty million dollars had been paid out to seventy-five of us. While my portion wasn't a great deal of money compared to the more senior partners, for me it was a great deal. It was an enormous source of pride that I had achieved that at a relatively young age.

I've always been frugal. I always save a substantial amount of my bonus every year, and I would never take a first-class carriage on a train or consider flying club class or first class in private life. I never drove a Mercedes or a fancy car. I felt it was very important to live a modest life-style, which meant living no differently after I received the money than before in terms of the cars I drove or the houses I lived in or the restaurants I ate in or whatever. I felt very strongly about that and I tried to maintain that position. I believe that modesty is an enormously attractive quality in people who are successful.

Until Big Bang, we, as a foreign firm, had been precluded by regulation from becoming involved in the Stock Market. Suddenly those barriers to entry were down. I became Chairman in 1987. Last year, 1993, we would have been the most profitable merchant bank in the United Kingdom.

David King (b. 1945)
I joined the London Metal Exchange in 1987. The LME had been a sleeping giant and hadn't realized its own potential. It had been successful for a long time but kept a low profile and was perceived to be a bit clubbish and old-fashioned. In the last five years it has quadrupled its turnover and activity which, for an Exchange over a hundred years old, is surprising.

The Tin Crisis occurred in '85 and had weakened the Exchange psychologically. It was perceived by the City to be in disfavour and have its back to the wall so it had to look at itself and restructure. Bearing in mind this background and the emergence of the Financial Services Act, the Exchange called in Price Waterhouse to advise it and they recommended a new management be brought in to run the Exchange centrally rather than by committees as in the past. A new constitution was evolved and it was felt necessary to have a proper, organized financial and administrative system. I was recruited as part of the new set-up and was initially taken on as the first director of Finance and Administration. I became Chief Executive in November 1989.

We run a tight ship, the entire LME secretariat staff is twenty-nine. When I arrived I was the only person with a professional qualification and, of the original staff, about a third are still with us. The people who left had been here for decades – in one case for four decades – and were excellent, competent, nice people but the world had moved on and we needed people with fresh ideas. We dropped the retirement age from sixty-five to sixty and bolstered the pension scheme to enable some people to leave earlier. It was all done in a gentlemanly fashion and not in a shallow way. One of the strengths of the Exchange is that we treat people well. All the senior people now have either got a degree or a professional accountancy qualification or an MBA.

The perfect role for an exchange, if one looks at page one of an economics book, is an open price discovery situation where there are lots of buyers and sellers with equal information and the result of that is that they will identify the true price. That's classically what happens on the Metal Exchange because, although there may be only a few brokers down there, they represent three-quarters or more of the world's industry in that particular metal and they will be buying and selling on behalf of the globe. The Exchange tends to be very frenzied because it's open outcry trading. There's a trend to computerize this activity, as happened in the Stock Exchange, but I think that won't affect us for a number of years.

The Ring Dealing Members are the inner circle. There's an outer circle, psychologically, of other users of the LME who can trade on behalf of clients. Some Ring firms go back to having founded the Exchange more than a hundred and fifteen years ago. Latterly, American commission houses have joined the Exchange and they bring a very different culture, more financially orientated, whereas the older London firms are more merchant orientated. Our brokers can deal twenty-four hours a day. Another role of the Exchange is as a reference on pricing medium and about ninety per cent of the world's pricing activities are based on the LME for copper, aluminium, zinc, lead, nickel and tin. We have a computer network of five thousand locations all over the world where at any time of the day or night anybody involved can know the true price of the six metals.

About ninety-five per cent of our business comes from overseas and travelling is an integral part of what we all do. I was in Hungary last week and about a month ago I was in California speaking at a conference. Recently I was in Atlanta and Florida, and I have people this week in Paris and Brussels and last week one of my people was in Brazil. We are forever receiving global visitors at the Exchange. Yesterday, for example, we had the Bolivian ambassador, to whom we showed the Exchange, followed by lunch at the Savoy. Last night I was at a function at Leighton House, courtesy of the German ambassador, followed by dinner at

Langan's. This does not mean that life is one big social whirl. I work long hours, typically forty to fifty hours a week.

The LME's lease in Plantation House expires in 1994 but I don't foresee us moving outside of the Square Mile. Between the morning and afternoon sessions in the Exchange, most of the traders on the floor will go back to their offices, which need to be in walking distance. As well as two or three hundred traders and clerks on the floor, there are probably two thousand support staff in their back offices, which is one reason why we couldn't move to a green-field site – we'd need to move all these other firms. The City of London is a unique institution. It's grown by accident on the back of the Industrial Revolution but it is here because the financial industry is here; the shipping, the insurance, the banking. The shipping for a lot of our metal will be arranged in London through Lloyd's; the insurance of it will all be arranged here, as will the banking – seven hundred billion a year. If we were to go somewhere else, that infrastructure would still be required. All of this could be done by phone but the fact that it is essentially in the Square Mile is an integral part of the great strength that London has. It may be eroded by time, but it won't easily be taken away by Frankfurt or New York.

I would like to stay in the City because I like the environment, the concept. This is actually the first job I have liked. The City is still a thriving community. You can almost feel the business atmosphere and I like that.

Haruko Fukuda (b. 1946)
When I joined Vickers da Costa in 1972, I said, 'I don't know anything about stocks and shares', and they said, 'It's all right. You can write a two-page economic report on Japan every two weeks, a fortnightly newsletter on the Japanese economy.' I thought that was terribly easy. The rest of the time I was writing my book.

I had been aware of some of the early dealings between the Japanese stock market and London because my father was the Japanese Ministry of Finance official here in the early 1960s. In 1961 the Chairman of the Foreign and Colonial Investment Trust, who was a great horticulturalist, wanted to go to Japan to look at camellias. He thought he should have a look at investment opportunities at the same time! As a result, Foreign and Colonial was one of the first to invest in Japan. (I am now a director of that company.) Foreigners' investment in Japan had to be made through various vehicles such as EDRs (English Depository Receipts), the very first of which were issued in London and New York. It was considered to be an important step forward and British merchant banks, which were involved in underwriting the new issues, took it as the basis for enormous opportunities for the future. The British–Japanese Commercial Accord was signed in 1963, and in 1964, for the first time in fifty years, a Japanese government bond denominated in sterling was issued in London. This latter was my father's achievement. He was given the fountain pen which signed the agreement; it was a black Parker pen with a gold cap and he gave it to me and I used it for my exams throughout my time at Cambridge. It was very much the beginning of Japan's participation in the international financial community. The other landmark in 1964 was that Japan's Big Four securities companies, Nomura, Nikko, Daiwa and Yamaichi, opened their offices in London.

Vickers da Costa was among the first British firms to invest in Japan. When I joined, it had about a hundred and fifty people in total. Its offices were down by the Monument in Regis House. It was frightfully scruffy. They had about ten people in a room, with desks close together and telephones ringing the entire time: a great contrast to the calm of the World Bank. Suddenly I was working with people who were very much at the sharp end of commerce. They were robust, they followed their intuition much more than reasoned argument, they were jumping around, always going out for long lunches and coming back having had five brandies and carrying on in the afternoon talking on the telephone. After work, many of us went to the pub called El Vino's (I didn't always go) and had wine or whisky until late in the evening, chatting about the market and the deals done that day.

I didn't think I would actually stay in stockbroking, partly because it never occurred to me that I would work in anything like finance before – certainly not in commerce. In Japan stockbrokers were considered to be absolutely the lowest echelons of society and I couldn't bring myself to tell my family what I was doing for about six months because I knew they would be absolutely horrified. After my books were published, I was going to leave the City but some of my colleagues at Vickers said, 'We're negotiating to go to James Capel and set up a Japanese department there. Why don't you come with us?' James Capel offered me a much improved salary and so in the end I said, 'All right. Perhaps I'll do it for a couple of years.' It seemed a rather appealing interlude in my life after having worked very intensively on my writing. There were five people in the team that left Vickers.

Capels was bigger than Vickers and it was a more established firm in the sense that it was, for example, the Queen's broker and very much more up-market in terms of image, and of course it was one of the largest firms in the UK equity market. It was in a modern 1960s building, Winchester

House, with air-conditioned offices, with a plush, luxurious feel and the people in it were a slightly different type, much more public school. We arrived in the spring of 1974, which was the beginning of the bear market, perhaps the worst bear market of the last two or three decades. Almost every day in the summer, one or two firms went bust. My attitude was if we didn't make enough money in the Japanese department and were all thrown out, it wouldn't matter to me too much. The others also took the same sort of attitude because in those days we were fairly carefree. If it happened today it would be rather worrying, but somehow we all felt we could get other jobs.

It was not done in those days in the City to move from one firm to another and start speaking to clients from the previous firm. We had to generate new clients; there were some people in the City that we started to do business with, but we also very much relied on the Continental client-base, so we went to Switzerland and France and Germany and Belgium for new business. My role in the team was to write the economic reviews, but one of the people in the team became unwell and as a result I was asked whether I would speak to one or two clients. I wrote a report on the banking sector in Japan, which I thought was tremendously over-valued at that time and probably going to fall, so I telephoned a few clients who had bank shares and said I thought they should sell them. They were all rather astonished to hear from me because they had never heard of me before, but one or two of them telephoned later in the afternoon and accepted my advice and I got some large orders. That was really the beginning of my success. From that start I went around visiting clients in Switzerland and so on, partly to talk about the economy and partly to talk a little about stocks. But I really didn't know a great deal about the market at all at that time.

The market bottomed out and started to rise in the autumn of 1974. At the end of 1974 I went to Japan to visit some companies. Although I was Japanese, I didn't actually speak Japanese very well then and certainly not the technical language of the markets. I had to write out for myself a little dictionary at the front of my notebook (in Roman characters phonetically, because I couldn't write Japanese) and used to refer to it. You learned the technique after a while of how to ask the same question four times in different ways to get an answer if they weren't forthcoming. In the next two or three years I became quite good at getting all the salient information in thirty or forty minutes of interview. By 1977 my Japanese got greatly better. I don't think I had any kind of patriotic loyalty or love for my own country. The process of discovery would have been equally interesting in a different country.

By about '78 we were contributing quite a lot to the firm's earnings and

1980 was a breakthrough year because I became a partner of James Capel and a Member of the Stock Exchange. In that year there was an unusual development in the Japanese market: mysterious mammoth buy orders were coming in from abroad. There were many rumours about where they were coming from, but of course it was oil money. We discovered who was putting out these vast orders and for several years we were able to receive really huge orders even by today's standards. Every day it was a race to get to the office to get to the telex machine in time to be able to get through to the client before the other brokers jammed the telexes and telephones. In the end we had a direct line to them and they gave me a secret telex number which was not used by anybody else. Secrecy was absolute and we set up coded account names and all sorts of things for them. In the morning I would speak to them on the direct line and they would read out a list of orders and it would be in tens of millions of pounds, so this was a very exciting time. But it was not just oil money. Virtually every London institution was investing in the Japanese market in the first half of the 1980s and we were playing a major role in that process.

In 1979 Mrs Thatcher removed foreign exchange controls, as a result of which all the pension funds and life insurance companies started investing in Japan. Until then most of our clients were specialist fund managers in London and on the Continent, but from 1980 onwards the client base widened substantially and the business got greatly larger. Between 1979 and 1985 I was really deep into stockbroking. My father once said, 'I think you should give up because it's not your sort of thing. You should go back to a more genteel life-style.' By then it was too late! I couldn't possibly give it up. There was no other way of living! I was up often all night dealing and brokers from Tokyo used to ring at midnight and I talked to them from bed. I don't think I was really doing it for James Capel, I was doing it for my own satisfaction. We did something like two or three per cent of the Tokyo Stock Exchange turnover by ourselves more or less every day from 1981 to 1984 and ten or twelve per cent of the foreign investment in the Japanese markets, so that was a very large amount.

Big Bang was a psychologically traumatic time for us because the abolition of minimum commission and introduction of dual capacity brought a totally new competitive element into our lives. The senior partner of James Capel was thinking, 'Under such competitive pressures we might not be able to survive in the same way as before. It is too dangerous to have unlimited liability; we need more capital if we are going to compete with the Merrill Lynches of this world.' It seemed imperative to sell our firm. In the end we sold it to the Hongkong Bank. We were paid for our shares in five or six tranches and were tied in and not able to

1. Gwilym Lewis

2. Lord O'Brien of Lothbury

3. Lord Benson

4. Michael Verey

5. Dundas Hamilton

6. Leonard Toomey

7. Sir Brian Corby

8. Sir Martin Jacomb

9. George Nissen

10. Hugh Peppiatt

11. Peter Spira

12. Jack Spall

13. Sir Kenneth Kleinwort

14. Lord Rothschild

15. Sir John Craven

16. John Wolff

17. Charles McVeigh

18. David King

19. Haruko Fukuda

20. Jane Partington

21. Nick Durlacher

22. David Verey

23. Davina Walter

24. Valerie Thompson

25. Philippa Rose

26. Ross Jones

leave until we were fully paid for several years. It was called 'golden handcuffs'.

Certainly, the financial advantage was enormous. I made fifteen times what I had invested in the firm when I became a partner. We made a windfall gain which we could never have *saved* in our lifetime. Selling our firm changed our lives; we were no longer a partnership, the whole ethos changed. The fact that we had to stay in the firm for five or six years at first seemed to be all right but as time went on people began to feel very uncomfortable. Even if you didn't have any wish to leave before, when somebody puts a handcuff on you, you desperately want to leave. The effects of the take-over and the sudden expansion of the firm were that there were enormous strains and tensions, and the firm became rather divided and by 1987 it was a rather unhappy place. There was no longer the same kind of commitment which prevailed under the partnership arrangement. Some people just walked out and said, 'I don't care about my money, I'm just going because I'm unhappy.'

It was an unsettling time. Big Bang brought many new firms into the Stock Exchange and they were recruiting good people. Once you are approached by one or two major firms for important jobs it becomes impossible to stop thinking about it. When Nikko came to me (I was actually approached at that time by two other firms, one Japanese, one American) I thought, 'I am going to do it this time.' I spent nine months negotiating with the Hongkong Bank to be released from the 'handcuffs' and they had to agree to rescind the contract.

It was unprecedented for a woman to be offered a job at such a senior level in a Japanese firm from outside. There's no other woman in a similar position in the Japanese financial services sector. I don't think it was a conscious decision on Nikko's part to employ a woman; I just happened to be there and they thought, 'Ah, here is a person who crosses cultures well. She is Japanese but she seems to be accepted by the British and it would be an advantage to Nikko to have somebody of that kind of seniority.' I was there to inject a bit of Britishism into Nikko but at the same time they didn't have to contend with somebody actually British. I could speak Japanese and understood their ways a little better than a Brit would. But I also had an established reputation in the Japanese equities market.

Nikko Europe is the European headquarters of Nikko Securities and the chairman of this company is chairman of all the group companies and offices in Europe, of which there are thirteen. At every level, in every department, we are in daily, constant contact with Tokyo. The whole organization of the company, the ethos and mores are completely different. At Capels a small number of people did a lot of things but at Nikko, a much larger firm (ten thousand in the group worldwide), I found masses and masses of people, each with his own tasks, and they seemed not to know or care much about what others did. One of the reasons why Japan has been so successful in the post-war period has been attributed to the single-minded corporate culture. In terms of the sort of people this corporate culture produced, the Japanese businessmen are very unkeen to make instant decisions, they have to build a consensus amongst colleagues before they decide to do the simplest thing. I have learned to work within that system without it affecting too much my own scale of values, but I have also learned from the Japanese the skills of consensus management. It has its advantages as well as disadvantages. But at first I felt as though I had come to the Soviet Union.

Nikko's office is outside the Square Mile, which added to my feelings of strangeness. It's in Victoria Street and all the people in the streets look different and have different expressions on their faces from those in the City. Also if you walk down the street in the City you are bound to bump into someone you know and, of course, that doesn't happen in Victoria because there are not many investment people here. And we've got a street market next door, shoppers. I am now thoroughly used to it and I like being here very much indeed. I am a director of the Foreign and Colonial Trust and also of the First Ireland Investment Company so I go to the City often for their meetings quite apart from visiting clients of Nikko. Socially, I am of course always in touch with innumerable friends from the City.

David Verey (b. 1950)
Lazards, when I joined in 1972, was very much at the top of the tree. It was a firm of movement and excitement. It was a very recognizable British merchant bank with an investment management business, a banking business and an 'issues business', which was the beginnings of an advisory corporate finance business. It had a relatively small board of people, who had probably worked all their lives here.

I was one of three starting with the firm on the same day, their first graduate intake. I was sent to the Stocks Department (attached to the Investment Management Department) which was based in Houndsditch and I was mainly transcribing one lot of information from one book to another. Over six months I worked my way round that department. When the place was idle there was an underlying anarchy about it. There was the inevitable joker in the department and one day when they had all been in the pub he was wandering around in a girl's dress and high heels and everyone thought it terribly funny. There was another character who wore the most beautiful clothes and put his feet on the desk and read the *Daily Express* all day; he didn't last long. I have clear memories of the Winter of Discontent when the place was completely dark with everyone huddled over with little blowlamps on the desks.

One day Lord Tryon, who was head of the Private Client Department, loomed over my desk and asked if I would like to join his department? The Private Client Department took a very snobbish attitude to what they called 'gross funds' – the department looking after pension funds – they thought the people there were barrow-boys behind a sort of green baize door. They had decided the Private Client Department shouldn't have overhead lights and they had strip desk lights which threw a limited beam of light so when I went in I saw big oak desks with piles of paper and strips of light and at least two people smoking large cigars. It looked absolutely thrilling. The entire department was male. In those days it was a splendid atmosphere and in the morning a variety of stockbrokers would come into the office – today there would be at least fourteen rules to stop that happening – and would chat about buying and selling shares and no doubt fix their fishing for the weekend. They had known each other for a long time. (Not any stockbroker would come to Lazards, it was a tradition that some did and some didn't.) The brokers would then go down to the Exchange floor – we were just over the road from the Stock Exchange – and find out what the market was doing. A lot of that generation of stockbrokers are utterly miserable now. They were partners in small stockbroking firms and had a position and a good life which was fun and then, all of a sudden, post-Big Bang, it disappeared and everything was done on the telephone or became electronic and lost its personality.

I left the Private Client Department in the spring of 1974 to go into Research and Planning and then joined Corporate Finance in the winter of the same year. At that stage there were maybe eight teams of two in Corporate Finance, all male, and a secretarial pool. In the Private Client Department we were doing valuations and looking at stocks and shares, so quite a lot of the day was taken up having a chin-wag but there was very little chin-wagging in Corporate Finance. You got there around eight in the morning and you worked; there were urgent tasks that had to be right first time, needing real thought and imagination. You produced your piece of paper and had to get it typed, and the secretarial input into the process was of a different order in those pre-computer days. Cutting and pasting was an art; those guys who did not get on with their secretaries definitely slipped backwards. We were a small department with tremendous pride and saw ourselves as the shock troops of Lazards; the secretaries were very much a part of the team. No piece of paper could leave the department without the head of department or his deputy having read it. From a technical point of view, a young corporate financier needs a commitment to quality and getting things right. Unless the work is absolutely first class, you can expect to lose the client. Not only has it to be high quality, it has to be done extremely fast.

At this stage in my career, people at my level were still known as juniors. The title explosion came somewhat later. We don't have juniors any more. I became a senior around 1977–8. Later, I spent three months at Harvard Business School on a senior management programme which put an academic framework on the instincts I had about how to run or not run a firm. I became a director on 1 January 1985. As a director in Corporate Finance you are encouraged to secure your own clients. Whilst you are a team player, in the end you are trying to persuade the client not only to ring the bank but to ring *you*. It's important that the client can talk to you because, outside their love life, these transactions are often the most emotional part of their lives – it may be a once-in-a-lifetime event for them.

It was the days when beauty contesting started and you had to go and make presentations, which we were all very bad at to begin with, but we learned. For example, the client will call in six banks and each will be given three-quarters of an hour to show their beautiful slide presentation and prove they know their subject backwards and are frightfully energetic. The whole idea was shoved forward by the privatization process because the government couldn't afford to be seen to be just picking so they had to have a beauty contest system through the Treasury. That set the tone for business, it's a bit of a fashion and there's been a flood recently – we do about thirty a year. It doesn't always happen. We still get asked to do things because people say, 'Because of your relationship with x, y, or z, you seem to be the right people to handle this.' Then we have to weigh up whether we want the client and quite often we decide that we don't. On the other side, we do a tremendous amount of marketing and taking ideas to companies who are not yet clients. We try and steer things into a softer process than a presentation by arranging a dinner or a series of lunches because that's a better way of allowing people to express their personalities. A lot of it is to do with personalities – do you fit in the way you work and the way that you think? A lot of thought goes into which individual is going to fit with which individual.

In the run-up to Big Bang, many of us at Lazards were very anti the idea of buying a broker and jobber. The opposition in the marketplace said we would lose our clients if we couldn't offer an integrated service but they were wrong and I don't think anybody who is honest would disagree now. Everybody had written us off but we had just created Lazard

Partners and we had a new and energetic Chairman and Chief Executive in John Nott, who had previously been Secretary of Defence for Mrs Thatcher. I jumped a generation of people (I was thirty-six) and was appointed Deputy Chief Executive. We realized that we needed to jack up our act and hire one or two really good people and take advantage of the fact that, after Big Bang, there were good people inside other organizations willing to make a move. We took someone from Kleinworts, someone from Schroders, someone from BZW and someone from Citibank. We concentrated on our Corporate Finance business and it went 'p'choom'!

Another thing we did was get a new Finance Director who started a long and slow haul on improving the IT and computer side. We also got in a training guy. We did a lot of internal management improvement. It was particularly good fun because we were winning in the marketplace. In 1986 profits were fifteen or sixteen million but by 1990 they were nearly seventy million. It was a period of tremendous boom in the financial markets, particularly in Mergers and Acquisitions, and we got a very decent share of things. In 1989, probably the height of take-over activity, we were number one. That was partly because we hadn't joined in Big Bang, we had focused and had minimal distraction. 1989 was quite a year for me because I headed our team on the Gateway bid (for which we earned about eight million) and on the BAT bid (for which our fees were about fifteen million).

When John Nott retired from Lazards in 1990, I was appointed Chief Executive and I took over as Chairman in January 1992. The first few months were nerve-racking. I had just turned forty, most of my senior colleagues were older than me and I had to find out if they would follow me and, if I needed to exercise it, submit to my authority. They were marvellous. It helped that 1990 was a good year. Most people in senior positions within the big institutions are twenty years older than me and if I meet them at dinner they say, 'What do you do?' I tell them I'm at Lazards and they say, 'What do you do there?' I say, 'I run it', and they look at me and frown and you can see 'Can that really be right?' is ticking through their minds.

The last two years have been difficult because the markets on the whole turned against us. I have worked hard to upgrade people generally and I've had to make quite a lot of people redundant. We've had some successes in winning new business and likewise some set-backs. Since I joined Lazards, the three traditional businesses have been through dramatic changes. The Banking Division has gone from being the powerhouse of the place in terms of profit and clout to having to shift away from their traditional business into new businesses where brains rather than clout apply. It's gone from a hundred and fifty people to sixty-five. The

Investment Management Division in the early seventies was, broadly speaking, equivalent to those at Schroders, Rothschilds, Barings, Warburgs, etc., but was badly managed and consequently whilst Schroders manage twenty-five plus billion and Warburg's thirty to forty billion, we manage five billion (which has doubled in the last year). It's a hell of a long way to claw back but we're moving in the right direction. It's down to just over a hundred people from a hundred and sixty-five. When I joined, the Corporate Finance Department was probably ten strong and it's now a hundred and thirty. We have added a capital markets business and Stock Exchange money broking. We added a real estate team and also a venture capital division. John Nott and I got carried away with our success and went into oil trading but after it lost a million pounds, we decided to stop!

Davina Walter (b. 1954)

Cazenove, which I joined in 1974, had a lovely atmosphere and was (and still is) unique. The senior partners worked in a wonderful wood-panelled room with portraits on the walls and beautiful desks. It was always said that all the partners had never met together and that the senior partners carried the vote of the remainder and made all the decisions. There was a lighting system throughout the office for calling a partner. In the days of old, when there were only twelve partners, there was an old clock and each partner had a number and, if the number flashed red, would pick up the telephone. There were about twenty partners when I started and you had to be a real stand-out person to make the grade.

I spent three months in the back office and three weeks in Cazenove's Box on the Stock Exchange floor and was then offered a proper training programme and spent two years doing the rounds of each department. The hub of Cazenove's has always been corporate finance, although it was never known as such, and there was the fund-management side as well as a huge private client base.

During my training period, business was incredibly slack, everyone thought the market was going to disappear into a black hole so there was no turnover and we were twiddling our thumbs. In the final quarter of 1974 the partners paid our bonus out of their own pocket and Cazenove's were the only stockbroking firm not to lay anybody off. I went round in a slight pink cloud, not realizing quite how bad things were. The seriousness of the situation was brought home to me when I saw Coleman Street cordoned off because someone had jumped out of the window, committing suicide. I felt so sick at that. There were quite a few suicides. What reversed it all were a couple of big rights issues, the Commercial Union being one. It triggered a lot of activity and the market had a phenomenal lift.

I was told I was going into the American research side and I worked with three other people. Just before Christmas 1976 the head of our department and one of the others left suddenly, leaving me with someone I'd known since I was about eight years old, Christian Kindersley, as the American department. I'd had all of three months' experience. Exchange controls were in place, making investing overseas an expensive process so it was a quiet time to be learning. A typical client would be a UK pension fund who would say to us, 'What do you think of these twenty companies?' and I'd go through the statistics and stuff and form an opinion. It's hard to imagine now, but even in 1976 the information flow was not what it is now, so a lot of clients wouldn't even have a screen and wouldn't know how any of their stocks were doing. American companies would send us their Report and Accounts and the *FT* had a library of those, too. Things like couriers were incredibly expensive so you depended on the postal system. Cazenove's had a New York office – with only three men and a dog in it – and a regular pouch went back and forwards with London.

From 1978 I made infrequent trips to America. I needed to go because clients would say, 'When were you last in America?' and I'd say, 'I haven't been for a while', meaning I hadn't been since I was twelve and went with my parents. Cazenove's were concerned about whether I would survive in America. The trips sound glamorous but it's jolly hard work and a bit lonely travelling by yourself. In a two-week trip I'd probably visit thirty companies and you have to do homework beforehand. The best experience I had travelling in the States was when I went with Richard Henderson, who was in charge of the US desk at Henderson Administration, and I learned a lot from that in terms of his line of questioning the companies we visited. Cazenove's were brokers, looking after clients, whereas Hendersons was a fund-management group, looking for ideas.

Cazenove's was a wonderful place to work but I was churning out reports on the same old companies and needed more stimulation. I was having lunch with Richard Henderson one day and he asked me if I knew anybody who had experience of US stocks and might be interested in coming to work with him in the fund-management department at Hendersons? I suddenly realized that was what I wanted to be – a fund manager. I said, a bit jokingly, 'Me, perhaps?'

It was a tricky situation because there's a very tight relationship between Cazenove's and Hendersons. At the time the chairman of Hendersons was Johnny Henderson, who was a partner at Cazenove's, and the connections go the whole way down. (Richard is Johnny Henderson's nephew.)

Hendersons didn't want to seem to poach me and said, 'It's got to be you who says to Cazenove there's a job at Hendersons you want to apply for.' I found it extremely difficult to psych myself up to go and see my boss; in fact he was extremely nice about it and totally understood. He's married to a Henderson.

I was with Cazenove's for eleven and a half years. The firm has been a fantastic success and has survived when other people said they couldn't go it alone. The partners could have sold out at the time of Big Bang and become instant millionaires but they opted not to sell what they regarded as their children's heritage. There was very much the attitude, 'This is not our business to sell.' They cherish whatever it is that makes them so special and feel they should carry on with that tradition, which is great and commendable.

I joined Hendersons on 1 June 1985, at the offices in Finsbury Square, sandwiched between Merrill Lynch and Enskilda Securities. Richard Henderson had launched the American Small Companies Fund, very much his baby, and he handed it to me on day one and watched me decimate the portfolio. I sold all his favourite stocks and put in stocks that I liked. That was my testing-ground and in a matter of months I was given a number of other funds to run. It was no different from what I was doing at Cazenove's except that I had to make the decision about investments rather than making suggestions to clients about what they might do. Speed is of the essence. People who over-analyse can't make a decision. If you waver, you don't make a good fund manager.

I love what I do. I'm ambitious but not overly ambitious. I want to do a good job and be involved in things at a senior level but I don't have a burning ambition to run the company, maybe in part because I want to keep the balance I've got and be able to spend time with my husband and two sons. I certainly don't have any illusions that I might become Chairman, that's not where my skills lie and I haven't got broad enough experience.

When I joined Hendersons, I was employee one hundred and seventy-nine or eighty. Within two years there were over six hundred people and instead of having our Monday morning meetings of the investment department round a single table, we have a big room and sit in rows on chairs, so it's a different atmosphere. We moved into our new building, 3, Finsbury Avenue, part of the Broadgate development, in August 1985. I'm a tiny fish in a huge pond. One thing I'm very conscious of is that previously I would always know people in the back office and go and see them, whereas now I never get the chance to go to other floors in our office. I feel sad that I only see people when I bump into them in the lift. There's a slightly different culture and that was probably inevitable, a tougher exterior to the whole way of doing business. Having said that, at Hendersons we work very much as a team and are kept posted of everything as it progresses.

Valerie Thompson (b. 1956)

I started at Hitchens Harrison in 1971 and earned twelve pounds a week doing filing and helping with the switchboard. I started going to typing classes in Chadwell Heath every Wednesday night. I was with the firm for ten months or so. It was a boom time and I ended up getting a huge bonus of about a hundred and ninety pounds. I'd never had that much money in my entire life, but the work at Hitchens Harrison was boring so, through an agency, I went to another stockbroking firm, Vickers da Costa, as a telex operator. I didn't know how to operate the telex but the recruitment agency said, 'Don't worry. Just tell them you can do it.' On the first day, I was in a complete sweat and the supervisor was just terrifying. I didn't know what I was doing. A stockbroker asked me to get a price in Peugeot – this shows my ignorance – and was screaming and kicking the bin because he was frantically trying to trade in Peugeot and I'd asked for the price of Persia because I didn't know what he was saying. He must have thought, 'Oh my God, what have we hired?' I was sitting there shaking. After that, I learned quite quickly. It was very exciting, my first introduction to buying and selling in the City. I loved that job and the guys liked me because I would work all hours, but the supervisor – a woman – gave me a really hard time. I remember thinking, 'I can't cope with this', because I was in knots before I went in every day. I resigned a month before my bonus was due to be paid and she wouldn't let me have it. I walked away. I didn't have a job to go to but I couldn't stand it any more.

I went and did temporary work and then I saw an advertisement in the *Evening Standard* for a job at Salomon Brothers. It said, 'Telex operator – thirty-two pounds a week', which was eight pounds more than I was earning before. I went for an interview at Number One, Moorgate and saw the girl and the guy who were running the telex area. I went for a couple of interviews but they felt I was too young. I can't believe I did it, but I rang and said, 'Who runs Salomon Brothers?' and was told it was Eddie Aronson. I asked to speak to him and said, 'I've come in for two interviews and they've knocked me back and I know I can do this job.' He said, 'Come and see me right now.' I went in that afternoon and he said, 'You've got the job.' I would never do that now but I got away with it. I was desperate for the money. That thirty-two pounds was like winning the pools! I joined Salomon in June '73.

It was all live telex communication, buying and selling stocks and bonds to various banks on the Continent. We had a Siemens telex machine on line to New York the whole time and the other ones were just dialled up. The guys were sitting in the middle of this open-plan, oblong-shaped room and they'd shout to me to type live on to the telex. I was in at eight o'clock in the morning until late and I seem to remember working Christmas Eve and Boxing Day. I didn't mind because the money was excellent. I got a raise and good bonuses and after six months or so I was in charge of the telexes and a lot of direct phone-lines to counter-parties the guys were dealing with in the City. I had a lot of responsibility. I was about eighteen. At weekends I used to work in a pub called the Ash Grove.

I got married in 1974 (I had met my husband when I was fifteen) and my daughter was born in 1977. I was running the telex department by then and was regarded highly and well-compensated financially. I was earning more than my husband, an electrician, and he didn't like the idea of my stopping work when my daughter was born – he's never been a lover of responsibility. When I came back to work after ten weeks' maternity leave they'd started to computerize the department and I've never been keen on computers. I said I wanted to stay with the firm but didn't want to carry on doing what I was doing. I wasn't in a rush but I said I'd look for an outside job if nothing else had come up at Salomon's within six months. They suggested I went on the trading floor on the support, making the tea and being a dogsbody. By then I was on about six thousand a year.

I went on to the dealing floor at the beginning of '78 and started off making the tea and answering the phones, checking the tickets and helping a man called Sheldon Prentice – keeping notes for him as to what clients wanted to buy at what amounts. After a while they said to me, 'You don't want to do this all your life. How about trading?' I went away and thought about it and said, 'I'll try it.' What terrified me was that they announced to New York that they now had a new Deutschmark trader in London and that was me! I just thought, 'These guys are mad!'

It's amazing what you can do when you have to. At this point I didn't know what a yield was, what a rate of return on a security was or how to work out an interest amount. I was so ignorant about general matters. The guy in charge said, 'Don't take any positions more than five million dollars.' I couldn't even work out the noughts for five million dollars. He said, 'These are the names you can play.' In hindsight, I can see what he did was sensible because the downside was limited and the credit risk was more or less insignificant. I came up with swaps in small amounts like two hundred and fifty thousand dollars. It seemed like so much money but if you're talking about major investors that have maybe a billion dollars under management, two hundred and fifty thousand dollars is nothing.

All I ever knew was what I didn't know. I used to think, 'One day, they're going to wake up and I'm going to be completely exposed.' I used to get terrible indigestion pains in meetings because I thought, 'If anyone asks me a question, I'm just going to die.' I didn't know the first thing about the basis of economics. I never looked at the *Financial Times* – I couldn't even read the *Daily Mirror*. But I learned it. I learned it and I made money.

There came a point when I was taking positions in Deutschmarks and guilders and I had the idea that I would sell short and it went badly, horribly wrong. I sat there thinking, 'God! I've got to tell someone about this.' I sat down with my boss and said, 'I've lost a hell of a lot of money. One hundred thousand dollars in total.' I thought he was going to fire me, but he didn't. I can't remember exactly what he said at the time but he handled it brilliantly. He said, 'There's obviously something you've missed. Go back and find out what it was that you missed.' I learned something very valuable. In fact, it's good to lose money early on in your career – it's good for any trader to get used to cutting when you know you're wrong and then just starting again.

About a year after I started trading my husband said, 'We're OK now. You can stop work if you want.' I said, 'You must be joking! I never want to stop!' In 1980 I went to the States to do my Registered Rep exam. Because Salomon Brothers are an American firm they require every employee managing their money to take the exam. I took my daughter, who was a couple of years old, and my nanny and we stayed in these fabulous apartments in the Surrey Hotel on Fifth Avenue. I worked and worked for the exam and I was very scared. I didn't think I would get through. Getting through must have helped my confidence but I didn't read too much into it.

When I got back to London – Salomon had just moved to Angel Court – the guy who traded Floating Rate Notes was just leaving for New York. I said, 'Who's going to trade the FRNs?' and he said, 'There's a delay in the guy coming to take over so I guess you'll pick it up.' It threw me in at the deep end and I knew nothing about it. It was the worst two weeks of my life. By twelve o'clock that first day I couldn't get out of the chair because I was totally soaked in sweat. I was dripping, my skirt and everything. Dealing in FRNs changed my life because I had all the other major houses – our competitors – ringing me up. I'm sure they were saying to one another, 'God, they've got some daft cow at Salomon that's never done this before. Ring her up and see.' It was as if they were the big boys who understood the rules of the game. I had to stand up and be counted. I was given a hard time but I managed not to lose money.

When the guy arrived from America to take over, I handed the FRNs back and carried on with Deutschmarks and Euros and guilders – which I was much more comfortable with – but my appetite was whetted and towards the end of 1980 I began to become a specialist in the FRN market and later took over responsibility for it. It was a period of tremendous growth – when I first got involved in FRNs there was a total of ten or fifteen billion dollars' worth of debt outstanding and maybe a hundred issues and by 1986 there was a total of about a hundred and fifty billion dollars and many more issuers including a lot of governments and banks worldwide.

I used to get up early but I wouldn't get to work until eight at the earliest. I've always worked better at the end of the day. Before I went to bed I would ring Tokyo and find out what had gone on in the Far East and I would ring New York. You'd trade in the night. You'd do it in your sleep. When you know the market inside out, you can do it with confidence. You just have to ask the right questions. If you don't ask, no one's going to volunteer stuff. I never minded the calls in the night but I wouldn't want to keep up the same pace now. I used to see my children in the mornings and at night and at weekends.

Salomon were very good to me. They knew I was a bit of a different animal. I wasn't a graduate who had gone through the programme with certain expectations. They didn't look on me as if I were a freak and they were forgiving and accommodating. As long as the results were there, they left you free to apply yourself in the way you felt comfortable. I took trading very seriously. If there was a chance to do a trade and make the investor happy and the salesman happy, I'd be doing it. I guess my desire to make people happy was balanced out because I could also get my anger out. Emotionally, it was the best thing for me because all my pent-up anger against men and life that came from my childhood, I could express in trading with the other houses; I could kill the other houses, decimate them, wipe them out. I would swear more than most of the guys because it was a way of expressing something I felt deeply about. It was healthy stuff for me.

By the time I left Salomon in 1987, I had ultimate pricing authority for all the money that they committed in the bond market. I never found the risk-assessment hard. What I found harder was adjusting to the growth of the firm in the eighties and to its becoming more structured. When I first joined Salomon I was working with about six people and by the time I left there were something like eight hundred and six and we had moved to Victoria Plaza. Salomons is very different now because of its size and because the industry has changed. That's true of every firm. I'm very driven by my feelings. I didn't feel happy and I was getting more anxious and I thought, 'I can't stay here doing this.'

I left Salomon after I had been there nearly fourteen years. The firm was like a family to me because I had started when I was sixteen, but it was necessary for me to leave to develop completely. No one job is enough to express the whole of a person. I wasn't even quite sure what the whole of the person consisted of, so I had to find out. Leaving was like getting divorced in a way. There have been times when I've really ached for the feeling and the fun but you can't go back and you can't recreate it.

When I left Salomon I didn't know what I was going to do. Although I had earned a lot, I was never really good with my own money at all. I have a nice house and a decent pension from Salomon but other than that it just came in and went out. I saved some, but getting divorced cost me a lot. And I've got complete financial responsibility for my two children, who are in private schools.

I decided to go on my own. I put together a company, Euromarket Trading Consultants, now based in Shoreditch. My present line of work is primarily head-hunting in the capital markets. What I find most satisfying is that I know what I believe in and what I will and won't do. I won't compromise. I will say to people, 'Don't want the work. Don't want the business. Wouldn't even represent you.' I don't say it like that but that's how I feel – that they don't deserve us. I'm not in the business of sucking up to clients. We know the business we're in and they need to use us properly. We're not just a machine.

Philippa Rose (b. 1958)
I wanted to participate in the buzz and power and stimulation of the City. All the nasty things *The Bonfire of the Vanities* wrote about appealed to me: big amounts of money changing hands, secret conversations. The fact that it was a male-dominated environment seemed an extra challenge. I wanted to be a woman in a man's world, to succeed where men have traditionally succeeded before me.

The germ of Philippa Rose & Partners was born in 1980 and it was launched in 1981. We began with three parties of about seventy people each at the Ironmongers' Hall. I wanted to access as many people in the City as possible. I sent invitations to ninety people I vaguely knew, telling them they could only come if they brought a colleague with them and that, in their reply, they had to give me the name of that person. That bed of first contacts paid off and over the years I've had further contact with well over a quarter of the people who came to the parties.

I was a twenty-two-year-old with no experience, so I wasn't going to compete with the director-level assignments that every head-hunter goes for. I intended to focus on the younger end of the investment banking market because that was where I saw a niche. My pitch was to represent the first-time movers, people who had gone into the City, done a couple of years and found they were unsuited to their role, just as I had done at Kleinwort Benson. I was targeting the people who were considering a move but wouldn't be comfortable going to an agency.

The first assignment I remember was from Fielding Newson-Smith, a firm I got in to see through my father. At that time I was recruiting by advertisement. The Fieldings ad was the first ad I ran and it was a thrill to see 'Philippa Rose & Partners' on the bottom of the advertisement. My father cut it out, framed it and had it signed by all the family and it's still in our downstairs loo, so I can't forget it! The assignment was for a stockbroker for twenty thousand pounds a year to work in the corporate finance department of Fielding Newson-Smith, now part of County NatWest. I can't remember who I recruited, I've no idea. It was a simplistic business in those days. Now we never advertise because the people who answer ads aren't the very best.

I dropped advertising as soon as I could and started head-hunting properly. People don't come to me to find them a job. I go to them and try and persuade them to move. Our clients are the chief executive or the heads of divisions. You've got to deal with the key decision-makers. It was a battle to start with because every time I approached a head of division the tendency was to shove me off to meet the personnel people, which I fought tooth and nail.

I wanted a chance to prove myself and didn't charge the client anything up front for the first assignment. Almost to fob me off, they told me the profile of the person they were looking for. Of course, none of them thought I would deliver, but I came back every time with the goods and got quite a lot of repeat business. One reason why I've been successful is that I'm not easily intimidated and don't find senior people remotely frightening. I don't talk up to powerful men – I face them as equals. I'm not interested in power. I'm interested in excellence, which is different.

The run-up to Big Bang, 1985, was a record year, there was enormous demand from all sorts of different banks who were developing their business in capital markets, structured lending and corporate finance; I was active in every area. My big clients then were County Bank, SBCI, Goldman Sachs, Paribas and Samuel Montagu. It wasn't a big deal finding good people, they were still spread all over the City. In the past it was easy to find good people in second- or even third-tier banks. Now the talent has found its own level – the top people are employed in the top banks, etc. In order to lift people from these banks, I'm having to produce a very sophisticated argument. One really has to go into fine details about the difference between two houses.

Ms A (b. 1959)

My first job in the City was in 1983 when I went to work for a Japanese securities house. I was the first girl they had employed. The first year felt completely mad to me; I was in a department of warring men who were all stabbing each other madly in the back, yabbering on in Japanese all the time, and I didn't know what the hell was going on. They hated the fact that they needed you because their clients were Western.

When I arrived there were a hundred and eighty employed in the firm and by the time I left, two-and-a-half years later, there were four hundred and fifty. I was paid the going rate for a graduate and our pay rises were good. I started on seven thousand a year and was on about nineteen thousand when I left. The work became fantastic fun because I was travelling every week for two-and-a-half years. On the first business trip I went on, I stayed in a suite at the Bristol in Paris and couldn't sleep a wink because I was so intimidated by the rooms; I was still relatively untravelled and naïve.

At that time, the Japanese were trying to win business and they used to offer terms on deals which we knew were uneconomic, so they were basically writing blank cheques. The headquarters was prepared to take a loss just to be able to say they had got a prestigious piece of business. They were obsessed about competition, particularly between themselves and other Japanese securities houses. The Japanese are well-known for giving presents and Westerners come to expect and enjoy it. I remember stopping off – three limos and all the rest – to buy seven Sony ghetto-blasters for the management team of a car manufacturer. It was not an approach I felt I could adopt as Westerner to Westerner – there was no way people could accept gifts from me.

I was sent on an eight-week 'training' tour of the Tokyo, Singapore and Hong Kong offices. When I came back, my job had changed and I then had a superb time developing corporate relationships in Europe. There was a huge opening up of opportunities in Japan in late '85 and '86. I'd never been taught how to read a balance sheet so I went off and did the work for the Stock Exchange exams but wasn't able to take the actual exam because I had to take four Japanese analysts from Tokyo to Holland that day, which was frustrating. The other problem I had was that my boss was often away and I got worried because there was nobody else between me and the companies we were dealing with; I felt totally inexperienced, having had no training for the sort of work that was asked of me. I got rather wound up and would go home at night and scream at my boyfriend. I was working to the exclusion of looking after my private life and in retrospect I feel bitter about that. I talked to my parents more than anybody else about the pressures I was under.

I was very conscious of not wanting to look like a job-hopper, I wanted to have a good solid base in my first job. What brought things to a head for me was that my boss was sent back to Japan and I was offered a job working with a team where I didn't get on with or like the person in charge. I didn't want to be shunted somewhere where I would have to make my name again – I had quite enjoyed having my head.

I felt it was time for a change. Through my boyfriend, who worked for a recruitment agency, I got an interview with a British merchant bank and after a month moved there. I was doing similar work to what I was doing before, but I was introduced to a lot of different methods I hadn't come across, so it was a good learning experience.

It was the first time I'd worked with English people. Most of them were of a type; public-school, fairly upper-crust, but with a humanity that you don't find in all the British banks. There were a number of female directors and there was a feeling that the path was clearer for women, which was a great change from my previous company. I could set myself goals and see a possible future. We had yearly appraisals and a lot of informal appraisals. There was a sense of alliance between myself and the other women.

After about nine months with the firm, I became a salesperson in bonds. It was a small dealing room about the area of a squash court, one desk, oblong with two 'T's at either end, and about fifteen people seated round to hear all the conversation and it became second nature to tune in and tune out when you needed to. The average age was about twenty-five. It was a position where I could show my strengths and make something of the City; I felt that I had to prove myself. There were days when I lost confidence and couldn't pick up the phone and just sat there feeling miserable. It happens to everybody.

Selling is about getting on the telephone and using a variety of different techniques – involving charm and bullying and knowledge and whatever else you can muster – to get a fund manager to buy something from you. There wasn't any training. I was just given a telephone. I'd phone the appropriate fund manager and after a while I got a good rapport with some of them and a very bad rapport with others, whom I didn't call again.

You had to be incredibly positive and aggressive every morning. In the competitive market in which I was working, anything was fair play. I developed two distinct styles. One was the pushy style, which worked quite often, and the other was my charming tactic, playing on my femininity with a male fund manager.

Until the Crash came, when there was a real slow-down, I was working nearly a hundred per cent of the time. There were days when I didn't even stop for lunch. I would get to work at a quarter-to-eight and then it became a quarter-past-seven. I used to get pains in my neck and shoulders from being hunched over the telephone and tense, so I would have massages; once I bummed the whole day off work and went to the Sanctuary and pampered myself.

The October '87 Crash was a nightmare. We had a historical precedent in the thirties but the system was so different, much slower and fewer people involved and less money. The 1987 Crash was cataclysmic psychologically for a lot of people. You tend to get optimists working in the City and they can't cope in a crash because it's outside their normal psychological boundaries.

We were lucky, we had a flat book on the Friday night so we had no risk. Gradually during the day, Black Monday, people from the rest of the bank were coming and standing behind us, glued to our screens, making wry comments mostly about their own personal stocks. I could only think, 'My God, I sold x to so-and-so at ninety-three last week. It's sixty-seven now!' I had sold the tiny holdings I personally had on 11 October – by this time I was reading the *Financial Times* every day and also the *Independent* because they had a very good financial section. We quickly started to think, 'Hang on. Everything goes in cycles. This is going to turn round and there's going to be a bonanza, you're going to be able to make fortunes. The question is, where is the bottom?' That was what everyone was working on.

There was a rally in '88 but not much of one. The Crash was the start of the major sackings. I stayed with the bank until the spring of '89. I was on forty-two thousand a year when I left after two-and-a-half years.

At a certain point, you started to get head-hunted. I got approached by a great 'name' on the capital markets because a fund manager talked to someone else. He was always looking after my career – he fell in love with me and I went out with him later, but that was a disaster and another story! It was virtually in the bag that I would go to this firm when I went to a drinks party and was introduced to someone from an American bank. He had tremendous charm and I made the decision to go to his firm after a series of interviews and because of a personal liking and respect for this man. I joined on fifty thousand pounds a year with a promise of a fifty-thousand-dollar bonus for the first year. In the event, I got virtually no bonus so I was badly screwed as I'd given up a bonus of around twenty thousand pounds by leaving my previous job.

I was philosophical about the loss of the bonus money. I was getting to the point where money was starting to be rather important, and in a way I'm glad it happened. I had got sucked into a spiral of thinking I could get money for doing nothing, and I might never have made the decision to leave the City if the American bank had paid my promised bonus. I might have become a horrible person, or miserable, or both.

I stayed with the Americans for just under a year and then was head-hunted by another bank and went there for a while but I wasn't happy. I didn't feel my brain was being used. I saw myself as a tiny cog. A lot of people start to feel they're terribly important – the Square Mile has more egos in it than anywhere else and it becomes a wearying experience. People should be more humble because the real doers and shakers are not in the City, they're actually making things and running hospitals. I was on seventy thousand a year when I left. I would have survived in the City but I would have had to put up with the stress of horrible, arrogant people stabbing me in the back the whole time.

In the last three or four years of my time in the City I never went out or stayed up late or got completely pissed or went out dancing – I didn't have time. You get hooked and you don't think beyond what you're doing. I wasn't hooked on the money but I was hooked on the excitement for a bit. I kept thinking, 'I don't know how I can stand this', and yet I carried on. It took me until I was thirty to make the break and get out of the City.

A lot of us were affected by the image of the City in the early eighties and got sucked in. If you are very ambitious and good at what you do, you can still make a lot of money in the City but the price you have to pay is a tremendous amount of stress, probably a ragged social and home life, and for what in the end? In my case, it has given me enough money to retrain and be able to do something else. But for other people it may be different. If you're an ambitious person in the City you may not have other things you want to do, you may want to do it for its own sake and that's where it becomes dangerous. I came across enough people like that to know I didn't want to rub shoulders with them too much longer. It creates an imbalance in a person's life and on their outlook. These people had the potential to make a great deal more out of other sides of their personalities because, on the whole, they were incredibly bright. When they were at university they were the movers and groovers – they weren't the creeps – but because they met the challenge of the City and became so totally focused, the other elements of their capabilities just withered and died.

At the end the City was killing my self-respect and now that I've left,

I'm beginning to recover. I don't quarrel with having lots of money. It's what you have to do to get it and what you have to put up with. If I'd been a man, I think it would have been even worse. At least I can come out and say, 'I'm a woman and yet I made it.'

Ross Jones (b. 1959)

I had no idea what a discount house did when I joined Gerrard & National in 1977. I knew it was something to do with gambling. There were about seventy staff when I arrived. After two or three weeks I looked round at the place and the people and had an ambition to be a director by the time I was thirty. That's what I set myself.

In my first year I was doing settlements, which is all parrot-fashion and accuracy. There's nothing nicer than balancing the books and I liked the idea of the routine. It's an exact science, very black and white, and I love to be able to say, 'Tie the knot in that, that's done.' I worked from about eight-thirty to five-thirty. The beginning of the day was the busy bit and in the afternoon you were preparing work for the next day. We worked in a big general office at a long desk and there was a lot of joviality. One thing that struck me was that when people didn't have any work to do, they didn't hide the fact. I don't mind somebody sitting reading the newspaper or standing chatting if there's no work to do. Our job tends to be either intense pressure or no pressure.

When I joined the firm I was on three months' probation and it didn't cross my mind that I might fail. I got called into the chairman's office just before Christmas and he gave me a six-hundred-pound pay rise, which I couldn't believe. He told me I was now a permanent member of staff, which made me very happy. I bought myself another suit – I only had one – and a nice coat and some smart shirts. I wanted to look the part. I never had anything that I really wanted to go out and buy. I've never had an overdraft in my life and I believe in living within one's means if you can.

Then I went on to the dealing desk and for the first two years I did struggle. In my second year I was a glorified bookkeeper, keeping the Money Book. Every buy and sell the company did had to be written in a big ledger and balanced at the end of the day. People would be shouting at you the whole time and you had to make sure you kept up to date. It used to get quite exciting sometimes because at two-thirty you might be five hundred million short and we would have to borrow five hundred million in the last half-hour of business. You had to get the cheque in by a quarter-past-three and in those days you had physically to go and get the cheque and plug it into Barclays Bank. I went home at about four-thirty, it wasn't exactly tough.

In my third year in the mornings I went and visited different banks in the City who had money to lend us, a sort of social visit. I was still quite young and the people I was seeing were senior. The vast majority were very kind, they made you feel important and pretended to be genuinely interested in your views. They would say, 'What's the shortage today?' or 'What's going to happen to interest rates?' It was very narrow in those days, we might just have known what American interest rates were doing but no one looked at sterling-deutschmarks or had any idea when the Bundesbank were meeting. London was still a little island. The great thing about going on those rounds was that if ever we had a problem we could just phone up the chap and sort it out. He knew your face and he trusted you.

One came back and had a jolly good lunch and then squared the book off between two-fifteen and three o'clock. In the afternoons I was back on the dealing desk. I was quite slow in dealing-desk terms and after about one-and-a-half years they were probably worried that I was a bit thick. I remember when I found my feet. Before that, if someone said, 'What do you think interest rates are going to do?' I didn't really know. I'd just be sitting there watching other people and saying, 'Well, they say buy, so I'll buy.' I can't pinpoint what it was, but one day someone said, 'Buy', and I said, 'No, sell.' It was the first time I was contributing other than a clerk's role. It got to the point where I was working under Tommy Fellowes and he used to phone from the boardroom and he'd want to buy but I would think, 'We don't want to buy down here', so when he said, 'What's the price?' I gave him a false price. I'd just shade it so that it would put him off. I told him about two years ago that I'd done that and he thought it was quite funny. He probably knew. He might have been testing.

The next major thing that happened to me was being sent off to Spain for a year in 1983 when Gerrard & National took a small stake in a bank there that was running a discount house that wasn't working very well. My first reaction was, 'This is a career opportunity', and I said I would go without even thinking about it. It was a chance to get some experience of my own and get my fingers burned a little. I learned to stand up for myself in Spain because I had to. It made me a lot tougher.

I came back to London in 1984 and was immediately promoted to an assistant to the director, which gave me a level of seniority in the company and put me above some of the people who'd been my bosses before I went to Spain. I was put on to the gilt desk to learn about gilts. It was very exciting. I'd got a huge increase in salary. I bought a flat and I got my first car, which was a Porsche. Six months later, my salary went up again and six months after that it more than doubled. Big Bang was a year and a half away and all the preparations for it had to be made because it was a major change in the way the City operated. The pay-structure in the City exploded and we had to keep our staff.

Under Brian Williamson, who succeeded Roger Gibbs as Chairman, the structure of the firm altered. When I first came to Gerrard & National it was purely a discount house with a small presence in the Eurodollar market but since then it has changed a great deal, partly because of Big Bang. We now deal in the French and German markets, wherever, as well as in the American markets, and we own seventy-five per cent of GNI, who are commodities dealers in the futures market, a very dynamic company. There is also GVG, Gerrard Vivian Gray, who are a stock-broker, predominantly private client.

For me, the important development was Gerrard & National Securities, which is the gilt-edged market maker. After Big Bang we effectively set up as a jobber (i.e. a market maker in gilts). We were at one stage going into partnership with a major stockbroker, a joint venture, but we became more and more confident that we didn't need them and could do it ourselves. I was very pleased – I wouldn't be where I am now if it wasn't for that decision. There was a shortage of people who had experience and although I'd only joined the gilt desk at the end of 1984 it was at this time that I went on the board of Gerrard & National. I was just twenty-seven, so I'd got my target.

It's fun setting up something new; you're in exactly the same position as everyone else, no one's got an advantage. I was running the sales operation and the dealing operation. We had to work hard. Everyone thought we would lose a fortune within the first six months and get closed down. There was a survey done of who were going to be the first casualties and we were always named. That was a huge incentive.

I started working directly with Henry Askew in about 1990. He has been at Gerrard & National for some thirty years and is a wily old bird with a great market nose. He's a nice counterfoil to me. Henry either backs me whole-heartedly or doesn't go against me. When he backs me we'll be more aggressive but when I'm overstepping the mark he'll come in and say so.

This job is about having ideas and bouncing them. As long as you have six good ideas to four bad ones, you're OK. That's why you have a team of dealers around you; everybody should be bouncing ideas and you need a bit of disagreement. Your emotions are very much out in the open in the dealing room and you're vulnerable because you're putting your neck on the line the whole time. I get very excited when it's going right. I don't like sitting in a chair, I jump up and down, I rant and rave. I'm probably far more emotional than some people on the board would like, but the business is all about getting the feel of the markets. If you get it right you want to get the dealing room a bit pumped up and if you get it wrong you want to show you know you got it wrong. You can't bear a grudge on the dealing desk. Occasionally you get very angry with people and I sometimes go home livid. The next morning we'll have a good laugh. I'm probably a bigger gambler than most of my colleagues.

The key is to understand when the markets are just about to change because the real money's made when you see a dramatic move in the marketplace – it's normally because the majority of people had a view and suddenly all at the same time changed their mind. I very much believe in taking the contraview for most of the time – when everybody else is buying, I'd much rather sell a bit. The majority of the time, the majority are wrong.

The 1987 Crash was terrific for us, we made a lot of money because we were a fixed-interest house and not an equity house. On the night of Black Monday there was a dinner at the Savoy Hotel, the Lords Taverners' Annual Dinner, and we had a table. Roger Gibbs came in and said something like, 'Wall Street's down seven hundred points.' We rubbed our hands and said, 'Terrific. Suits our book.' If we'd been long of equities, we'd have been buried, but we weren't involved in the equity market. The next morning the money supply figures were really bad and the gilt market fell further. The equity markets were nervous and going down. A member of our board, who is at the LSE and used to be chief economic adviser to the Bank of England, phoned up and said, 'For God's sake, buy everything you can. They're going to slash interest rates.' We bought everything we could get our hands on. Within an hour and a half the American bond market had gone up five points, the gilt market had gone up three points. It was very exciting.

I was driving back along the Embankment in the rush hour that night with a colleague – I had an XJS Convertible – and a German car came up alongside and wound down the window and shouted, 'You yuppies, you are all finished. It serves you right.' He thought it was the funniest thing. We just sat there roaring with laughter. He'd got the wrong people.

The Crash pricked the bubble of Big Bang and brought the whole thing down to reality. It was all too much and everyone was far too pleased with themselves and being paid too much. Now, in 1992, there are about ninety-five staff in Lombard Street. Post-Big Bang, we got up to about a hundred and fifty and I felt uncomfortable because there were suddenly about eight people whose names I didn't even know and that really worried me. Like everybody else, we made experiments at the time of Big Bang that didn't work and had to close down those operations. I sit on the Staff Committee, which meets once a month, and we do a full staff review every three months. People feel the company is losing its paternal way. Two weeks ago we made two people redundant and that was the fourth year running that there have been redundancies. One of the two got a job within three days and the other's got lots of offers; both were in their twenties.

I'm extremely ambitious to create a successful dealing operation and I'm also very ambitious in terms of Gerrard & National Holdings, in terms of where we're going as a group. I've got to get a lot better at my job if I'm going to make the dealing room successful. I've got to become more disciplined in myself, in my trading and how I view things.

What is so tiring is that since Big Bang it's become so difficult to make money. We haven't done badly – we had one bad year – and have performed above average but in doing that it's taken a heck of a lot out of you. It's too long a day. I've tried to fight the way the City is going because I think it's wrong. They keep moving the hour back when the market opens. It used to be nine o'clock, then it was eight-thirty, then eight-fifteen and now five-past-eight. Somebody will make it seven-thirty sooner or later. I get up at a quarter-past-six. I go and say good morning to my little boy, Felix, and then I get in my car and arrive at Gerrards by seven. The markets are now open until six in the evening and there are lots of other things one has to do – admin, committees, whatever. You can't expect people to work those hours. I'm very ambitious but I'm just becoming aware of the sacrifice you're having to make to do it.

It's a game. The discount houses play a role in making sure that there is liquidity in the banking system and smooth out the money flows between the Bank of England – or the government – and the market. But what do we actually achieve here in Lombard Street? We don't. We're a punting operation, it's as simple as that.

Part Three

Issues and Opinions

Ethics and Control

Peter Spira (b. 1930)

Before the First World War, certain things weren't done and you heard phrases like 'people knew their place in life'. The First World War swept all that away and you began to get much more emancipation between the wars. The Second World War swept away another layer of cobwebs and things which were considered 'not done' suddenly became 'done'. For instance, one of the things 'not done' when I entered the City was that you didn't call on other merchant banks' clients to solicit the business away from them because it was a rather ungentlemanly thing to do. That was precisely how Warburgs made a name for themselves, because they went after the clients of other merchant banks. We would, perhaps, offer new, ingenious services. If we were dealing with a new and more open-minded chairman compared with the previous one who had been a friend of the chairman of Lazards, you might find him saying, 'Yes, we would like Warburg to act for us.' Of course, Lazards absolutely hated it.

In the early years after the war, there was a strong personal linkage between bankers like Olaf Hambro, the Kleinworts, Bicester, Kindersley and the Schroder family. They had probably all been at school together, they belonged to the same clubs, dined in each other's houses. The war still had a very strong effect because that had formed tremendous friendships and many of them had been in the same regiments, either the Brigade of Guards or the Green Jackets. Then there were a few outstandingly successful people in the broking world, Kit Hoare, Antony Hornby, Herbert Ingram at Cazenove's – Cazenove's has always been amongst the élite. It was a close-knit group of wealthy, cultured people who had art collections, who shot and raced and did all those sorts of things. The Governor of the Bank of England was the captain of the team. There were unwritten rules, you behaved in a certain way and people on the whole didn't overstep the mark. Life was very agreeable. Then Siegmund Warburg came along and upset the apple-cart.

The British Aluminium Battle was a watershed in the market. It went back to a business relationship between Siegmund and Henry Grunfeld at

Warburgs and the Reynolds family who controlled Reynolds Metals in America. Reynolds were interested in acquiring British Aluminium, a rather sleepy company of which the Chairman was Air Chief Marshal Lord Portal, who was a war hero. It was a typical post-war event that you had ex-generals and admirals and airmen as chairmen of companies about which they knew little. It was very much an old boy network with managers running the companies.

It was felt that a British entity needed to be formed if Reynolds were to acquire British Aluminium, so talks started with Lionel Fraser of Helbert, Wagg, who were advisers to a company called Tube Investments. Lionel was a charming, self-made man and not part of the Establishment at all. A UK company, RTIA (Reynolds Tube Investments Associated), was formed and made an offer for British Aluminium. I would imagine an approach was made to the board of British Aluminium who said, 'Rubbish, we'll have nothing to do with it.' As a defensive measure, the board announced they were going to offer new shares to the Aluminium Company of America (ALCOA), who were friends of theirs and which would give them an effective controlling holding of the enlarged shareholding.

Therefore, you had a board of directors who, perhaps because they were scared of losing their jobs, were not prepared to put before their shareholders the bona fide offer from RTIA which would give the shareholders a better price than selling to ALCOA. RTIA said, 'We will write direct to the shareholders of British Aluminium and make them an offer to buy their shares for cash.' I'm not sure that had ever been done before – an offer to the actual owners of the company (the shareholders) over the heads of the board – and it had certainly not been done on such a big scale in a hostile situation where the board was actively trying to fight off the offer and do a deal that was generally believed to effectively deprive the shareholders of the choice.

The offer went out to the shareholders and while it was happening, Warburgs went into the market on behalf of RTIA and bought millions of shares – the key was to get fifty-one per cent – and this was an absolutely new element. I was in hospital at the time and my colleague, Billy Straker-Smith, would visit me and say, 'We've bought a million shares in the market today', which was big stuff in those days. There were meetings taking place at the Bank of England trying to calm things down. There were leading articles in *The Times*. It was a *cause célèbre* all over the world. *Au fond*, Warburgs were thoroughly enjoying it. The adrenalin was pumping in their veins like mad and they were winning. There's nothing more exciting than being a member of a winning football team, particularly when you're David and there are an awful lot of Goliaths around and the big battalions are lined up against you. You can feel quite smug when you know right is on your side as well, because what we were doing was in the interests of the shareholders in a completely objective sense.

The combination of buying shares plus the acceptances of the offer we got from the shareholders meant Warburgs were able to announce at a pretty early stage that we had over fifty-one per cent, which gave RTIA control. They ended up with one hundred per cent and the old board of British Aluminium retired to their country estates. I don't think golden parachutes had been invented in those days – where directors get paid large sums in compensation for loss of office.

It was a tremendous stepping-stone in putting Warburgs on the map. We were fairly gung-ho-ish and there was a feeling of 'We've arrived. We are now a factor to be taken note of.' Many companies who had been contemplating buying other companies but were nervous of making hostile bids said, 'Maybe this is something we can do. Let's go and talk to Warburgs.' Warburgs became the leading experts in the hostile take-over field. There was a famous meeting between Siegmund and Jack Hambro where Siegmund said, 'We fought a professional war. It's over now, let's behave like civilized people.' The shook hands and it was all patched up. I won't say the Establishment banks actually liked Warburgs for the next few years, but they respected them.

Hambros would never have behaved as Warburgs did because Jack Hambro would have had a word with Hugh Kindersley at Lazards and they would have said, 'No, we don't want to upset the apple-cart. Let's try and do a deal behind the scenes.' If they had, out of character, acted as Warburg's did, there would have been less fuss because there wouldn't have been the xenophobic and anti-Semitic element thrown in.

Michael Verey (b. 1912)

The merchant banks were at total loggerheads, that is to say Warburgs versus Hambros and Lazards. We at Helbert, Wagg were on the same side as Warburgs and there was tremendous anti-Warburg feeling. The telephone never stopped ringing. For six weeks you couldn't call your life your own. It was quite good fun, looking back. Siggy was intensely tenacious and clever over it all.

There was an effort to get a syndicate together by Lazards and Hambros to make a bid for the remainder of the outstanding shares. They got together a consortium in the City to support them. It didn't look much of a starter to me. Then various people wouldn't join, of which I suppose the most eminent was Barings. I went round to see them and they said first of all they disapproved of this ganging up together and Evelyn Baring said to me, 'And secondly and probably more important, we would never do anything ever, Michael, against Alfred Wagg.' That rather weakened the syndicate's position but they went gaily on. There was a moment when the Governor of the Bank of England, Kim Cobbold, intervened and tried to get everybody together to have a truce but it was just a fight to the finish.

There were rows at every turn. Hugh Kindersley said that he had met Warburg in the street and said, 'Are you buying shares?' – which was a very improper question – and Warburg said 'No'. It was probably true that Warburg was not buying shares but his firm certainly were. There has been a dispute which continues to this day as to whether Warburg lied or not and what Hugh Kindersley precisely said to him. Warburg would have done better to have said, 'That's my business', and walked on.

George Nissen (b. 1930)
We were all agog during the Aluminium Battle. It was said that the Chairman of Tube Investments had a signed letter of resignation from all his directors – undated – in his drawer. I remember thinking how unbelievable it was and what an absolute shit he was! Yet, nowadays, I've no doubt those kind of things are quite common.

Michael Verey (b. 1912)
The Aluminium Battle helped Helbert, Wagg's reputation. We really made no enemies. We made perfectly good terms with Lazards and Hambros and the others who sided against us. But Warburgs were in the doghouse for a long time.

We all thought it was a marvellous earth-shattering deal, but in a funny way that was a lot of nonsense. The shares of British Aluminium were sold at something like eighty-five shillings and everybody cheered and said, 'Too marvellous!' About six years later, from my memory, Reynolds and Tube Investments were happy to sell the shares at forty-five bob.

The papers wrote a lot of drivel about changing the City irrevocably. The City was changing anyway. Warburgs were professional, we were professional, Morgan Grenfell were professional, some of the other firms weren't very professional. We had turned professional long before. Instead of partners doing everything on the back of an envelope, there were actually some chaps who had passed a chartered accountancy exam.

The difference was that until then there weren't really any unfriendly take-overs. You went along to the merchant banker, say Barings, to say, 'We have plans and intend to make a take-over bid for your customer, Bloggins.' You then delivered a letter and all the rest of it. In the same way that if a client of Barings wished to leave Barings we would go and say, 'Smiths have approached us and wish to leave you and come to us and we wish you to know.' All very polite and gentlemanly. After the British Aluminium business, take-over bids were made by letter slammed on a table at eight o'clock in the morning without so much as a by-your-leave. Nobody went round to another merchant bank any longer and had a friendly discussion about it. So there was a deterioration in manners.

Sir Martin Jacomb (b. 1929)
The charge that the British Aluminium Battle changed City ethics is simplistic and incorrect. There was plenty of questionable behaviour in the old days among the old guard, most of it smothered in a veneer of respectability so it never came to light. It's very interesting reading the 1957 Bank Rate Tribunal evidence. There had been a sterling crisis and the Bank Rate had been raised from five per cent to seven per cent. In between the decision being announced to the directors of the Bank of England and the public announcement of it, firms associated with two of the directors sold a great deal of gilt-edged securities which, of course, were going to go down in value a lot as soon as the public announcement was made. It looked like good old insider trading. The two individuals were both eminent City figures and were completely exonerated by the subsequent tribunal. But today the issue would have looked different .

Nick Durlacher (b. 1946)
The Stock Exchange motto was 'My word is my bond', so the concept was that no one did lie. But you found out that people did lie. You had to accommodate that in the way you dealt with them. You might challenge them if it was very serious. The consequences of challenging someone for lying was that you might be right and you might have some short-term gain in it, but there would be such a blooming awful fracas that you would have to weigh that up against whether it was really worth it in the long term. So if you found out that someone was an inveterate liar, part of your skill as a dealer was accommodating that.

Sir Martin Jacomb (b. 1929)
When people are working for foreign firms, you can't rely on old traditions and you have to have a much more formalized regulation and more international methods of doing business, methods which fit in with what happens in the United States and on the Continent. The old-fashioned British methods of doing business are no longer what prevails.

Peter Spira (b. 1930)
The market got too big and, as it became international, practices which we thought were over the top but which were perfectly normal in other

markets began creeping in here. Different people have different views on what's right and proper. The Chinese in Hong Kong think we're mad when they see our insider dealing rule and say, 'Basically, you're saying you can only buy and sell shares about which you know absolutely nothing.' In Hong Kong insider dealing is perfectly normal. Even in Switzerland it wasn't made illegal until about two years ago; I mean real insider trading, people dealing in shares of their own company with insider knowledge.

When I came back into the City after eight years at Sotheby's, I found standards had changed. Practices were going on that were considered normal which to me, in my rather old-fashioned way because I was from a different era, were immoral. For example, when company A makes a bid for company B, it's not illegal for the merchant bank adviser of the company to buy shares in company A provided no arrangement is made to reimburse them for any loss they make (as in the Guinness affair) and provided proper disclosure is made. I consider that manipulation of share prices is a practice that ought to be banned. It certainly happened in the past but it was not the norm it became in bids of the eighties.

You have to be ruthless against your competitors and it is difficult not to keep pruning your firm so that you have only people of the highest quality in terms of winning business. It doesn't necessarily mean they're particularly nice people – you go for effective people and that tends to mean you pick up a few unpleasant people on the way. It's one of the reasons why I was quite glad to get out of the City. I and a number of my colleagues didn't like the attitude that there isn't time to spend with your staff and for relaxed human relations. I don't see that changing.

People get worn out after a time and the great secret is to be wise enough to know when you're worn out or the world has changed. Standards may change and you may say, 'I don't like these standards any more. I would rather get off this bus.'

Nick Durlacher (b. 1946)

There has been a social structural change that's taken place which has moved City businesses from a strictly hierarchical structure where age and seniority meant you were at the top of the pyramid to a willingness now to pass responsibilities on to much younger men and women than in the past.

In many cases firms got rid of experienced talent at around the age of fifty. That may be a good or a bad thing, but there was a certain innate discipline in the old hierarchical structure. Particularly in the City of London, an awful lot of the businesses were partnerships where the senior people had their own money on the line rather than the more remote shareholders' or charities' money – that gave a certain urgency to management supervision.

Ross Jones (b. 1959)
The City is going back to raw capitalism. In the old days the old boys in the stock market used to make an absolute fortune but there was still a certain structure. We're losing structure. It's going to get nastier. I look at the people retiring and I find it distressing that the people coming up don't have the same values.

Hugh Peppiatt (b. 1930)
In the 1960s, there was not the regulatory work in the sense that we understand it today. The Bank of England had power to make regulations to compel the banks to act in a particular way and at Freshfields we did an enormous amount of work on how we might implement the Bank of England Act. Suffice it to say, the arrangements were made but certainly never saw the light of day.

The other significant feature was that I set myself to do all the Bank of England work myself over the mid- to late-sixties because I understood every facet of it. (I had good support from the managing clerks and another partner later took on responsibility for the work on the government stocks.) Contrast that with three years ago when Freshfields had at one time twenty-four partners involved with Bank of England work. It's an obvious commentary on the increasing complexity of the work and the whole addition of regulatory work. Formally, the change came with the 1986 Finance Act.

Michael Verey (b. 1912)
There's been a lot of people packing up and moving from one place to another, no two ways about it. It was almost unheard of at Helbert, Wagg – the partners didn't move for better jobs. It wasn't a problem when the firm was small. These people who swap about, you can't really rely on them. They may be perfectly honest, but if you're going to have a continuing relationship with a company, the last thing they want is a new face. If they've got accustomed to the first bloke and like him, they might get to like him too much and if he moves from A firm to B firm, they might want to follow him so you've lost a good customer. One always had to watch out that somebody didn't become too influential with a particular company if you thought the chap wasn't really tied to you. You can get blackmailed. One young man said if he wasn't made a partner he would go and take this or that client with him. I said, 'The best of luck.'

Peter Spira (b. 1930)
Anyone going into the big merchant banks is in it for what they can get out of it now. That's partly the spirit of the age and partly because I'm not

sure top management spends a great deal of time trying to engender loyalty. Because volatility is so generally recognized as being acceptable and because of the way the world is, you don't know whether the firm you are joining will be there in x years' time, which engenders the feeling that you'll stay as long as it's fun and the pay cheque's sufficient, but that if something better comes along you'll go.

Nick Durlacher (b. 1946)

One of the consequences of Big Bang was that, as a generality, the banks got into businesses which they hadn't been in before and didn't understand it. To some extent, they still don't understand it. A lot of the time you see great tension in banks between their traditional activities and their securities business. They don't understand how the money is made in securities, why they have to pay such big salaries to the people who apparently make the money. They've had great trouble coming to terms with the fact that earnings are extremely volatile and that people move jobs very easily.

Ross Jones (b. 1959)

Psychologically, we are still suffering from the excesses of the 1980s. Everyone had a go at the yuppies but I think one wants to look fifteen or twenty years older than that to where the blame lies. The Stock Exchange was a closed shop and it was greed in holding on to the fixed commission structure that caused Big Bang to happen as it did rather than in an evolutionary way. The management made decisions to pay fortunes to stockbrokers and those brokers made sure they got every penny they could at Big Bang and then ran. That was a generation of greed.

Charles McVeigh III (b. 1942)

The sort of family atmosphere that existed in our business – merchant banks and investment banks alike – was largely shattered by the drive for performance and the meritocratic undercurrent that has crept in everywhere. If business got tough, management in firms let people go. That had a profound effect on the atmosphere.

We've bred a very mercenary type of young person who comes to make the most amount of money he can in as short a period of time as he can, who doesn't feel a great deal of loyalty to the organization. He is grateful for the training he's had and for the opportunity to make a great deal of money, but he doesn't feel he really owes you anything. So there's a tremendous turnover today. It's a by-product of the business. It's sad when people don't try to balance the monetary reward with a sort of psychic reward of trying to build something in a business that goes beyond their own wealth.

Ross Jones (b. 1959)
Just prior to Big Bang we interviewed a chap to come on our sales side who had only three years' experience. He was expecting to be paid a good twenty-five thousand pounds more than I was being paid. (I was going to be running the department on a day-to-day basis and I felt I was overpaid.) We didn't offer him the job. I think he got that level of pay elsewhere. It was a stupid time. A friend of mine was working for another gilt-edged market maker and I know they made a huge loss but he was still paid a bonus. He was earning more than double the rate I got and we were the top two gilt-edged market makers that year.

Charles McVeigh III (b. 1942)
Wall Street is controlled today by people in their thirties. By the standards of Wall Street and by City standards, I'm old at fifty-one.

Davina Walter (b. 1954)
Retirement age in the City has come down so much. There are all the young ambitious people wanting to get into position. Somebody in their late fifties is thrown out now; that seems to be very much 'retirement age' in the City. In terms of the slightly younger people, there's either those in their mid-forties who are working incredibly hard (probably earning a lot of money but, my goodness, probably they deserve that because of what they're sacrificing in terms of family life) or there is the person who is seriously worried about keeping his job.

In fact, I would say all mid-forty-year-olds working in the City are worried about keeping their job. Firms have yet to tackle this. It is piling on more and more pressures on us all without seeing what effect it's having. People are having health problems. It's live by the sword, die by the sword.

Ross Jones (b. 1959)
The City should be self-governing. The politicians got involved and brought in a legal structure and the problem with that is if someone sails close to the wind but hasn't broken the law, there's nothing you can do about it. The lawyers have been a disaster – look at all the cases that get thrown out on technicalities.

There's two ways of playing the rules. Do you take a legalistic point and stretch it to its maximum and say, 'I'm within the law, therefore it's OK?' or are you taking a moral standpoint? I think a moral standpoint is very important. It should be embedded in the way people work and their whole attitude as opposed to saying, 'You must do this, you must do that.'

There's a different type of person coming into the City and, to be frank, they don't know how to behave. If you go back ten years, people could phone up the chairman of the other banks and say, 'You've come across so-and-so? Not the right sort of chap.' And it worked because these people then couldn't come and work in the City. The club system worked, provided the people running the committees were the right people. The trouble was that the City got too greedy.

Disputes develop within banks. For example, say we'd agreed on three-eighths and they thought it was an eighth. In the old days, you'd phone up the chief dealer and settle on a quarter, in the middle. Now you phone up and he says, 'Hold on. I'll put you on to my in-house lawyer.' It's nothing to do with a lawyer.

Peter Spira (b. 1930)

Regulations can never be wholly effective, in the same way that you can never stop terrorism. They have done an enormous amount to diminish insider trading but the fact is, there are dishonest people around. I have little doubt that a great deal of money has been made in the past few months in certain shares where people put out a rumour that such-and-such a company is going to announce a loss or a fraction of the profits the market was expecting – the market being as fragile as it is, that can knock twenty-five to thirty per cent off the share price overnight. It doesn't take much imagination to sell short of a few hundred thousand shares of Company X, spread rumours that it's going to come out with disastrous figures, let the shares drop the price a pound and then buy your shares back the next day. There have been some names where exactly that happened in the last few months and I have no doubt that some of it is dishonest. They may just be sharks who sell shares they don't have, which is called 'shorting the shares'. We're talking about professional crooks; amateurs would probably slip up.

It's amazing how many Stock Exchange enquiries there are where you never hear the results. It isn't because the Stock Exchange haven't got their suspicions as to who's behind the scam but if they haven't got proof ... The vast mass of people are honest but it's always the few who are dishonest who bring the system into abuse.

Sir John Craven (b. 1940)

I was asked by the Governor of the Bank of England if I would sit on the SIB [Securities and Investments Board, a regulatory body] for a three-year term. The SIB doesn't carry the kudos of, say, the Court of the Bank of England or the board of ICI. And the meat of regulation is as boring as hell.

The idea of having a board made up of practitioners in the financial services and investment industry and then having a staff who do the work has not, in my opinion, worked, because the non-executive director, going in once every three months to a board meeting, just gets a quick sort of photograph of what the concerns are. One is not involved in the affairs in the way in which the public think we are.

Insider/Outsider

George Nissen (b. 1930)

The way in which Smith Brothers were treated in the old days was rather horrifying. They were regarded as outsiders. They were strongly Jewish and regarded as rather spivvy. They were slightly hot. As a Blue Button in the Stock Exchange it was thought you had to be very much more careful when you went to Smith Brothers than if you went to some other houses.

Smith Brothers decided to open up in the gilt-edged market, which was surprising as this was regarded as the aristocratic part of the market. The key to the market was your relationship with the Bank of England through the Government Broker, through whom you needed a channel of conversational communication to get the flavour of what was happening. More importantly, the major jobbers were dealing with the Government Broker all the time, transacting business for him and using him to help them out if they got into difficulties. Smith Brothers came in and probably committed quite a lot of capital but it was said their conversations with the Government Broker were completely inadequate. His willingness to deal with other jobbers remained as it always had been and he was quite unwilling to do business with Smith Brothers. They were not accepted. After six months they simply packed it in. People were not entirely surprised.

When Pinchin Denny decided to have a go at the gilt-edged market, they prepared the ground much more carefully and talked to the Bank of England and to the Government Broker and eased themselves in much more slowly.

Jeremy Wormell (b. 1943)

The gilt-edged market was always its own rather peculiar little place. It was always said that Akroyd, one of the big jobbers, were gentlemen, whereas Wedd, the other big jobbers, were always said to be Harrovians. It was said unless you were a Mason you couldn't be a participant in the gilt-edged market at one stage. That has been thoroughly broken by Big Bang now. I was never invited to be a Mason, I made my views very clear on that kind of thing. Fred Althaus and George Nissen were typical of two people who would not have considered joining the Masons. You could smell a Mason a mile away.

Leonard Toomey (b. 1924)
Masonry is poison to me. There were three Lodges in Lloyd's. I would never, ever join. And it didn't do me any good, not joining. Their influence? Great. Not so much now. Masonry is in disarray. I don't believe in secret societies. I've lost Names because I wasn't a Mason. I had Names that were coming on the syndicate and giving me the old handshake and when they didn't get one back, that was that.

Mr B (b. 1944)
It wasn't until I was about twenty-six and went into the City that I began to know anyone who was brought up in the mainstream of British culture. I found it extraordinary. I'd never met an Old Etonian until I went into the City. I came to my first interview and met this fellow, John, who was so like something out of Wodehouse you couldn't believe it. He was the boss of the department in which I started my City life and he was one of the oddest characters I ever met. He was about thirty-five.

My first interview was with John and another, rather nasty little man who was very different. As they left me, John waved his umbrella, kissed it and said, 'Cheerie bye'. I blinked. It was the kind of thing that nowadays I take in my stride but then I'd never come across anything like it. John was related to half the important people in the country. He gambled a lot. He's the only Mason I know who seems to take it very lightly. He was a generous soul. The thing that always struck me about Old Etonians is how well they get on with one another, what a large number of people they know who were also at Eton and how these people filter through life.

Sir Martin Jacomb (b. 1929)
I am not conscious of whether people have been to Eton or not. When I first became mature it was universally considered to be a big advantage to have been there and people occasionally even wore the Old Etonian tie. Several decades have gone by since then and that has changed in a most fundamental way. We have been through a period when it was almost a disadvantage to have been there because people mistrusted any inherited advantage. Certainly the flaunting of being an Old Etonian as if it were a worthwhile attribute has completely disappeared. I have not seen anybody wear the Old Etonian tie or overtly refer to the fact that they were there with a view to gaining credit for years and years and years.

What was a factor for at least a decade after I arrived in the City was the difference between the old-fashioned people based on inheritance and family and tradition and the people who relied on brains and ability. As the years went by the former were made to look more and more ridiculous – the idea that you gave business to somebody because he was at school with you and all that kind of crap. It was essential that that went. It was complete anathema to me as well as being bad business.

Mr D (b. 1944)

I won't say I was obsessed, but I was concerned that I didn't have the right old school tie for the City when I began working there in the 1960s. Whether you'd been at public school or not mattered. It was quite common for a client to ask you where you'd been to school; they wanted to put you in a box. I became quite proud of having been a grammar-school boy after a while because it was different. They would say, 'Gosh, I've never met one of you before.' You didn't have the current regulatory regime and, as a consequence, they were more prepared to trust people they knew or had been to school with, mistakenly, because many of the problems that have arisen have been because of misplaced trust.

There was a certain arrogance about a group of Old Etonians. I used to take great pleasure in having Etonians work for me and making them work like hell. I used to run them very hard indeed. I'd never make their life miserable, but we'd be on an out-of-town job and I would say, 'Right, we're going to cut a week out of this.' You always got bonus points for finishing early because we were resource constrained, so I'd make them work until ten o'clock every night instead of going down the boozer. One of them, who's now a good friend of mine, would tell me, 'I've got a Debs' Delight dance tonight', and I'd say, 'I'm afraid you can't go, you've got to work late tonight.' I've used that technique on a number of occasions. I'm more relaxed about it now; once you've demonstrated that you can achieve, it doesn't become important any more.

Michael Verey (b. 1912)

The City has always been a place of very mixed blokes because a great many people, which includes oneself, were climbing up a fairly greasy ladder and the object of a great many of us was to get to the top if we could. It depended what means you used, whether you trod on people's hands or kicked them in the face to get there, or whether you decided you would only get there in a decent, well-behaved manner, something which other people would applaud. It's sort of how you were brought up as to which way you wanted to go.

As for Etonians in the City, it only makes a difference if they have maintained the Eton standards, which most of them have. During my time in the City, those who hadn't been to Eton were striving for Eton standards and the Eton ethos dominated from Kim Cobbold, Governor of the Bank of England, downwards. Good Etonian standards means a total trust – if you say you'll do something, you'll do it. A great many people say they will see you at a quarter-to-twelve and then turn up at half-past-one. On the whole, dealing with Etonians in the City, you had a sense of confidence that they would behave impeccably. People like us would never have had anything to do with Hatry. Kit Hoare, who was at Harrow, was very much in with Hatry, but my old firm wouldn't have touched Hatry with a barge-pole.

Within the Accepting Houses Committee, the standards were roughly the same. Those were the people one really came into contact with, or brokers of equivalent standard – the top half-dozen brokers. If you had gone to the bottom half-dozen brokers you would have found a very different life, but we never did.

The influence of the old accepting houses has diminished tremendously now because they don't cut the ice they did due to the enormous increase in foreign banks. The accepting houses have merged into something called the Bankers' Association. I'm not sure there is much loss to the City, the loss probably comes between the merchant banks because the Committee helped make us all friends. If you meet and discuss, you may have rows but you tend to see that the other chap has got a point. When you don't meet, if there are animosities they brew and grow. Curiously, that relatively small group from the Accepting Houses Committee still very much stick together – Barings, Warburgs, Schroders, Lazards, Kleinworts and Morgan Grenfell (less so now they are part of the Deutsche Bank). All the people are different and the businesses are different, but they have a regard for each other and it's rather like a forum which represents them because it's fairly powerful in terms of money and it's probably fairly good on moral grounds. But it's swamped now by the hundred and five foreign banks who work in London.

Sir Nicholas Goodison (b. 1934)

When I became Chairman of the Stock Exchange there were several things which I thought needed to be done. The most important was the opening-up of the Membership at the right moment to the overseas securities houses, because it seemed fairly obvious that the London Stock Exchange would not capture the business in overseas securities – and might even lose business in securities like BP and ICI that were traded freely in New York and other places – if it did not bring into the community the houses that were able to compete outside the Stock Exchange. That may have seemed obvious. It certainly was not obvious how it could be solved because clearly the Members of the Exchange would regard any bringing-in of powerful overseas houses as a serious threat to their own business. I also saw that, in order to make it possible for our Member firms to compete in overseas securities, they would have to be freed of the London restrictions of minimum commissions and single capacity when dealing in overseas markets.

Opponents of change came from three angles. The first category would be a number of practitioners in the government bond market, the gilt-edged market, who would have seen the erosion of the single-capacity rules, the erosion of the minimum commission rules as a very serious threat to their standard of living and to their somewhat large incomes. Other opponents would have come from people dealing only in the domestic market who would have seen the threat from overseas and the freeing of the restrictions as a threat to their livelihoods, particularly smaller firms who depended on a range of domestic customers for their revenue. There was a third general line of opposition from people who had just generally got used to carrying on their lives under the restrictive rules of the Stock Exchange, which I have heard many people call a club. As time went by, more and more came to realize that the competitive pressures from outside were going to erode their livelihoods anyway and took the very correct view that 'if you cannot beat them, join them'.

Sir Martin Jacomb (b. 1929)
When Big Bang came and abolished single capacity, the Accepting Houses Committee had to be reformed and rechristened. Evelyn Rothschild became the first Chairman of the British Merchant Bankers Association, directly in succession to his having been Chairman of the Accepting Houses Committee. I took over from him when he retired.

We focused the organization on pressuring the British government (mainly the Civil Servants of the DTI and the Treasury), Brussels and the Bank of England, as and when necessary. We wanted to do everything possible to bring business to London. We expanded the membership to include the major foreign firms, because by then it was clear that the prosperity of us all depended on everybody being in London and not on preferring British firms. Peter Baring eventually became my successor.

Valerie Thompson (b. 1956)
I couldn't have wished for a better employer than Salomon Brothers. I would never have got the breaks with a British company. A British company wouldn't have hired me because I didn't speak properly. They wouldn't have thought I had any brains. There isn't the flexibility in the British system, which plays it by the book. Salomons was unique because it was such a mixed bag and it didn't matter what creed or colour or

background you were because it was a meritocracy. It was the ideal place for me because unlike a lot of firms where you have to eat, breathe, sleep and interact in the Bloggs Brothers mode, Salomon were more cognizant of each personality. Usually they were very driven people so they needed to retain a sense of self and to express it positively rather than shut it down.

Peter Spira (b. 1930)

Traditionally, pre-Big Bang, the bankers were the people who tended to have a cultural life. They would go to the opera, they would collect works of art, tend to have a few musical friends, whereas securities people would tend towards sport, fishing and shooting in the lodges in Scotland. Now the difference is getting blurred. Bankers used to despise stockbrokers. When I was at Warburgs, the idea of ever calling on a stockbroker was absolute anathema. As a junior director you would summon the senior partner of Sebags or even Cazenove to Warburgs. You would never dream of going to a broker. Jobbers – you didn't even know jobbers. Big Bang forced the change. It was a shock change.

There was a period when young stockbrokers were making so much money for their firms that they acquired a spurious status that was largely, probably, with their yuppie girlfriends who admired their Porsches and their yuppie ties and bank accounts and all that went with it. Speaking snobbishly, I never regarded a whiz-kid with a great deal of admiration. I thought he was a splendid whiz-kid but that was about it.

Valerie Thompson (b. 1956)

In the last twenty years when all the markets have been growing up and there's been massive expansion and loads of financial products and lots of competition, of the people that have succeeded, most have probably come from dysfunctional backgrounds. They might be moneyed, and some not, but there's a common thread in that they're used to things being bleak and are forever, endlessly trying. People that are more contented souls still make a good living in the City but they're not as desperate or plagued by as many anxieties and not so inclined to go for the jugular and fight. The City really does attract a rich mix of characters.

Mr E (b. 1954)

Basically the management has moved from being a typical public-school-type management to grammar-school, northern origins and fiercely proud of it and regarding anyone who had a private education as being really not up to the grade. It really counted against one of my colleagues, which is disgraceful. You should employ people to be the best in their field and that's it, full stop. It doesn't matter if they went to Manchester Grammar. Who cares? It's irrelevant.

Mr D (b. 1944)

Many of the people at the top of our firm are not public-schoolboys today. Nowadays what matters much more is where you went to university. Oxbridge has a much bigger cachet that it ever had before, certainly in my mind. What we're looking for is demonstration of achievement; if you want to go to Oxbridge today, you have to set your mind to it and then do it. That's more important today than where you went to school. You have to have a good class of degree before we even start talking to you. You certainly won't get an interview with us if you've got anything worse than a 2:2.

If I wanted to join my firm today I wouldn't get an interview because I didn't go to university. When I joined the profession, the graduate intake for accountancy was five per cent so they were quite unusual and they all went to the big firms, but the majority of people training in accountancy were A-level applicants. Now the graduate intake is one hundred per cent. We have over 12,000 applications a year for training with our firm and we take on five hundred. We look at university degree class and O and A level results. The consequence of not getting good enough A levels to go to university today is not worthy of contemplation; the pressure on people at school is infinitely greater, which is bad, and it's moving down the age scale. If you haven't got an 'A' in Maths and English at O level and you didn't do them at A level, you won't be interviewed by us. If you got good grades in, say, History, Geography and Art at A level and a good degree but you got a 'C' and a 'D' in Maths and English at O level, you'd be screened out and not interviewed.

We interview very rigorously. You don't get an offer here for a training contract until you've spent a whole day at an assessment centre. About twenty per cent of our graduate intake is from Oxbridge and it's increasing.

Peter Spira (b. 1930)

You will read in the press about a 'forty-seven-year-old Jewish banker'. It has a perjorative sense attached to it. You won't read about a 'Forty-seven-year-old Protestant banker' or a 'Roman Catholic banker' or a 'Buddhist banker'. If you take the Guinness trial, there has been comment that the four defendants who were eventually found guilty were Jewish or had Jewish connections. That that was worthy of comment is interesting.

Sir John Craven (b. 1930)

I can't think of one black man on any of the boards in the City. In Morgan Grenfell, having a black skin wouldn't be in any sense an obstacle to promotion, but we don't have one.

Sir Martin Jacomb (b. 1929)

There's no prejudice that I've ever discerned on colour or ethnic grounds in the City but it's true they're not there on the boards. One reason is that until you've succeeded to that degree, you don't succeed; it's self-fulfilling and extremely difficult to gain reputation and break into the level of business and level of acceptability which would lead to black or coloured people being appointed to boards.

There is another reason, which is that the successful ethnic business communities depend very closely on each other and feel most comfortable in their own circle. For instance, you will find that Pakistani firms like dealing with Pakistani firms and that it's a close-knit community. It's a sort of freemasonry and it's similar to other communities with strong internal bonds – it's a complaint made, of course, about the old boy network, which is another form of freemasonry. Freemasonries are difficult to break down because they are extremely powerful.

When you find a community supporting each other in business it lends a tremendous strength to each member of it. They don't struggle to compete against each other but only to compete together against the outside world. Because of the closed community feeling, when you're trying to raise capital for a client who is a member of such a community, it can be difficult to get into the innermost details of their business, and this leads to an absence of total and complete confidence by the firm raising the capital. That in turn means that the terms on which the capital is available from the investment markets tend to be significantly less good than where there is total knowledge and total trust.

I think things will improve over time, very much like the arrival of the Jewish community all those centuries ago. Eventually it happens. When the ethnic communities are rich enough and confident enough to be much franker and let the rest of the world in, it will change.

Peter Spira (b. 1930)

I am sure there are places in the City where coloured people would be cold-shouldered. I would think there are a few black people on the boards of British institutions but I can't actually name one.

I've done a great deal of interviewing in all the firms I've worked for and I've rarely had a black candidate. I haven't actually met many black people. Because of the way things are and the way the education system works, you don't find many applying for the sort of business I've been in.

It's interesting to look at the next generation. My son, who is just leaving Eton, had in his house a number of black boys who were outstanding athletes. They were treated with no difference whatsoever from any of the white boys; they were members of the top societies, captain of this, keeper of that. You're seeing in that generation more black people getting higher education, so things will change. We're still way behind America. I worked for an American investment bank in London for five years and certainly there were people who were black, who were as intelligent and charming as anybody else.

Mr F (b. 1962)

Generally speaking in the summer of 1985, when I was first working in the City, there were two types of people. There was the classical pin-stripe brigade of people who were generally educated at public schools in the UK and had gone to either Oxford or Cambridge. The other group was more of the rough-and-tumble barrow-boy variety who made it as traders, people that hustled in the City. There weren't very many people in the middle.

When I was leaving Cambridge and was interviewing on the milk-round for jobs in the City, I chose not to apply to many English merchant banks. I wanted to be in Corporate Finance and the logical place would have been an English firm. I found the English firms were much more closed-minded and class-conscious, and they were certainly more race-conscious. The American firms were more meritocratic and prepared to let young people take on responsibilty more quickly.

The racism in the City in the mid- to late-1980s was not overt. There's a big difference between dealing with equal opportunity at a very junior level and when you become more senior. If you look around today in the City, you will find very few non-white, non-Anglo-Saxon people in positions of influence in British institutions. It may be because there's self-selection and those who are non-white, non-Anglo-Saxon don't choose to go and work at Barings and Warburgs and Schroders. Maybe it's partly because those organizations are not as meritocratic and not so able to let people rise to the top based on their capabilities.

There are some barriers that are in many ways the same for women, but today there's a whole element of positive discrimination for women which doesn't exist for minorities. Whilst I personally do not favour any type of positive discrimination, if you have a man and a woman of equal capability in contention for a very senior position, you may well find in many institutions there will be a bias in favour of the woman in order to prove they are an equal opportunities employer. I don't think that exists for Asians or Chinese or black people in the City. If you had two men and one was Asian and one English, I don't think you would have a board of directors saying, 'We'd really like to have an Asian to show we're an equal opportunities employer.' That wouldn't happen.

The City's changed even in the ten years that I've been working there and even the older, more traditional British institutions have become more open and meritocratic. This may be because of the influence of the American and European firms whose culture has become more widespread in the City. However, there are still very few Asians who have been there for a significant period of time and reached senior positions. There are also still quite a lot of people in their fifties and sixties who have a problem dealing with successful, well-educated, professional Asians. The most important thing that can happen over a period of time is that Asian people are successful on their merits and get into important positions of influence and decision-making capability and are role models for more people to do the same. After a while, it won't matter what colour they are or what country they came from or what school they went to. What will matter is their capability.

In ten years the analysis might be different because over the last ten years there have been many more non-white people who've come through university in this country and gone into the City. That generation will be very succesful in the long term.

Men and Women

Michael Verey (b. 1912)

My wife was an absolute asset when I went abroad. Wives were always included. Again, Helbert, Wagg were in the forefront of it. Older partners decided it was an advantage to the firm that the wife should go with the husband and see the people and form a judgement and all the rest of it. Wives were encouraged to go even when they had small babies; you know, 'Hire someone and we'll pay.'

It wasn't any use asking my wife's opinion on whether it should be seven per cent at twenty-one or nine per cent at eighty-two but I would say, 'What did you think of the man on my right?' and she would say, 'Absolutely unspeakable', or 'Most awfully nice', or 'Biggest crook I ever looked at'. It was on the people really and the life-style of the people that you were involved with. She's a very shrewd judge of character. It was usually restaurant work but we had various times when we were asked to people's homes and she would probably have lunch with the wives at somebody's house the next day. (Most of them were perfectly nice, hard-working mums with families and children problems, whether they were French or anything else.) It firmed up or unfirmed relationships. After you had done it several times you decided you did like so-and-so or that you really didn't like so-and-so.

Gwilym Lewis (b. 1897)

You don't want women messing about in a business if they're not in it. It's a bit different now – women are in the game all over the shop. You can't go into a bank now and you don't have your money shovelled out to you by a woman. Never used to have women in a place like that. Mentally, they can be quite good.

Michael Verey (b. 1912)

Women were totally disregarded when I started in the City. They were typists or bookkeepers, there was no question of them becoming partners or any nonsense of that sort. We respected them in the sense they were frightfully good at their job. Miss Muller, who was head of our girls, was a

Swiss lady and spoke five languages and could do shorthand and typing in all of them. She was an absolutely splendid person at recruiting and nearly always picked winners. But we would never have thought of her for one second as becoming a partner. She was very humble. She didn't realize how good she was at her job. She lived in Swiss Cottage with her mother, to whom she was devoted. If you wanted anybody to stay late or get there early, she was utterly dependable. She retired at sixty and went to live with her mama.

Sir Brian Corby (b. 1929)
If you go back long enough in the Prudential, there were separate entrances and exits for male and female staff. I believe they came in at different times and left at different times. Against that background, it always seemed slightly surprising that there were so many marriages taking place between Prudential staff – no doubt they were always meeting notwithstanding all the precautions taken within the building.

Michael Verey (b. 1912)
At Helbert, Wagg, there was an office dinner at either the Savoy or the Ritz, men only. The ladies in the office were given two stalls for the theatre of their choice.

Jack Spall (b. 1930)
When I first worked in the City I tended to go to lunch with the men from the office because although there were a lot of young girls in the typing pool, they were presided over by a tyrant and when you took work into the room it was almost as if she considered you'd committed statutory rape simply because she thought these young men were too much for these girls. I was probably scared stiff of her. Boys became clerks, girls became typists. Janet and John stuff.

Sir Kenneth Kleinwort (b. 1935)
The secretariat that did the typing was female. I think they were just there to do the typist's job, so to speak. I don't think they had any aspirations of anything different.

Philippa Rose (b. 1958)
The only thing that would change the status of secretaries is if more men became secretaries. There's no very good reason why men aren't secretaries. It's the old-fashioned belief that a woman is more suited to the role than a man.

The market for twenty-eight-year-old secretaries is twice as buoyant as for forty-five-year-old secretaries. Despite the fact that the latter group are hugely more experienced and generally more dependable, every man wants a secretary fluttering around him that he likes to look at and thinks is sexy.

Ms B (b. 1962)
I find dealing with secretaries awkward. You're both women and there's a sense that she's prepared to take orders from a man but she doesn't see why she should take orders from a woman. If you're like me, you over-compensate and are terribly nice to them and they feel patronized.

John Wolff (b. 1940)
There were no women when I joined the London Metal Exchange. It was against the rules of the Exchange. The first women I ever saw there were visitors from the Eastern bloc delegations which came in the 1960s.

George Nissen (b. 1930)
The arrival of women on the Stock Exchange floor was a very controversial matter. It happened in the early seventies or perhaps the end of the sixties. There were passionately held views that it was quite inappropriate for women to subject themselves to the rough-and-tumble of life on the floor. There were not violent scenes but you needed to be resourceful and to be able to look after yourself. If a new issue had opened in a particularly interesting security, dealing would start when the House opened and there would be an enormous crowd of people around the two or three jobbers who were dealing in the share – everyone would have their orders and would want to get their business done. There would be a scramble and if you were at the back of the crowd or you weren't good at catching that jobber's eye or pushing yourself to the front, it might be five minutes before you could get your deal done, by which time prices might have changed. Some people thought it quite inappropriate for women to subject themselves to that kind of hurly-burly.

Nick Durlacher (b. 1946)
I never felt it was a huge burning issue whether women should be allowed on to the Stock Exchange, but funnily enough I'd been through an educational system of one-sex schools and then to a Cambridge college which was very firmly of one sex in those days, so the fact that I then came into the Stock Exchange where women were not admitted as Members didn't strike me particularly as odd because I had been conditioned through my life thus far in thinking, 'This is the way of the world.' It never struck me as likely to pose problems. In the broad sense, the older people

were, the more likely they tended to think the admission of women to the Stock Exchange (and, when it was relevant, Lloyd's) would be likely to change in some sense the character and workings of the place. The people who didn't like it thought it would damage those workings.

I remember when women came on to the floor of the Stock Exchange that it was a curiosity. Even to its dying day, they remained rather a strange minority. At LIFFE (London's Futures Exchange, which opened in 1982) there were boys and girls from day one. Although the majority of the people on the floor are men, at the point of recruitment it's about fifty–fifty.

Jane Partington (b. 1956)

I went on to the floor of the Stock Exchange in 1975 and was about the third or fourth girl there. I was a nurse before I went into the City and I'd seen an advertisement for a Blue Button and didn't even know what that was. The first time I went to the Stock Exchange as part of my interview, I looked down from the Visitors' Gallery and saw men in top hats with white collars and not a woman in sight. When I joined, the young man who I was assigned to to teach me where the pitches were didn't want to be seen with a woman.

The girls all got given nicknames by the men – I was the Night Nurse, there was Sweaty Betty, Super Bum, the Grimsby Trawler, the Road Runner, Stop Me And Pick One. They were very cruel. Stop Me And Pick One was because she had acne. You had to have broad shoulders and a good sense of humour because you would be the butt of a lot of jokes. They would even suggest that you had changed your bra from one day to the next. If you were dressed in red from head to foot they'd call you Pillar-box all day and try to post letters. You'd think carefully about what you wore. They'd sit ripping up newspapers and sticking it all together and then creep up and clip it on to your skirt so you'd walk off and have a thirty-yard tail behind you.

The thing that struck me so hard was that the women didn't stick together as I would have expected. They resented each other quite a lot, it was a little like sibling rivalry. Two or three would pair off and be friends but basically they all wanted to be Queen Bee. I was a Blue Button when a girl in the market had just been made up to be a dealer. She had been invited to lunch with a group of jobbers and when she heard that I had been invited too, she refused to go because she said she didn't want to have lunch with a Blue Button. I offered not to go. They sat her next to the empty chair.

There were various approaches with men on the Stock Exchange. You could go out and say, 'I'm a woman, you must accept me this way', which was the way a lot of feminists felt we should go. You could be a gold-digger and a good-time girl and offer your favours around. Or you could have standards and be a proper human being. You had to win their confidence and their friendship. Life got considerably easier for me when I got engaged and then married. I was no longer in contention, somebody who had to be chatted up.

Ross Jones (b. 1959)
I'll make myself unpopular by saying that I do not think that women are generally suited to a dealing-room environment. You have to have ego to be a dealer and a bit of aggression. You need to be very hard and very tough. It's very intense and you have to be very quick. People shout at each other, they get very emotional and say nasty things. I don't think it is the environment for women to work in. Maybe that is an old-fashioned view.

Lord O'Brien (b. 1908)
I did notice a year or two back that the Equal Opportunities Commission had some effect on the Bank of England recruiting and I saw some people there who I would never have allowed into the Bank. I've got nothing against them but they are not in my opinion Bank of England types. They are rather rough people; not, I would have thought, completely civilized. This may be an old-fashioned view; after all, I'm no longer young and my standards were learned in my youth. But the style of many females in the Bank has altered a great deal from my day. There are a great many now who are far from being from the educated middle classes. They say it's because they cannot get women to come into the Bank. They have to look to the East End rather than the West End for female staff. I think perhaps the character of the staff has changed more among the women than it has amongst the men since I retired from the Bank.

Peter Spira (b. 1930)
There is a prejudice against women in industry and women in the financial world. A City career is not one that many women choose as it tends to be regarded as a masculine preserve. They choose not to go into business because it's very disruptive of domestic life, it's jolly difficult to have children and to see much of them. There's always a tendency for men to think, 'This woman's doing frightfully well but it's only a question of time before she starts having babies.' Even if she goes on working there are going to be crises with the children. There's always at the back of your mind the thought that they're not going to be able to give, for practical reasons, a total commitment. Of course, that doesn't apply to single

women or women who don't have children, but the prejudice is still there. It's a combination of women not choosing those particular careers and it still being a fairly masculine world.

I'm a great believer in having women in organizations because they bring a different viewpoint. They're often brighter and they have wiles which men don't have. I can think of occasions when clients have absolutely lapped it up – if you take an attractive girl as an assistant rather than some heavy rugger-playing man, the client is probably far more disposed to see you than otherwise. You choose the right person for the job. The Japanese would be surprised if we said, 'Our colleague will call on you about various things and she is a woman.' I don't think they would be comfortable with that. Women are at a disadvantage pretty well in any country in the financial services world. They have to have something extra compared with a man because of these prejudices.

Michael Verey (b. 1912)

Once the universities started opening up to female entrants and they were getting degrees just as good as men or better, why shouldn't a woman be just as good as a potential account supervisor or partner as any man? Much more of it happened after I left Schroders, which is now fifteen years ago. We were taking girls and if they turned out to be bright, all right, they got another leg up the ladder. But we weren't looking for girls. If they applied and appeared to be jolly good, they got a chance. There were no women partners when I was Chairman but there were some female assistant directors and they were just as bright as the chaps.

I didn't want to take women just because they were women. They had to be as good or better than the men. We were more likely to lose them because they would marry and have babies and go away somewhere, so they weren't a long-term bet for our sort of business. My principal worry was having too many of them. Whereas a lot of the men come and stay for forty years – and for them, unless they get an inheritance, it's a career which they are going on with until they are sixty – not many of the women look upon it as something they are going to be pensioned off from at sixty.

Ms B (b. 1962)

The men I was working with were highly competitive Euroshits who felt threatened because they didn't know anything about me. They'd heard what a terrific reputation I had and were worried that I was going to write more tickets than them, and wouldn't that be terrible because I was a woman and their masculinity would be undermined? The better your reputation, the more threatened they are and the worse they behave. A female colleague of theirs told me that in their old firm they felt secure and had been just about bearable but in the new environment they became intolerable – arrogant, rude, unhelpful. It wasn't just me. The other girl had been working with them for ages and had the same problem.

Ms C (b. 1956)
I was the first woman to be made a manager of men in my particular area – UK institutional sales – which is probably the last bastion of maleness left in the City. I've recently had a man refuse to work for me. He point-blank refused to work for a woman. He was thirty and belligerent. It was immaturity and insecurity – a wish for a world which doesn't exist any more except in his mind – a beer-swilling, rugby-playing world where I wouldn't fit in. After a year, he was transferred away from my team. I don't think he'll succeed in the City, he'll self-destruct unless he grows up.

Ms A (b. 1959)
He was this highly stressed person. He would always leave it till the last minute before going to the airport and we'd have to run. In Japan, the junior person always carries the bags and the fact that I was Western and female made no difference. I carried everything. We're talking about ton-weights of paper. The classic time was in Paris when I was running after him and my heel broke. I wandered around for the rest of the day on tip-toe and my leg hurt like mad. He'd always fit in too many meetings and you'd be exhausted by the end of the day.

Peter Spira (b. 1930)
Philippa Rose's success has nothing to do with her father having been in the City. She is a remarkable, dynamic and incredibly efficient woman. She has a very masculine mind. She thinks like a man, whereas women, including successful businesswomen, often partially think like women. This may be in the eye of the observer. Philippa Rose's timing is immaculate and she follows a sensible policy of only working for four or five major houses. I introduced her to Goldman Sachs and she has produced remarkable results for them.

Philippa Rose (b. 1958)
When Peter Spira described me as having a masculine mind, I suspect he meant goal-orientated, forceful, aggressive, outspoken – I guess he is right. I seem to have a reputation in the City for being hard-nosed and forceful; the word 'tough' comes up over and over again. I think 'tough' and 'aggressive' are not words they would use if I was a man. In a businessman, a certain level of forcefulness and toughness is accepted as normal. That

same level in a woman, particularly a British woman, seems less usual and therefore more noteworthy.

Ms B (b. 1962)
The team of women in the fund-management department at one of the banks called themselves 'The Tampax Team'.

Jane Partington (b. 1956)
Men always attribute a loss of temper to your femininity. I bit someone's head off one day and still think it was justifiable. One of my male colleagues looked up and said, 'Wrong time of the month, is it dear?' Actually, no, it wasn't.

Any woman worth her salt knows she's got to concentrate a lot harder if she's prone to PMT. Men go out and get drunk and come in with hangovers, they're not going to be brilliant in the morning. They have financial worries. They have problems with marriages. Women can have all those things too, but they don't occur every month. I wish there was some kind of willy disease we could attribute to men at certain stages of the moon, but we can't. Most women are sensible enough to know when they're likely to be under stress from that area and they make allowances.

Ms B (b. 1962)
I found one of my colleagues extremely difficult and I let fly at him a couple of times and once was particularly bad because I swore at him, which is a sacking offence. I was hauled in front of the boss and was also asked to see the personnel manager. Unfortunately, as is always the case, the personnel manager was a woman. She said, 'Do you suffer from PMT?' I was utterly livid. I knew my difficult colleague had come to see her as well and I didn't know whether the question came from him or from both of them cooking it up. I wanted the real problems to be addressed.

I do suffer from PMT quite badly. Its main symptom is not fury, it's a sense of not being able to cope and having over-emotional reactions. It's a real bugger.

I was trying to poach a team from another bank and there were various meetings at the RAC because one person was a member of it. There was a classic occasion, a meeting with the heavyweights from the bank and the three of us. It was organized at the RAC for seven o'clock in the evening and a sort of fourteen-year-old bellboy stood in my way and said, 'You can't go in there. It's men only.' The person from the bank was excruciatingly embarrassed. I thought it was hilarious. They bent the rules.

David Verey (b. 1950)

My father comes from a generation where women were definitely in a different category of human being, which is not to say they wouldn't be dealt with extremely politely and with great care. If he was honest, he would say, 'Of course, it's a complete waste of time hiring these women because they come in and leave us. They have children.' In his defence, I would say his logic is impeccable. It's very difficult to cope in business if you invest a lot of time in training someone and they leave you. Nowadays you don't actually have to ask the question because if you're talking about a senior role, girls in their thirties and forties will say, 'I'm married. I have two children. I have the usual hassles over nannies, but it's fine. I may easily want to have another child.' They're very up-front about it, it's not something you have to winkle out of them.

My wife's got a friend who now has three children under two, the last pair being twins that came five months ago. She is pleased to be going back to work. She's going to do a four-day week. She works in another bank in the City and she's designed her own job. She's very bright, she's done a lot of training and is an experienced pair of hands. But she's going to work in a small team and doesn't have the risk of having to stay there all night. She has stepped back from the challenge of getting to the very top and somewhere in there lies the nub of the issue.

One of our women staff struck a deal when she joined us that she would have an especially long summer holiday because she was a mother. Quite a lot of the chaps said, 'This is intolerable. We are fathers, we would like to be with our children. Why shouldn't we have that?' It's an issue not far under the surface. The male conditioning is still sufficiently strong to stop people pushing at that door but I can see a time when it will happen. As a father of three children and three stepchildren, I understand it very well. But there are jobs and jobs. The other night one of the guys here on the Corporate Finance side was working until eleven o'clock at night, went to the hospital, the baby was born at three o'clock in the morning and he was back to the deal and up all night trying to conclude it. That tends to be how it happens. They work very hard and don't see enough of their families and find it difficult to wrestle the two.

There's an attitude of mind that says, 'I am the breadwinner.' I remember after having the third child – and I think a lot of men feel this – that the feeling of responsibility is considerably greater than the first two. A lot of men get depressed after the third child. It's, 'Golly, look what I have created. I can't afford to lose my job. We've got to think about the future.' It's not the school fees. It's a large responsibility which you, the male, are having to carry.

Ms C (b. 1956)

Women working and having children has been the hidden agenda in the City. Everybody tiptoes about this delicate land-mine. You hear, 'Oh well, when you get married, you're probably going to have children?' said. They know they shouldn't ask you, but they're dying to know. The Catch-22 is that she wants to discuss it with her boss so it can be done in the best possible way but if she wants to get promoted, she's hardly going to say, 'I'm going to have children.'

In the back of my mind, I knew two or three years ago that if I was going to have a family I would have to start quite soon. I worked very hard to establish myself as a valued member of the team so that I could do this with a great deal more confidence than I might otherwise have had. You know you're going to have to ask for some leniency, some kind of understanding. I was terrified of talking to my bosses about the fact that I was pregnant. My immediate boss didn't want to make any decision about it and I had to talk to the Vice-Chairman. All I knew was that I would get the minimum government maternity leave but I wanted longer and I knew the firm should have a better policy than that. I wrote a paper saying what I thought would be sensible. I gave it to the boss of my division and he took it to our foreign bosses and got it signed. I managed to negotiate sixteen weeks at full pay. It was clearly stated to me that this was not a precedent. I was very conscious of being a role model for a lot of other girls and of the fact that I was breaking new ground. If I had mishandled it, it would have been disastrous. I worked until about thirty-nine weeks. Towards the end I was not firing on all cylinders but I was managing to keep a presence and maintain the rapport with the clients.

The City has never been particularly generous about leave (unless you are very ill, when they've always been very supportive). Maternity leave is not an issue which has bothered the City until quite recently because most of the women employed there were in their twenties and not wanting to switch to motherhood. My boss was very fair and sensible. There is a tranche of men coming through the system who do appreciate how difficult it is for working mothers because their wives are going through it. It's not just me fighting a battle – paternity leave is also very important. Men in our firm get one day. It would be useful if a man stood up and said he wanted a week or two off.

Sir Nicholas Goodison (b. 1934)

When my wife was producing our second child, Adam, I remember when I was standing at her bedside holding the gas over her nose, I was on the telephone placing some shares.

Davina Walter (b. 1954)

When I joined Hendersons, the wonderful thing was my immediate boss, Richard Henderson, just assumed I'd get married and have children but he also assumed I wouldn't let him down. Indeed, that's exactly what happened. Poor chap, within minutes of my joining I got engaged. And within minutes of getting married, I was pregnant. I wasn't feeling well when I got back from honeymoon and I went to a presentation for a food company and sat there watching the slides on food thinking, 'God, I feel ill.' I went to a chemist and bought a pregnancy test and just couldn't believe it. Hendersons were fantastic. Richard Henderson had three children and he totally understood. I didn't want to be one of those women going round in a smock, looking vast. I was determined to disguise it because I didn't feel it appropriate for me to go into meetings panting and heaving. I bought myself a size 14 black jacket and some skirts with elasticated waists.

Among my friends from school, remarkably few have wanted to maintain a career as well as juggling family life. I'd never been in close contact with babies but you do get the most wonderful maternal feelings and you think, 'I can't leave this little bundle with somebody I don't know and go off and work.' But I didn't want to let Richard Henderson down and it was the crazy markets of 1987, an extraordinary time. We've had two fantastic people looking after our children so I can do the job without having to worry if the boys are well and cared for. I couldn't just sit at home and think about what I'm going to give them for lunch or go and meet my friends with other children. That's not the life I could lead. I seem to be one of the older generation of women in the City and it's amazing how many younger women ask me about having babies and carrying on working.

Philippa Rose (b. 1958)

I suppose the biggest challenge I had was having to go back into hospital for a small operation the week after I had had little Fred, which coincided with an extremely important meeting with one of our clients who was considering giving us a major piece of business. I had been wondering if I could have the baby induced so that I would be free for the meeting but apparently a mother can't influence the timing of the delivery unless she has a recognized medical problem. When I had the baby three weeks early my first thought was that I would be free to go to the meeting.

The meeting was on a Tuesday afternoon at three o'clock. When I was taken into hospital unexpectedly in the middle of Monday night, my first thought was, 'Help, how am I going to get to the meeting?' I asked the doctors whether they could delay the operation for a couple of days and they advised me strongly not to do that and said I was due to be operated on at twelve o'clock on Tuesday morning. I realized it was going to be tight to get to the City by three o'clock. I managed to persuade them to bump me up the theatre list to a ten-thirty appointment. The anaesthetist in the end agreed not to give me a pre-med, which would have slowed my coming round, and I thought that by the skin of my teeth I could make the meeting. All went according to plan – until I was told that my surgeon couldn't check me out until three o'clock because he was on theatre duty. I kicked up a bit of a stink with the nurses and said it was really critical that I left the hospital by two o'clock. They managed to persuade the surgeon to come to the ward between operations to check me out. I don't think he understood why it was so urgent.

At two o'clock I was released but I didn't have time to go home and get my clothes (I had only a nightdress) and get back to the City by three. I rang my husband on the portable phone and he shot off with a list of clothes, jewellery and make-up and arrived at the hospital at a quarter-past-two. I dressed at breakneck speed while being checked out (in the oddest combination of clothes) and got to the City with about five minutes to spare. The meeting went extremely well and we got the business. It was all very satisfactory.

Mr G (b. 1951)
I used to work with X and it was just awful. Her children would ring at six o'clock and say, 'Mummy are you coming home soon?' 'Yes, darling. I'll be home soon.' Seven o'clock, 'Mummy, you said you'd be home soon.' 'I'm sorry, I will be there soon.' Eight o'clock. 'Look darling, could you ask Nanny to give you supper and put you to bed? I will be there very soon and I will read you a story, I promise.' Nine o'clock. 'Mummy . . .' It tore her apart. But she always said, 'I am absolutely clear where my priorities lie. They lie with my work.'

Ms D (b. 1954)
On Monday, I'm going to leave the office at about quarter-past-three to watch my younger son do his judo gradings. That's not necessarily the serious-minded female executive, but I want to do it and it's very important. Luckily, being senior, I'm arrogant about it and say, 'That's what I'm going to do and you knew that when you employed me.'

Valerie Thompson (b. 1956)
When I left Salomon it was partly because I wanted a private life with the children. When you're a mother, you never lose sight of the fact and in some ways I riddled myself with guilt at having left them. But I realized

that, had I not shut down and focused and been very cold at certain times in order to pursue my career and stay at Salomon, my children would not have had the life they've got now, which is vastly different to the life I had. They would have been to bog-standard schools with bog-standard ideas and would have ended up being grown-ups with very limited options. I would have been perpetuating the past.

My decision to leave was greeted with amazement. Most men in my position wouldn't have done the same. They thought, 'Is this woman mad?' Different things drive different people and men find it harder to break the mould because of all the expectations on them, whereas women have this emotional side, which gives them more scope.

I'm not sure I was driven by finance. The whole thing about being a mother and working and feeling guilty is a big issue. My daughter has said a number of times recently, 'Mummy, I would like you to go back and work in the City', because she enjoyed the glamorous part of it.

Peter Spira (b. 1930)
There are very high rates of divorce in this industry. If you work for a firm like Goldman Sachs or Warburgs, it's going to take a toll on your home life. Not much thought is paid to the fact that people have personal lives. There are trainees at Goldman who work until three o'clock in the morning, night after night, but the adrenalin pumps through their blood, they're young, they don't have ties, they're getting well paid and it's very exciting. Similarly, the investment banking business has always been fairly disastrous for marriages and much more so in the Mergers and Acquisitons business in the 1980s. At today's frenetic pace, if you are involved in a major merger, it can go on for weeks on end with meetings that last twenty-four hours a day. It's nothing odd to hear of people who don't have a free weekend for months.

It was clear to me once that an individual was working so hard that it was having a bad effect on his home life. I said, 'You've been overdoing it with all your travels. Take Friday and Monday off and take your wife away for a long weekend.' It came back to me through a third party that the last thing in the world he wanted to do was to spend a weekend with his wife. That taught me a lesson; not to interfere in private matters.

Mr H (b. 1941)
My ex-wife would claim that my bank and my dedication to the work ethic was the core of the collapse of our marriage. I've debated that endlessly. I don't believe it. There is so much to be said for loving what you do and coming home full of enthusiasm and having that permeate the rest of your life. The other way round, if you're bored and idle you may have more

time for your family but you are dissatisfied with your lot in life. My wife was the force in the family while I was spending a great deal of time at the office. She was a tremendous mother to our children and created a great home life. In a curious way it was a good balance. Being successful also meant we could travel a great deal more and take holidays. We never had great concern over whether we could send our children to the best schools. We could live better than we might otherwise.

One of the things my wife found difficult was the total dedication to a number of people who were not part of our private lives but were enormously important from a business perspective. For instance, we'd be sitting at home on Christmas Eve and I would get a call from one of my colleagues who had a problem and I would take the time to treat him in a way that was supportive. It might take an hour or longer and my children would be sitting in the other room and my wife would be boiling that the office had invaded the inner sanctum yet again. My reaction was that if somebody in the office needed my guidance, they deserved it because it was important for their careers and my management of the office. If I was wrong, it was that I wasn't tough enough in making people think for themselves and did not impose greater discipline on that kind of imposition in my personal life.

Gwilym Lewis (b. 1897)

My wife was very supportive of me when I left Sedgwicks. She turned to me and said, 'Now's your chance to do something worthwhile with your life.' Looking back, I suppose I was a bit of a workaholic. My work was my pleasure and my pleasure was my work.

Mr A (b. 1932)

The day of the '87 Crash was appalling. I went home in the evening and there were my mother and sister busy discussing some bloody dress or other that they hadn't been able to buy. I personally had lost a hundred and fifty thousand pounds that day and the thought of whether they were paying twenty-five or thirty quid for a dress was somewhat trivial. It merely serves to underline that other people don't understand one's business and that we're all different. You get involved in your own little world and there's a great big world outside where people are wondering whether to buy a dress at C&A or Marks and Sparks.

Philippa Rose (b. 1958)

I fear what happens is that men give up trying to involve their wives in their work lives. They often don't take the trouble to explain to their wives what it is they're working on and the problem snowballs. If you invest the time at the beginning to teach your wife what it means to have won such a big mandate, the next time you have a major *coup* or disappointment it becomes much easier for her to share it. Eventually the wife is so much in the picture that she can appreciate even the day-to-day developments and feels genuinely involved – and can better suffer her husband's varying moods and energy levels. But if the men don't make that initial investment, after a number of years it's too hard to break the habit and communication gradually breaks down.

Michael Verey (b. 1912)
In the City it was really essential having a wife. Generally speaking, the partners much preferred to have married chaps. They felt, I think rightly, that they were more stable, more committed, and with a growing female staff it was better from every point of view. They judged married men were a better bet. People were very old-fashioned on the whole and we would all have felt that if we had got a very obviously homosexual partner, there would be certain clients – important businessmen – who wouldn't like it. You wouldn't be able to say, 'You take this on', because you'd say to yourself, 'Gosh, old X at Tube Investments or Burma Oil, will they like a homosexual?' It would have been a disadvantage. Not if he were a bachelor, not if he were unmarried, but if he were an obvious homosexual. I don't know about now but I expect it's still true. If somebody sent one round to me I don't think I would mind particularly but I wouldn't be impressed by it. I wouldn't think it very clever of the people who sent him. The only ones I've known have, in fact, been unreliable. That's my principal recollection, that they are unreliable blokes. You can't depend on them. You can't be sure. It very likely came out afterwards. First of all you realized they were unreliable and then later that they were homosexual.

Peter Spira (b. 1930)
I have no recollection of the matter of homosexuality ever having been raised in the City. Obviously one has come across the odd individual who one thought might be homosexual but my impression would be that it would not be prejudicial in any way at all and that it's not as rife as it is, for instance, in the art world.

Jane Partington (b. 1956)
Homosexuality was more pin-downable when we had the old Stock Market because there were two-and-a-half thousand men there and a certain percentage were going to be homosexual and they had their own sub-culture. They would know each other. They would proposition young boys

as they came into the Market as Blue Buttons. I would take the prettier ones that worked with me aside and say, 'If he asks you for a drink, if you're homosexual, fine. If not, take your girlfriend along.' I didn't want them to get into a situation they couldn't handle. It wasn't so heavy and obvious as the approaches the men made towards women.

David Verey (b. 1950)
There was a man in the Stocks Department who had a desk close to mine and used to spend the whole of his lunch-time on the telephone. He would witter on. Some little time later, I noticed there was a woman at the back of the department who also spent her entire lunch-time on the telephone. It took me some further time to discover they were talking to one another and were conducting a love affair across this open-plan office.

George Nissen (b. 1930)
We would have been slightly shocked at Pember & Boyle if a married man was known to be carrying on with one of the secretaries. We wouldn't have regarded that as quite the thing.

Leonard Toomey (b. 1924)
I never placed Names with Mr X at Lloyd's because I didn't approve of his morals. It had nothing to do with underwriting. I knew his first wife and she was a super lady and she helped him build up. Then he got shacked up with this girl from one of the broking houses and got rid of his wife and married her. His wife was treated badly. That would stop me going on a syndicate. It's got nothing to do with making money.

Ms E (b. 1963)
It's amazing that I got through six years without having an affair with somebody at my firm. The work is all-consuming. Your whole life is spent thinking about work and doing the work and getting there and getting home. During the years in the City I couldn't even manage TV dinners, I didn't use to eat really in the evenings. You just lived in the City and breathed it and if you met anybody it was likely that they were connected with your work.

Ms B (b. 1962)
I very unwisely started having an affair with a client. I handed his account to somebody else as soon as I started going out with him because I have certain ethics I wouldn't want to compromise. It's one of those areas not covered by regulation and that's one of the major holes in the City – and it's rife.

The affair was going swimmingly and then out of the blue he ended it in a cruel manner. I was extremely upset and spent most of December going into work and doing nothing apart from crying into the telephone to my various friends. In January I started getting over it and had a very hard look at everything. I equated his behaviour with behaviour I detested in the City generally. I woke up one morning planning a new career and knowing I was going to do it.

I feel that someone like me shouldn't be compromising her chosen career for a man. On the other hand, if you're going to compromise your career for something, then it should be for a man.

Mr H (b. 1940)

There were always a certain number of office love affairs but I was always the last to know. At the end of the day I would have taken a rather dim view. We had a basic policy at our firm of not going out with the staff. There are endless relationships that evolve into marriage. The reason is that a lot of young ladies come to work for us and often work six days a week till eleven o'clock at night, and there are a lot of young men who work similar hours and similar days. As a result, about the only relationships they have exist within that office. There's been an acceptance that that's probably the case.

The problem comes more in the senior–junior relationship. There are legal issues in terms of whether it can be proved that somebody got ahead because they were having a relationship with the boss – if so, they can sue you and win. Or, if you have an affair with somebody and they get fired, they can claim discrimination.

Having two people have an affair who work on the same desk is a problem. I'd probably place them on separate desks and explain why. Anybody having an affair in the office should know what the policy is. If it became open as opposed to clandestine, then the consequences in the early days were that one would have to leave. But nowadays one would tend to separate them by department.

Jane Partington (b. 1956)

When I was in the Stock Market, one of my fellow dealers came and said, 'I don't know how to put this, but you've been offered two hundred and fifty pounds for the night.' The person who wished to buy me for the night didn't like to ask direct so he sent my colleague to see if I would consider the proposition. I've often wondered about their relationships with women outside the market. Probably they were the kind of people who have compartments for themselves and their home life and their wives and family. I was always high-minded about things like that. You had to work quite hard to get a good name and keep it but once you got it, it tended to follow you. If you stuck it out long enough, you became a human being rather than a piece of meat to be looked at, but when you first arrived you were undressed mentally every day by several thousand men. A lot of girls came and went because they thought the market would be a hunting ground for rich husbands.

Valerie Thompson (b. 1956)
I've got a very earthy perspective so the sexual passes at work never bothered me. I was flattered. In many ways I'd give as good as I got. There were probably plenty of times where – if you hear some of the cases going on in the States now – I could have been done for sexual harassment. I wouldn't touch anyone but I'd make remarks.

Ms B (b. 1962)
A lot of girl salesmen do flirt and a lot of male fund managers expect it although quite a few hate it, particularly the married ones who aren't interested and just want to find out if you're going to help them make money. I preferred the latter type because I didn't like compromising my ability by overlaying it with a flirtatious veneer. There were a lot of girls who compromised themselves a good deal more than I did – lots of late nights and short skirts. There are far more male fund managers than women and it's probably easier to sell to men because they are more impulsive and have more gambling instincts. My charm tactics would work on some men but irritate others. Some men would find it impossible to work with a woman and only trusted other men. You become very close friends with quite a few because you speak to them every day, sometimes in greater depth than you do with your partner.

I didn't meet men in the City I could have relationships with even though I was surrounded by them. The men in the City were arrogant horrors. I was breaking traditional female moulds all over the place and in my personal relationships I didn't play the female game, and I was always up-front about my feelings, which would put people off and scare them.

Ms D (b. 1956)
I know of men who've been caught literally with their trousers down making love within the confines of the office. The woman's sacked. The man is given a reprimand and then patted on the back for being a bit of a rogue. A woman is still considered a harlot if she does something like that.

City Dress

George Nissen (b. 1930)
When I first started as a clerk I certainly had a bowler hat, which I never regarded as a particularly comfortable hat. I had starched collars. We all used to send them to a thing called 'Collars Limited'. You put them in a box and posted them to Glasgow and it was cheaper and better quality than sending them to a laundry. They weren't very comfortable.

Nick Durlacher (b. 1946)
When I joined the City in 1967 all the men wore hats and there were still one or two people in tail-coats. People universally wore waistcoats with their suits.

Ross Jones (b. 1959)
I quite like tradition. In 1978, when I looked after the Money Book at Gerrard & National, I had to wear a top hat to go and visit the banks in the morning. (The company very kindly bought it.) I wore it with a normal suit. I felt a complete and utter prat. You get some funny looks. You got the contrast between the builder on the site who basically told you what you were feeling and the American tourist who wants you to pose for a photograph.

Peter Spira (b. 1930)
People's appearance does make a tremendous difference, how they dress, how they look. On one occasion I said to someone I thought that now he was going up the tree and getting to a level of seniority he ought to smarten himself up a bit. His tie was never knotted and was hanging loose around the first button, his trousers were never pressed, he looked a shambles. I would have said, 'Go along to Burtons', probably. It's the way the City is. In the culture of merchant banks, any individual who wants to be on the fast track would be sensitive enough to realize that he would need to conform. You will notice among the British executives in British merchant banks that nobody will be wearing brown shoes or a brown suit. For the British the tradition is that you wear brown shoes at weekends

with your country tweeds. I remember somebody turning up at Warburgs with brown shoes and it was like those cartoons with everybody pointing at 'The Man Who Wore Brown Shoes'.

What would I do if a man came to me with gold earrings? I wouldn't employ him. I'm allergic to men who wear gold earrings. It's not just a personal prejudice. I'm convinced that if I took him along to the Chairman of ICI, for example, there's a fair chance he would have a negative reaction. It's not something that goes down well in our industry. Gold earrings would be a bit like brown shoes.

Charles McVeigh III (b. 1942)
I remember feeling almost immediately I arrived in London from America that I was badly dressed. The most striking thing was that I always wore brown shoes. A friend commented on it. I didn't even own a pair of black shoes, except dancing shoes, so I scrambled around and got a pair.

David Verey (b. 1950)
There was no point in not wearing a suit because there was absolutely nothing to be done about it. I remember getting terribly bored with wearing a tie. The thing that made me most self-conscious was when I had my first briefcase. I don't know what the hell I put in it, but I had one.

Ms D (b. 1954)
It's very much a perception to the rest of the City that at Warburgs and Mercury Asset Management they're very much individuals rather than team-workers. There's this joke that you have to have two jackets to your suit if you work at Mercury: one is to leave on the back of your chair so that people think you're still in the office and one is to go home in. You must always seem to be working terribly hard otherwise you're not a serious person.

Philippa Rose (b. 1958)
I have a good feel for when to dress daring and when to dress formal. As an interviewer, I pay quite a lot of attention to what women are wearing who come to be interviewed. Their make-up says something, their jewellery also. Too much make-up, unsubtle jewellery is not favoured in certain areas of the City (corporate finance, relationship management) whereas in the 'markets' area it would be acceptable.

How men dress is also indicative. I wrote a very careful letter to one Australian guy who I knew was brilliant but who came to see me wearing a thin gold chain round his neck and a quite heavy silver bangle. I gently suggested he remove both for his interview at Lazards. He did, and he got the job. He sent me a big bouquet and a Hermès scarf to thank me for my directness. He didn't believe many people would have dared say it to him and it proved an invaluable piece of advice.

There was another guy who we had to get to shave off his moustache because we discovered that the bank that was thinking of employing him was reticent about making him an offer because he didn't look 'polished' enough. I pushed the bank to articulate what it was that was causing them to hesitate. It really irritated me – I knew damn well it was because he had a moustache. In the end they admitted it. I went back to the guy and told him. He shaved it off and he got the job.

Davina Walter (b. 1954)
At Cazenove I was emphatically not allowed to wear trousers, which was fair enough. I would quite often wear culottes as a slight rebellion. What has now evolved is more of a uniform in terms of wearing suits but I tend to put my stamp on whatever I wear.

Jane Partington (b. 1956)
At home I rarely wear the clothes I would wear to work. Different bits of me operate in different places. It's fun putting on my City clothes – the jacket and skirt – it's a good excuse to be a different person.

Valerie Thompson (b. 1956)
There were no rules about dress at Salomon but I never knew how to get it right. If you haven't grown up in that sort of environment you are always making attempts to change your image. I was probably quite a scruffy dresser because fashion has never been important to me. I've had moments when I've gone out and bought designer stuff but most of it I chucked away. I'm inclined to wear shirts with my sleeves rolled up and just a skirt, a bit of Essex in me. I like to look nice if the occasion justifies it but I'm not part of the beads and scarf brigade or the corporate pin-stripe suit. I'm sure there were times when people at Salomon thought, 'She could have dressed up a bit more', but no one ever said anything. If anyone had said, 'Wear a uniform', I would have said, 'I don't want the job.' I would have found it hard to be put into a mould.

Nick Durlacher (b. 1946)
There is a dress code on the floor of LIFFE which requires a certain standard. For instance, ladies must have jackets on with sleeves, men must wear ties and socks. It sounds bizarre but if you had no code at all, people might come in dressed in an inappropriate way. There's no requirement to wear a suit or semi or stiff collars, pretty well any shirt goes.

People wear brightly coloured jackets. The market supplies the yellow jackets to the trainees, a standard colour across the floor, and the red jackets of local traders are supplied by the market. There are corporate livery jackets. For instance, BZW being part of the Barclays group, has a red and white candy stripe with the Barclays logo – the eagle – on the back of it. Merrill Lynch has the bull, their corporate motif, on the back of their jackets, I think they might be black and yellow jackets. There are attempts by firms, some more successful than others, to use the dress code that is permitted on the floor of the Exchange – in particular the traders' jackets – to build a corporate ethos and create an identity.

When LIFFE opened in the Royal Exchange in the middle of the City in 1982, the vast predominance of people working in the City were wearing grey or blue suits of one design or another. Suddenly these brightly coloured dust jackets were seen right in the core of the City, round and about the Royal Exchange, the Stock Exchange and the Bank of England and some people thought it was at least as shocking as the new Lloyd's building.

Mr I (b. 1962)
I like wearing a suit and tie because in a sense it's a uniform; the toughest choice this morning was 'Which tie do I wear?' I've not been in favour of these 'casual days' which a lot of firms have mooted. We don't have them, but a lot of firms in the City now have 'Friday casual'. Normally it's casual but not jeans; it actually makes dress quite complicated. I quite like not having that choice.

A lot of American firms have casual days and it's much more rampant in New York. It was a phenomenon that sprang up in the late '80s for boutique-type firms, smaller companies, niche players who weren't so involved in the full service client business like we are. The problem we have is our trading floor is the focal point of our building so, for a client, it's not nice to have a trading floor of casually dressed people. There are probably only about four or five major firms in London who do it. Swiss Bank Corp is famous for it in London, I think they have casual every day.

I would have predicted that that's the way the City's going to go but I was interested about six months ago when there was a motion to our European Management Committee, which I sit on, and it was outvoted. Everybody thought it was the fuddy-duddies who had voted it out and that wasn't the case. It was pretty unanimously voted out. I was a fence-sitter, but I'm against it now because I think if clients come in, they expect to see us well turned out.

If I pop in sometimes on a Sunday in jeans, it's not got the same feel to it. It takes off the adrenalin a little bit.

Wining and Dining

John Castle (b. 1911)
I joined the City in 1919. At lunch-time maybe I'd buy a little bag of
cherries from the stand in Cornhill for two or three pence and then I
would go to the Lyons Tea Shop and my coffee would cost me a penny
ha'penny and my roll and butter might be another two pence and with a
piece of cheese, my lunch would cost about five pence.

Hermann Abs (b. 1901)
When I was in London in the 1920s, I tried all the kitchens of all the
private bankers. The best roast beef was in Lloyd's, the best fish was with
Olaf Hambro, the best coffee was with Schroder. The best general food, in
accordance with the season, was Kleinwort. I knew the quality of all the
luncheons in the City.

Sir John Craven (b. 1940)
I remember lunches in Hambros' partners' room. Partners would drift in
and out. There was wine and port and no business talked at all. It was the
atmosphere of a languid country-house lunch on a Sunday. Now, of course,
that's all changed.

Leonard Toomey (b. 1924)
When I joined Lloyd's I couldn't afford lunch so I used to walk the streets
during the lunch-hour. You had nowhere to go. Today a lot of people
bring food up and eat it in the office if they're a bit hard-up but you
weren't allowed to do that when I was a boy. You had to go out.

Jack Spall (b. 1930)
We had luncheon vouchers, not Luncheon Vouchers Limited, but actual
pieces of paper issued by the firm – I think they were half a crown. They
were available at Pimm's, a City restaurant, which was a bit pricey, and
there was Hill's, down by Liverpool Street Station, where you could just
about get away with half a crown – I mean, sitting down, a proper meal. It
shows how the world turns full circle – one of the directors of my firm,

before the war, had seen secretaries or clerks eating sandwiches in the street and thought they should have a hot meal every day and that's why we got luncheon vouchers. Now it's all sandwiches and almost nobody gets a hot meal at lunch-times. Hill's was taken over by the ABC later on. I think steak and kidney pudding was 1/9*d*. and you could have that with some potatoes and probably a sweet for half a crown or maybe 2/9*d*. It was one of those green-tiled places, rather like a loo today, it wasn't very inviting. A very nice waitress used to look after us, a kindly soul. And there used to be power cuts and sometimes it would be a candlelit lunch. It wasn't good food but it was adequate and quite cheap.

George Nissen (b. 1930)
Drinking was not regarded as a serious problem of its own, it was very much part of life. There was a huge amount going on all over. It seems to me that's part of the past. People were good at pacing themselves and could get accustomed to it. I don't think it led to horrendous errors although I'm sure it affected people's mental agility. On the Stock Exchange floor you were expected to go across to the bar and have several drinks at twelve o'clock in the morning and then have a heavy lunch. There was a lot of drinking in the lunch-room. Some people were known to enjoy several glasses of brandy after lunch, having had two gin and tonics before and several glasses of wine. That was pretty standard.

The senior dealing partner of Pember & Boyle, Brooks, used to drink far too much. One day when we were fixing a new issue for a local authority, which meant you had to be in touch with the Bank of England, Brooks disappeared to ring the Bank and his assistant was waiting for him to come back. Nothing happened until the assistant was rung by the Bank who said, 'What's happening?' Offending the Bank of England was a terrible thing. The assistant went flying round and finally found the door of one of the loos downstairs in the basement was locked and he could only assume Brooks was in there. He banged on the door loudly but he had to force the door open and there was Brooks, sound asleep in the lavatory. As he woke up he thought he was being roused by his wife; I don't know exactly what he said. That was the sort of thing he would do. There certainly wouldn't have been an apology.

Nick Durlacher (b. 1946)
The Stock Exchange could very fairly be described as a club and people in the club fairly understood who was good and who was bad and who drank too much and who didn't. There was always a sort of machismo that if you could hold your drink then you were somehow a better man than your neighbour who couldn't. People making judgements about whether to

employ someone or promote them would make their judgements in the light not so much of whether a person drank as to whether he could handle that drink or not.

At eleven-thirty when the pubs opened there would be an exodus from the Stock Exchange and everybody would go and have a drink. In summer they'd drink Pimm's. They would drink gin and tonic or gin and water, some would drink pink gins. A few of them might drink beer.

There were clubs, too, which weren't bound by licensing hours. There was the Angel Court Club, a drinking-club right opposite the Stock Exchange. My father, Jack, used to go there. A lot of the big deals got settled in the pubs or in the Angel Court Club. People like my father and Dick Wilkins used to go and have a drink with the Cazenove partners and they'd sort out some deals.

The City Club has a rule that you shouldn't do business in it. Each of my uncles and probably godfathers asked me out for lunch when I came to work in the City. I can remember the first day I joined and Dad and my godfather taking me to lunch in the City Club and saying, 'We'd better put your name down. It'll take ten years to become a member.'

In the late 1960s, when I joined the City, people were disciplined about the lunch-hour. The senior ones would go to lunch between one and two and they would go at one and be back at two. The juniors went between twelve and one and had to be back at five to one and people understood that very clearly. Very quickly that broke down so that the lunches became longer and longer. The juniors still went to lunch between twelve and one but the seniors wouldn't come back until two-thirty or three.

Peter Spira (b. 1930)
It was a bit of a joke in the City that there were two sessions for lunch at Warburgs, the 12.30 sitting and the 1.30 sitting. The more junior directors, if they invited clients to lunch, would be at the first sitting and at twenty past one the butler would come in with a note on a silver tray saying, 'Sir, the room is required for the next lunch.' It was embarrassing if you had someone arrive late from the airport and twenty minutes later you got a note, so occasionally there was the most ghastly panic.

What differentiated a Warburgs lunch from others in the City in those days was that in the majority of merchant banks there would be plenty of excellent wines and liqueurs and probably not much business discussed, whereas Siegmund would more or less say at the beginning, 'Gentlemen, you are all very busy and we are very busy, so we're sure you would like to plunge into your business problems right away. These are the points we would like to raise with you . . .' There would be proper business discussion over lunch. In subsequent careers, I have found nothing ever came up to the standard of Warburg lunches in terms of intellectual stimulation. Siegmund's policy was to have a group of non-executive directors of great distinction – men such as Lord Greenhill, who had been head of the Foreign Office, or George Jellicoe, who had been a Cabinet Minister. (We would use them as door openers for introductions.) To listen to Denis Greenhill reminiscing was fascinating and in that way Warburgs was unparalleled.

George Nissen (b. 1930)
Pember & Boyle had a notable lunch-room, one of the best in the City. We regarded it as an immensely important part of the business and got to know our clients extremely well inviting them to lunch. It was accepted as a worthwhile way to spend time from everybody's point of view. There was a lot of talk about sport, about national news, about politics, who was doing what in the City. We very often had MPs to lunch to talk about general affairs. John Betjeman came once, everyone said he was delightful and what a mess he looked and that his cuffs were undone.

The catering was done on the premises. There was a kitchen on the top floor at Prince's Street. Originally we had a housekeeper who had a wife who was an inspired cook. She was a real artist. She went on cooking for Pember & Boyle for ten or fifteen years and the quality was exceptional. There were marvellous lobster dishes. Wonderful beef, which we used to get down from Scotland every week. Soufflés. Always the very best ingredients. Very good wines, which came from Corney & Barrow, mostly. It was quite expensive but generally felt that the investment was worthwhile. There was a butler and an under-butler, not terribly formal but wearing a black jacket.

John Wolff (b. 1940)
You couldn't drink on the floor of the Metal Exchange (nor smoke except at certain times) but during lunch or at intervals in trading it was common practice for the senior members to go off to a pub in Leadenhall Market. The more senior ones went to the Half Moon and the junior ones to the Lamb. The publicans used to know you were coming in and tended to have the drinks already there – you had to be served quickly.

George Nissen (b. 1930)
One of the things which has been most enjoyable at the Stock Exchange is the fact that it's a sort of lunch club and whatever committee meetings are going on either you have a committee lunch or a general lunch and an enormous amount of exchanging of chat goes on all the time. Some of it is material to what you've been working on, some of it is much more general.

Some of it is what was going on at Ascot yesterday. It all adds to your understanding of the people you're working with and your general information about what's going on around the City.

Jane Partington (b. 1956)
When I was first at the Stock Exchange, it was very unusual for girls to be asked to lunch on a formal basis. The first time it happened to me was when I was asked to Akroyd & Smithers, where I was the only woman in the room. They all drank heavily. Nobody knew what to do with me – I had to go into the dining-room first, I had to sit down at the table first, I had to pick up my knife and fork first. It's quite daunting when you're a young girl in amongst twenty men.

David Verey (b. 1950)
There were no lunch facilities within Lazards so one had to go out clutching one's luncheon vouchers and seek food. Occasionally you had to cross a road but pretty much it was by alleyways in the back part of the City. Quite often I would try and arrange lunch with a chum, perhaps my cousin, Jeremy Wilson, who started at Barclays almost at the same time I joined the City, or with my brother-in-law at Arbuthnot Latham. I used to go to Simpsons in Cornhill and to the George & Vulture when I could afford it.

Jeremy Wormell (b. 1943)
When the Stock Exchange business turned down with a wallop in 1973–4, Pember & Boyle, a very solid business with plenty of money behind it, was just about breaking even for a couple of quarters. Grieveson Grant had just closed down their kitchen and Wedd Durlacher, very solidly financed, had decided to go over to a single course at lunch. There was a lengthy Pember & Boyle partners' debate about what they should do in order to cut back and save money. In the end it was decided that they would go from having four vegetables to three vegetables.

Charles McVeigh III (b. 1942)
When I first came to the City in 1973, everyone broke at around twelve-thirty for lunch, which became a major part of the day, whereas Americans tend to eat early and quickly and never drank anything at all. At Salomon in New York we would offer a drink to be courteous but by and large people never took it. People like Morgan Guaranty never even served a drink, it was against their internal rules. Lunch was over in an hour whereas in London it took two to two-and-a-half hours. People had at least one or two drinks before lunch, wine with the meal and thought

nothing of having port and at least one cigar afterwards. Interestingly, no business was done over lunch which, again, was completely different from America. You would wait until the end when you might, over a glass of port or as the dessert was being served, turn the conversation to some business area of mutual interest. Before that, one was positioning oneself socially with one's counterpart.

People were assessing very carefully the calibre of the person with whom they were lunching. They were assessing whether or not they could rely on them, whether they were men of integrity and whether the chemistry between the guest and yourself was right and would lead to a worthwhile business relationship. So there was very much an underlying business purpose. A great deal of conversation related to where I was from, where I'd been to school, what sport I enjoyed, what I did at the weekends. Then the conversation would inevitably turn to our view of interest rates in the United States or our view of the dollar–sterling relationship and to the markets in general. They were trying to gauge the person and get some sense of what Salomons was up to. A lot of my interests are similar to the people I was having lunch with. I'm afraid I'm in the shooting and fishing camp and as I was passionate about those activities as well as gardening, there was almost always a common denominator with the person I was with. My wife was keen on opera and theatre, so that opened another avenue of discussion. We were being entertained quite a bit in the evening and weekends, so one started developing one's own network.

David King (b. 1945)

Sadly, one of the very few City clubs demised recently. That was the Gresham Club, which had been around for some hundred and fifty years and we at the London Metal Exchange had used it for our monthly board meetings for probably a decade. In a way it underlines the changing face of the City because even in the last couple of years since I have been Chief Executive, the drinks bill as part of a lunch had dropped to such a level that we were having to pay extra just to sit there so that the Club could break even on providing monthly hospitality for us. There are more foreigners in the City now and the Americans and Japanese tend to have shorter lunches – an hour is the norm and not the exception, which didn't use to be the case in the City.

I was surprised the Gresham had stairs rather than ramps because I think you had to be dead ten years before you could become a member – you had to be chatted to by the committee to check that you were OK and could recognize a knife and fork, if not hold one. The building was quaint and seriously in need of decor. The gents in the basement was old-fashioned with old, clumpy masonry and a set of scales which you could sit on like a jockey to be weighed – the scales were auctioned for two or three thousand pounds when the Club was sold. On the ground floor was a large television where some members would watch cricket or things appropriate to a gentlemen's club. (Women could go to the Club, but I'm not sure they could be members.)

There were a couple of private dining-rooms, one of which the LME used, and also the main dining-room. There were little boxes where regular members could keep their napkins, which was a nice personal touch. The meals were very schoolboy-dinnerish and this is a trait of the City in some ways – spotted dick for dessert with dollops of custard. Recently French fries appeared, which was quite an innovation and didn't seem appropriate in a way. Because it was members only, it was unlikely that somebody from the LME would be sitting next to you, so you could talk freely – that was one of the problems of the City for us, because most of the restaurants nearby the Exchange would contain one or two LME-ites.

It was very sad to see the Gresham go, but, frankly, it hadn't moved with the times.

Sir John Craven (b. 1940)

I'm constantly being pressed by my colleagues to do more handshaking and cocktail-circuiting and that kind of stuff. I do an awful lot. I entertain at home quite a bit. I don't think that giving or attending big lunches and dinners is effective. I'm most effective on a one-to-one basis or in small gatherings where one can actually talk real strategy to one's clients rather than generalized nonsense.

I've been going to the IMF meetings for twenty-one years and I've never failed to learn something which I haven't needed or been able to use. Every single Minister of Finance is there, every Governor from a hundred and sixty-two countries comes, each one with a retinue of advisers. And every single commercial banker and investment banking firm of any importance in the world is represented. It's a constant series of lunches, receptions, dinners, parties and God knows what.

Davina Walter (b. 1954)

I'm teetotal because I've never found anything I like to drink. In the twenty years I've been in the City the attitude has changed. When I first started, people would press alcohol on you and thought you would change your mind. I didn't say I was teetotal, I said, 'I've got to keep a clear head today', or whatever. Now it's seldom that people have a glass of wine over lunch. In the early days it would have been spirits and wine, port and kümmel.

It's now 9 December 1994 and I've got a lunch every day until Christmas. It's not the archetypical City lunch, rolling back to your desk at five o'clock in the afternoon. It's the time of year when the brokers spoil us and take us to a lovely restaurant. Today it's La Pont de la Tour by Tower Bridge. Sometimes there's a department Christmas lunch, when they invite the whole of our US desk and we go to an American broker's office.

It's easier for a girl to eat less than a man. People think men are a bit odd if they say, 'I can't have bread ... I can't have potatoes ... I can't have a glass of wine.' I sometimes go without a starter because I love puddings. My husband isn't in a business where he has lunch every day. I try and cook him something in the evenings or 'Mr' Marks & Spencer might prepare the meal and I put it in the oven. I drive into the City each morning and *en route* quite often stop off at Marks & Spencer – it's full of women trying to pack that in first thing in the morning but there are quite a lot of men there, probably more in the City branch than if you went to a typical Sainsburys. Marks & Spencer has revolutionized a single man's life.

Ms A (b. 1959)
When I was working for the Japanese securities house, often we'd take somebody out to lunch or dinner and that was when I was very useful to them as an attractive, young, Western female. I know I got them business like that, in my own way. The entertaining side of the business – in the eighties more than now – was and is very important. In the competition between two of the big Japanese securities houses, something as minor as having a good dinner might swing it. I was conscious of playing a role which was politically unsound in the feminist sense. I wore business suits, not dolly long dresses or anything.

When we were being entertained by the French a couple of times we got taken to totally inappropriate places for a woman on a business night out, the Moulin Rouge and the Crazy Horse. The French don't tend to view these things in the way the British might, it's part of their heritage and therefore OK, even though there were stacks of women on stage with no clothes on. My Japanese boss and I took clients to a topless restaurant in London and I was the only woman there. I felt helpless really. It was outrageous but there was nothing I could do about it because if I made a scene it would be bad for my career. The only cool thing was to be completely blasé. I was very much the honorary man.

The Japanese probably weren't able to perceive that I was being put in an awkward situation. (In Japan, there's a code of behaviour in the workplace that the only place they can let off steam is after work when they go in groups and drink heavily in bars with topless shows. The

Japanese attitude to sex is very different and there are fewer taboos.) A Japanese would enjoy a topless restaurant in London because it was part of the social scene, not because he was being titillated. British businessmen, by and large products of the public-school system, have what I regard as a warped attitude to sex because from the cradle they're taught that it's furtive and naughty. Overlying that is the whole business of bravado, which comes out as they get into their rugby fifteen and is perpetuated through their lives in the City unless they happen to grow up. If they are the rugby players who have never grown up, they probably quite enjoy these places in the City where they get fed school food by girls in mini-skirts and no tops sitting on their laps. Those who have grown up must find it a complete bore but they probably still have to do it with their friends. I always assumed they weren't grown up because it was safer and I was usually right, sadly.

Technology

Dundas Hamilton (b. 1919)
My father, a stockbroker, came to London from Scotland at the turn of the century and at this time all the orders were sent by telegraph because people couldn't afford the telephone. He realized that if he put a telephone call in from London to Edinburgh to report what the market was doing, he could get some orders by phone, not only from his father's firm but from other Edinburgh firms as well. Everybody queued around his father's telephone and shouted their orders down and so he got a lot of business that way. At the end of the day he would call back and tell them what he'd done and the prices he'd dealt at.

Michael Verey (b. 1912)
The office manager at Helbert, Wagg was a Swiss. He was the original human computer. He worked out that it was cheaper to buy books of account unlined and, at my salary, to hire me to draw the lines with a ruler – a double line of red and then blue ink – and that this was quite a bargain. It was a difficult thing to do without smudging the blasted red because we didn't have biros.

Nick Durlacher (b. 1946)
I remember in the old days people were using sealing wax if they wanted to stamp something and make it absolutely secure in terms of delivery. There would be someone in the post-room who would have been responsible for that; there was a degree of trust because that person would have risen in the firm to the position he then occupied.

Sir Jeremy Morse (b. 1928)
I began my career in 1953 at Childs and went straight on to the ledgers. They had their own alphabet, which went back to the history of banking. You started on the same basis for the first letter as any other form of the alphabet, but after the first letter you then sorted by the first vowel. Let's say the first letter was 's', anything where the following vowel was an 'a' came before anything where the following vowel was an 'e', so 'Stanford'

would come before 'Sellars'. Within the 'Sa's you went in alphabetical order. This got quite complicated where the first letter was a vowel because you then went to the second vowel and the supreme glory of it was that, if there was only one vowel and it was the first letter, supposing you were called 'Orr', you went right to the front of the 'O's! All Souls' College came right at the front of the 'A's. The reason was said to be that when you were looking at a signature on a cheque, the vowels stood out at you. Whether that was true or not, I don't know. Of course, in those days, we really read the cheques, we really compared the signatures. The funny thing was, you got so used to this it was quite difficult to look things up in the telephone directory.

Dundas Hamilton (b. 1919)

In 1958 my stockbroking firm moved from handwritten ledgers to machine accounting. A few years later the computer was really going. We made our girls who worked the punch-card machines go on to feeding the computer. Between 1972 and 1985 we had roughly the same number of staff and we had ten times the turnover, so there was a ten times improvement in efficiency. (The staff were not the same kind of staff any more because many of the old clerical staff were now research staff.) When you get to the next stage – where no paper moves around at all, you don't have certificates and transfers and all those things but plastic cards that wire into the computer instead – then we shall reduce the size again and become enormously efficient.

Peter Spira (b. 1930)

In the 1960s, Eurobond certificates had to be signed manually. A normal sized issue was around twenty-five million dollars in denominations of dollars one thousand each, which meant that twenty-five thousand bonds had to be signed. There was one signing-machine in Brussels which could sign about twelve certificates at a time, with twelve pens attached to it, but basically the company had to send a team of three or four people to Luxembourg for a week to sign twenty-five thousand pieces of paper. That shows you the idiotic bureaucracy that existed in the days before facsimile signatures were accepted.

Nick Durlacher (b. 1946)

I remember being taken as a schoolboy in the early 1960s to my father's office in Basinghall Avenue (the office that the firm had right until Big Bang). At that time it was a brand new office on a large area of London that was still a bomb site, which looked across to the Barbican. We went to the seventh floor and I remember looking out and on one side being able to see Blackheath and on the other Hampstead Heath. Now, if you go to the same building you can see across the road in either direction and no further.

The offices were extremely smart and modern by the standards of those days because they were brand spanking new. The *Daily Express* ran a big photomontage because it was rather remarkable that there were forty or fifty telephone handsets; this was the largest installation at that time in London.

The earliest computers the firm used were made by Lions in the late 1950s and were called Leo Machines. The firm would have had a telex but essentially their business was done dealing with members of the Stock Exchange face-to-face so the necessity of communication other than that was pretty small. There was some necessity to use the telephone in terms of the settlement of that business, when a query arose, to talk to a broker's back office. But I don't think they would have been great users of telex or telegrams, although the headed notepaper certainly used to carry a telegram code.

In 1967, when I came into the City, all the communications between Stock Exchange Member firms were carried by messengers to a central clearing-point in Blossoms Inn. One of the reasons people had concentrated in the Square Mile was so that they could be part of this system. It meant you could have within-day delivery of inter-office mail and settlement transfers and cheques. Messengers were an important part of all City businesses and our firm, Durlacher, Oldham, Mordaunt, Godson, employed about twenty; an awful lot of paper was pushed around. There was a community of messengers. People didn't switch firms so there was probably more of a pride among the messenger fraternity in the firm they worked for than there might be now. I have a feeling that the old paper/messenger system may have been more secure than the electronic technology we have now and which can be hacked into.

The City was more of a rabbit warren than it is now. For instance, Warnford Court was a very big building complex which had an awful lot of tenants in it who had small suites. (A lot of the lifts still had attendants in them. There was an unwritten rule that you never took a lift to the first floor, you always walked.) They weren't skyscrapers but because they were big complexes they had enormously long passages and so in rainy weather you could almost get from our offices to the Stock Exchange without ever having to step outside. Instead of an office, you would occasionally come across a little tobacconist or a hairdresser in the corridors (Plantation House would perhaps be an analogy now). All the messengers were known to the porters of the buildings and although most used to have a sign saying, 'Admittance only on business' – i.e. you couldn't use it as a thoroughfare – they all did. There was an ethos in the City that you didn't attempt to overhear anything or look at something you weren't meant to read.

Most of the old passage buildings were torn down and replaced with tower blocks. Firms became bigger and tended to have complete floors. Gradually firms became conscious that financial espionage was something that people were prepared to embark on. The practice of having to go to a desk and announce yourself slowly came to pass and it became harder to casually walk through buildings and, in the end, downright impossible.

Dundas Hamilton (b. 1919)

The faster the means of communication, the worse the actual content. It's partly quantity but it's not only that. Mostly, the more quickly communication goes by satellite and other means, the less goes into people's minds and they understand less of what is happening. Thinking time and planning time seems to have gone by the board. People think they are communicating but they're not. Ultimately, people will get to use the equipment better and different priorities will be put.

Ross Jones (b. 1959)

I was known as 'Jones the Telex' because I used to have to telex lots of banks on the Continent to borrow money from them.

The first dealing room at Gerrard & National when I joined was a big 'H' structure. We had a keyboard and lots of buttons, each with the name of a bank on it – you had to physically press the button as opposed to touching a screen. We had far less lines out to people so you had to do a lot more normal dialling. We shared Reuters screens, so there wasn't as much equipment as now.

Nick Durlacher (b. 1946)

For us, screens for providing information began in the mid-1970s. It suddenly became more relevant for us to try and get information as quick as everybody else. That meant we started to have a dependence on things like Reuters screens and Telerate screens. We didn't use them for dealing, they were just for information purposes. In some senses it was like looking at a television screen to see what the weather forecast was, so it wasn't a big deal to adapt to that.

In those days we tended to have one or two quite big-format screens which could be viewed by four or five people rather than small individual information screens on each dealing desk. The very substantial change was when the dealing system changed from being face-to-face or on the telephone to being through SEAQ and using screens. That took place in 1986.

A lot of the settlement systems involved in buying and selling shares or bonds have themselves become electronic, so you don't need bits of paper representing ownership of the shares around between the buyer and the seller. You don't need to pass cheques between the buyer and the seller because it's book-entry transfer at the bank. That technology has been pretty slow for the Stock Exchange business because their last big effort on that dismally failed in respect of Taurus. Markets have to introduce the new technologies, otherwise they'll lose the business.

Charles McVeigh III (b. 1942)
We still use tester telexes because they are legally binding, whereas faxes (which today have completely eclipsed the telex) are not legal tender. There are real problems with faxes. I think the ordinary telexes stopped being used in the early 1980s.

Francis Holford (b. 1937)
In the last decade, there has been a continuous improvement in international communications which has revolutionized the business of the London Metal Exchange. In former times an important item of news that might affect the supply or demand of materials would take longer to be disseminated and, if you happened to get that news before a competitor or before it became generally known throughout the world, you had an advantage. These days everything is known in seconds via the Reuters network and news is flashed all over the world immediately on television, CNN, those kind of developments.

Reuters is the principal supplier of news and price changes to the metals and futures markets. They and services like them provide the screens in offices and dealing rooms with instant information of changes in price of every commodity and financial instrument that people are trading. One of the effects of the speed and volume of this information is to extend our working hours. Because of its place in the middle of the time zone between the United States and the Western hemisphere, London is acknowledged to be the financial centre of Europe. Information technology means firms like Rudolf Wolff are working from much earlier in the day until much later and that has an impact on people like me because I've got to be in control of the situation.

Ross Jones (b. 1959)
These days everybody has tapes. Every single conversation that takes place on the phone in our dealing room is recorded in case of disputes. I

should think once a week we have to go and listen to check what we said. If the technology's there, it makes sense to have it. We have a systems manager who looks after all the dealing desks and telephone systems and everything that's out there.

David King (b. 1945)

We dump all our records to an off-site repository every night. We've been doing that for a long time. It's partly terrorism, but we first did it because of the risk of fire getting at computer records. We've had a certain amount of disaster planning since the Baltic Exchange bomb.

Charles McVeigh III (b. 1942)

One reason I travel back and forth to New York less frequently is that today we have video conference facilities in London which are extraordinary. We have an enormous screen where the entire board room in New York can be seen on the video. In turn, in New York they have two enormous screens in the board room where Tokyo is on view on one and London on the other. It works brilliantly. You can interrupt the conversation. You can see who's looking at you and who's not looking at you. All your facial expressions and all the enthusiasm that you want to show in putting over a point are literally there. It's not better than being there, but it's the best substitute. The video conference didn't exist when I was first in London and you'd be having a telephone conference on poor equipment and lots of comments would be lost; you lost interest after about twenty minutes, and it became difficult to concentrate. You failed to get out of the meeting what you had intended to or what there was for the taking.

The first video conference facilities were available in London about seven years ago. The quality improved and the cost and equipment became affordable and available as recently as three years ago. At Salomon we have it on for about three or four hours a day. It's key for Tokyo because the trip from Tokyo to New York is brutal and to come all that way for a day conference is unbelievable. We had a conference call last Tuesday that lasted three hours and we could see Tokyo and New York whilst sitting in London. You get two or three hours' video conference for the cost of a first-class flight. The cost of technology will come down. You're not conscious of how much it's costing because the cumulative cost of all the people in the room is enormous in our business. Also, if it's a subject worth discussing, it's worth spending time on it. If the subject matter were to deteriorate into something relatively unimportant, you'd find it was a waste of time, but you'd be thinking about the time more than the money.

It only takes two or three years for technolgy to get a bit out of date. The speed of change is extraordinary and the investment that you make is quite large.

David King (b. 1945)
Electronics and automation mean that anyone could set up a metal exchange anywhere – they could set one up on a satellite and there would be no need for an exchange floor and so the whole culture of the London Metal Exchange would go. It's not unlikely that that will happen, maybe a decade away. There's a system called Globex which is likely to be introduced in the near future – its roots lie in the US – which will have screens in something like a hundred and fifty thousand locations and, in theory, anyone anywhere can trade via this system. This will be the catalyst which will determine the speed of automation because if this system works there will be a knee-jerk reaction from all the other exchanges.

One of the benefits of trading in open outcry – lots of people shouting at each other on the market floor – is that if somebody says 'Yes', they can say it hysterically or calmly or in a number of ways, which gives a signal to the other people around which is far more efficient than looking at a two-dimensional screen where you just see a symbol which says 'Yes'; you don't know how desperate, how sincere the person is. You lose the herd instinct.

Where technology wins over is it's cheaper, more efficient and, from a regulatory point of view, it provides a good audit trail. From a client's point of view, he can be able to trace second by second that his order was properly processed, it did have priority over another order and that he was properly and fairly dealt with. But of course every warm body on a market floor is against technological change.

I would feel sad if the London Metal Exchange ceased to exist because it has operated the way it has for over a century and, apart from stopping trading during the wars, has overcome all obstacles and flourished. But life moves on. I think the changes will be evolutionary and not revolutionary.

Sir Martin Jacomb (b. 1929)
I knew at the time I was living through a revolutionary epoch with masses of milestones posted around, and so it turned out. The main milestone has to be Big Bang but it only became the main milestone because of other changes which were occurring simultaneously round it – the ability to control a trading operation with computer technology and the telephone; the freedom from exchange controls. Because out of those flows the ability for capital to move without hindrance around the world.

Charles McVeigh III (b. 1942)

Compared to the early 1970s, the markets are infinitely more sophisticated. The information available globally is much greater now than in the past. If you go back to the period last year [1993] when the Exchange Rate Mechanism collapsed, it's certain that neither the Bank of England nor the Chancellor began to understand the cumulative weight of money that was driving that action. That cumulative weight isn't just UK speculators, George Soros or any single institution. It's every performance-orientated portfolio manager all over the world looking at the economic and interest rate news and taking daily decisions that ultimately translate into billions of dollars that will be bet against or for certain decisions. The Bank of England raised ten billion pounds (or ten billion dollars, I can't recall which) and ten years ago that would have seemed like an enormous war chest with which to defend itself against the weight of the money in the marketplace. It was nothing. It was like a tip to the hat-check girl in a bar.

Predictions

Peter Spira (b. 1930)
We are moving into a completely new era. Today, the first mortar attack on Downing Street took place, yet the market still goes up. It is based on a failure to understand what lies ahead, including a lot more redundancies in the City. If the Cabinet had been wiped out there would have been tremendous uncertainty as to what was going to happen and markets hate uncertainty more than anything else. Terrorism affects other industries – airlines, hotels – all of which depend on a cash-flow that's dried up. The tourist traffic has stopped and it has a disastrous effect on the retail trade. I think there will be a number of City firms which fold in the next year or two. We are in a different age and we will look back to 1945–1990 as the years of stability.

Valerie Thompson (b. 1956)
People have predicted that the City will become all screen-based and that there won't be so many people clustered under one roof. I agree to some extent, but I think at the end of the day what makes the markets go one way or another is still people. I don't see any great changes in people apart from them becoming more stressed. Money doesn't happen on its own, there are always people driving it.

God forbid that you'd get to a point where people just stayed in a little room with a screen. They'd go nuts. They'd kill themselves. The contact with other people makes the whole thing fun. It feeds our soul and we need it. I don't see anyone finding the City in the least bit attractive if all they're doing is crunching numbers. The biggest transactions are done through relationships. I think that will continue.

Nick Durlacher (b. 1946)
Some people have felt that electronic trades means that you will have no centre, you will just have a diffusion of marketplaces, ultimately in people's homes. In fact, the more correct analysis of electronics is that it enables a core centre to be even more effective at bringing in business than it was before. If you look at the introduction of the telephone for business

communications after the Second World War, what that did is destroy regional stock exchanges, which had had a *raison d'être* before.

Charles McVeigh III (b. 1942)

I think the role of the Square Mile is over. Salomon moved out of the Square Mile because of lousy City planning in the early eighties when the City completely failed to anticipate what was taking place and to grasp the international dimension of the City as it was evolving. Deregulation was taking place at a terrific pace and the opportunity to expand our business was enormous. We were adding staff very fast and Big Bang was on the horizon, so the demand to build our physical infrastructure was tremendous, spacewise.

We were in five different locations in 1985. The City had no alternative space at all. Broadgate was not more than a distant vision. We wandered around looking for some place that would house us for at least the short term (looking at Hammersmith, looking at Chiswick) until we found Victoria Plaza. We started work adapting it – it was nicknamed Victoria Palace because we spent about twenty-five million on it – and finished about a month before Big Bang. When we moved here we found the environment fantastic for all the staff and it became apparent pretty quickly that we should stay here.

The role of the geographic boundaries that used to dictate the City is over. Up until a year ago I would have said that London's pre-eminent position as the financial centre of Europe was its to lose – it didn't have to win it, it had it already in spades. It might lose it because the regulatory environment was too stringent or because some other city or region provided a compelling tax and economic incentive. But London has to fritter it away, it won't go naturally.

The next question is, in the last year or so has anything changed that view? Increasingly it's less necessary to be in one location to have a successful business. And the business has become truly European. The vast majority of work we're doing here in London is in Italian government bonds or German government bonds or Japanese government bonds or French government bonds or whatever. We're being encouraged, aggressively, to set up in Milan because the government of Milan is (a) trying to discipline us from operating our Italian government bond work from London and (b) trying to encourage us with incentives to set up in Milan. The French are doing the same. The Germans are doing the same.

We will entertain these overtures as everybody will; reluctantly, but we will. If there's an economic reason, fully costed, to put a team of people in Italy, and if the incentives the Italian government provide are compelling, we will do so. Conversely, if the disadvantages that they can insist on were we to remain in London are onerous, we would be inclined to move for these reasons.

By the time you've put twenty-five people in Milan and you've reinforced the Paris presence with your dealing and distribution capability and you've done the same thing in Frankfurt, you then ask yourself, 'What role is London now playing?' I presume, frankly, that London, for people like us, will remain the hub of the wheel but the spokes and the rim of the wheel will become larger and larger and the hub less important.

From the point of view of the Chancellor or the Treasury, they may well find that a great deal of the profits that were generated in London previously are being generated in those other centres. I think that's very possible.

Sir John Craven (b. 1940)

We are such a poor manufacturer these days. We are not good at building things and selling them. But Britain is good at inventing and adapting financial services and selling them and we have a strong internationalist trading history. We've been in the forefront of that and I don't think Frankfurt is a serious threat to the City at all. For example, Frankfurt has no Take-over Code, they have no law on insider dealing and no bank there has a compliance officer. It would be very difficult indeed for foreign institutions to move into Germany and obtain a significant market share of German business. If Germany had ambitions to become a major financial centre to rival London, it would have to have the same open-door policy that we've had here for years. We've positively encouraged foreign houses to come in.

Charles McVeigh III (b. 1942)

The American investment banks are the prototype of what the world may look like. That sounds arrogant, it's not designed to be at all. I genuinely believe that the American investment banks as a group have more capital, more vision, have created more decentralized, international operations, have done a better job in the Pacific, have done a better job in Europe than almost anybody else.

It's quite clear that the British government would love to see one British firm genuinely compete on a global basis. S. G. Warburg is the only merchant bank in the United Kingdom that has a global aspiration to compete on that scale although there are some who can compete in boutique structures in various markets. I won't suggest that Warburgs can't do it, but it will be very, very difficult for them.

The Japanese, who would have been odds-on favourites to be enor-mously powerful because of their sheer weight of earnings, have had an extraordinary setback in the last couple of years and I don't think anybody believes that any of the big Japanese securities firms will ever genuinely threaten the global capacity of the American investment banks. That's not a chauvinistic comment. The Japanese went from being enormously profitable to having almost no profitability at all. Salomon Brothers is consistently in the top five of all firms in Japan and the year before last I believe we made more money in Japan than any Japanese securities firm.

In the UK last year several of the leading US investment banks, including Salomon Brothers, were significantly more profitable solely in their London operations than any of the indigenous merchant banks competing on their own turf. That doesn't make us paragons of virtue and there's no God-given right for us to achieve global dominance by virtue of our profitability, but it sure as hell helps. It allows us to continue to build in the emerging markets of China, of Pacrim in Latin America and in Eastern Europe.

The ability to invest in the markets of tomorrow is infinitely easier with the level of profitability Salomon Brothers has. My Chairman in New York calls it the Big Squeeze. To compete with the top two or three firms in the global business, you have to incur the same cost base as they do. The top people are garnering more and more of a war chest of capital and profitability and have more to spend and so it's harder and harder for the competitors to catch up. The acceleration of the close of the circle has been faster in the last five years.

Sir Martin Jacomb (b. 1929)

Warburgs is certainly in with a chance. It is nothing like the size of Morgan Stanley or Goldman Sachs, but I don't think you measure these things solely on size. The question is, can you execute the biggest deals and can you execute them worldwide? Now, the big deals are given to a firm which has the muscle-power to say, 'OK, this deal is going to be done at such-and-such a price and we are going to raise y hundred million dollars.' To be able to make such a commitment, you have to be sure you can sell the stuff not just in London, but simultaneously in New York and Tokyo and to investors all over the world. If you can do that, the business is very profitable because very few people can do it and the margins are high. Certainly the biggest three or four US houses can do it and certainly Warburgs can do it.

Part Three

Postscripts

Postscript recordings were made with some of the 'City Lives' interviewees in the autumn of 1995 and early months of 1996. Since the original interviews were done, the troubles continued at Lloyd's, Barings fell, Warburgs lost its independence to the Swiss Bank Corporation and Kleinwort Benson became a member of the Dresdner Bank Group, Germany's second largest bank. In November 1995, UBS Phillips & Drew, NatWest Securities and Salomon all withdrew from the London Stock Exchange's SEAQ International system.

British Institutions in Trouble:
The Future of the City

Davina Walter (b. 1954)
I couldn't believe the news about Barings. I was staying with my parents and came down to breakfast and my mother said, 'Darling, did you know that Barings has gone bust?' Mothers sometimes tend to get things a little bit wrong (I'm a mother myself now) and I thought maybe she had. As the story came out, it was completely stunned amazement. It's totally shocking. And totally isolated to Barings.

David Verey (b. 1950)
We were asked to advise the Baring Foundation, which was the share-holder of Barings, at the point of the crash. On the Sunday evening, I left the Barings office to go round to the meeting at the Bank of England, where we were eventually told by the Governor that although the City had assembled some six hundred and seventy-five million pounds, there was no way of capping the risks associated with the futures contracts on the Tokyo Exchange and no outside party had been identified to come in with the money. The meeting broke up and I went back to Barings and told John Ashburton and Nicholas Baring the outcome. I remember John Ashburton saying, 'It's just impossible to believe that two hundred and fifty years of independence have come to an end literally over a weekend because of a rogue trader in Singapore.' I was standing on the twentieth floor of Barings with John and Nicholas and there was a beautiful sunset over the western part of the City and we just looked out into this great ball of fire and the sun sinking and it was rather an emotional moment.

Roger Gibbs (b. 1934)
Antony Gibbs, our family merchant bank, was next door to Barings in Bishopsgate from 1808, when it was founded, until 1979 when Antony Gibbs was bought by the Hongkong Bank. If you'd asked me two years ago, 'What are the undoubted merchant banks in the City?' Barings would certainly have been high on the list. One greeted its fall with incredulity and extreme sadness. The Baring family members have been terrific

friends of mine since my schooldays. They are very high principled, thoroughly decent, good people. John Baring was our main adviser throughout my time at Gerrard & National.

How could this happen to them? One writer said, 'Barings the Bank is a hundred and fifty yards away from Barings the Securities Company and their cultures are a hundred and fifty years apart.' I think that sums it up; neither understood the other.

The events at Warburgs were just as surprising. Warburgs was the great name in the City, the one British institution that could take on the rest of the world. It is very serious when Swiss Bank Corporation own Warburgs, Dresdner own Kleinworts, Deutsche own Morgan Grenfell and so on. It leaves us with very little strength in British merchant banks. I don't think it means anything bad for the future of the country, but it makes the British merchant bank fraternity look a bit thin.

Dundas Hamilton (b. 1919)
I've known the Barings all my life and I was an investor in the bank. In some ways its fall was inevitable. I was Chairman of the original Traded Options Committee, which brought in the first securities options of that kind, so that you could hedge the market. One fear that we always had was that things would get out of hand. The problem always on any market is that it's just as good as the individuals that are operating it.

Nick Durlacher (1946)
Barings was perceived to be a very solid, very conservative, well-run, prudent bank, which had not of itself got into some of the most flashy operations that perhaps some other people get into. I was surprised because I knew that Barings had withdrawn from our market at LIFFE more than two years ago. They hadn't been able to make any business sense of membership on the floor of our Exchange. I was surprised that they could have generated such enormous derivative exposure as to be threatening to the bank in a market when they seemed to have taken a rational and sensible decision in London.

Having done Economic History at Cambridge, I was vaguely aware that there had been a Baring Crisis in the nineteenth century but I don't think the present bank was tarred in any way by having been rescued in the 1890s.

The fact that there is less physical contact between people working in the City at whatever level or strata – whether it's messengers, dealers on the floor of the Stock Exchange (which has now disappeared), discount houses meeting because they used to walk round to the Bank of England or their brokers would visit the office every day – all of that in its totality probably reduces the social cohesiveness within the City. You could say this might be another reason why people in the generality haven't questioned that Barings wasn't saved. Fifty years ago, most people would have said it would be inconceivable that Barings wasn't saved.

Peter Spira (b. 1930)
I left Warburgs twenty-two years ago. All my contemporaries who left, we all felt exactly the same: shame, sadness. Why should we care after all these years? The strange thing about Warburgs is that it was like a club or a regiment and many of those of us who were there before Big Bang and helped build it up (some of us spending quite a few golden years of our youth with the firm) have always felt part of it and have had a nostalgic feeling for it. Frankly, we were appalled and dismayed indeed.

Ross Jones (b. 1959)
The City has lost a lot of credibility. Warburgs was a company that I admired hugely. They epitomized all the good things of London as a British house. It's terrifying how quickly they lost that and I still don't quite understand how they did it.

   Barings was extraordinary. Every institution in the City on the Monday morning after the Barings weekend must have gone through their systems and said, 'Could this happen to us?' The answer is, 'Yes, it could happen to anybody. But what would somebody have to do for it to happen to us?' We went through our checks at Gerrard & National. You would have to go to every single layer of the company and get somebody to play along with you. That's the key.

Nick Durlacher (b. 1946)
The amount of capital resources that any firm in the City has is vitally important to the business that it can and can't do. Little fish shouldn't swim with big fish; they can be a damn nuisance but eventually they'll get eaten. The recent mega-merger that two Japanese banks have constructed means they will be larger than the four British clearing banks put together. Size can count for a lot.

   There's an expression 'You punch above your weight'. Warburgs and Barings were able to be involved in business which was almost greater than probably their true net worth and capital resources. That's great when everything's running for you and brings a lot of success; it's the sort of gearing factor that works in your favour. But when things turn stormy, people see that the Emperor has no clothes.

Charles McVeigh III (b. 1942)

I mentioned in my recording that Warburgs was the only independent UK merchant bank that had the wherewithal to possibly compete on a global basis. The problem Warburgs had was severalfold. Quite simply, they didn't have the capital base or earnings power to meet their aspirations globally.

We went through a period in the late 1980s and early '90s of incredibly favourable markets – lower interest rates, an enormous amount of equity underwriting, significant fees being paid for M[ergers] and A[quisitions] advisory business. It was difficult to envision a more favourable period for the industry as a whole.

The question was always what happens when the music stops and the economic environment is a lot less favourable? That really happened in 1994 for a lot of us. My firm, for example, had an extremely disappointing year. For Warburgs, too, there was a significant profit decline during that period. The great challenge for Warburgs was the huge cost of trying to compete in America, in Japan, in Hong Kong, in the emerging markets, in Europe and in maintaining what had generically been a very profitable UK domestic business. It became increasingly obvious that this geographic platform could not be maintained. That's why they thought of trying to find a global alliance that would allow them to bring all of their talent to bear in a complementary link-up.

The original Morgan Stanley–Warburg alliance had, in most of our minds, formidable core strengths. But when a financial institution bets the shop on a merger and it then falls through, you have basically put a white flag up and said, 'We can't really survive on our own. We needed this alliance to be globally competitive.' When the transaction didn't occur, Warburgs really had no choice but to jump into the arms of somebody else. As the senior professionals started to haemorrhage, that decision became more and more urgent. The rest is history.

Barings was a tragedy. On the Saturday when the news broke, Salomon was asked by the Bank of England whether we and a few other investment banks familiar with the Japanese equity market would be prepared to underwrite or put a cap on the exposure that Barings had to the Nikkei and to the futures markets. What was immediately apparent was how extraordinarily difficult that was because of the apparent lack of ability to quantify the exposure and the losses there. It was extremely difficult based on our knowledge of the business to provide that type of cap and I understand that a number of firms were called. By Sunday the bank had collapsed. I was totally shocked.

You have a momentary flash of sympathy for all your friends at Barings, but your immediate reaction is, 'What does it mean for us in terms of our own risk exposure not only to Barings Bank but to the clients of Barings?' We called people in from their weekend and started to try to determine what our exposures were throughout the world to Barings in Singapore, in Tokyo, in New York and London. Fortunately our exposures were minimal.

What's happened since our last recording has been the awakening of a number of very powerful European commercial banks, recognizing that if they wish to play on an ever-consolidating global stage they have to have increasingly strong investment banking and commercial banking platforms. Therefore the strengths that a bank like Kleinwort Benson brings to a big German, Dutch or Swiss bank is clearly its UK perspective, a very strong equity perspective and an advisory and M. and A. perspective. It's fair to say that the Anglo-Saxon approach to merchant banking and investment banking is a lot more effective than is found elsewhere in the world. The acknowledged strength of the Anglo-Saxon approach to the advisory business and capital-raising means that anyone who starts life as a commercial bank and really wants to compete in Europe, in Asia and in North America has to acquire rather than build generically that presence. The only bank that's really built a generic presence in a variety of locations is J. P. Morgan.

The interesting missing piece in this picture is North America, which is clearly the largest securities market in the world. There, the appetite of the major Asian and European banks hasn't yet reached a point where there's a comfort level or a confidence level that they can bite off, chew and digest a big US investment bank. At the end of the day to compete as a European bank effectively on a global stage, one will have to acquire something in North America.

Sir John Craven (b. 1940)
Warburgs blew it in a major way. They adopted a strategy which was incapable of being realized. It simply did not have the capital or the stretch to compete with Morgan Stanley or Goldman Sachs as a globally integrated investment banking business, being all things to all men in all those marketplaces. They built up very substantial operations in both Tokyo and New York and overheads which were hard to justify in relation to the business.

When they got into negotiations with Morgan Stanley, they completely deluded themselves. They tried to tell their staff that it was a merger of equals. It was quite clear to everybody outside that this was a take-over. As far as I know, they had no formal external advice. There were a number of people, amongst them myself, who rang up when we heard about it and said, 'You cannot advise yourself. You need outside advisers.' They murdered themselves.

I was very sad. A lot of us were very cross. Warburgs was our spiritual home and it was competely screwed up. It was very sad indeed to see it being bought at a bargain-basement price by Swiss Bank Corporation, who were Warburgs' arch enemies. Having said that, I suspect that the two of them will get on with it and will build a formidable business. I don't think that story's over at all.

Michael Verey (b. 1912)

The City has been changed by the loss of Barings as an independent, very distinguished merchant bank. It is now a branch of a Dutch conglomerate insurance bank. It isn't the bank that we all knew. It is a great loss that both Barings and Warburgs have gone to foreign ownership. Warburgs tried to go too fast, too far and fell downstairs. Barings was a particular shock to me, I couldn't believe it when I heard it on the radio late at night. Warburgs wasn't a particular shock.

I don't know that British banks will be pre-eminent again, but I think we shall be able to hold our own without any trouble. To be really successful you don't need all that amount of capital. What you need is intelligence and competence. Quite often in the past, very large banks with very large capitals have promptly lost a very great deal of it and will probably do so again. One's only got to see the record of American banks in America itself.

John Wolff (b. 1940)

I wasn't as surprised about Barings as people who don't work in the City might have been. I know all about futures markets and one also knows about traders who don't keep to house rules and who hide things. I've seen that sort of thing happen quite often during my career but on a much lesser scale. In the modern day, with options and derivatives, there is the risk that managers don't understand what their traders are doing. Traders will baffle you with science and some are quite strong characters.

One of the best remarks I read after Barings was a man who is head of J. P. Morgan, an Englishman, who said he has a rule that if traders come to him asking permission to do certain strategies that may be very esoteric, he gives them three chances to explain to him what it is they want to do. If he doesn't understand it after three goes, they don't get the authority.

Sir Martin Jacomb (b. 1929)

Barings was an institution which represented British tradition, British integrity and the British way of doing things. If somebody wanted to discredit all those concepts, they couldn't have scored a more accurate bull's eye. It was a sadness for Britain, a turning-point in British history.

Jack Spall (b. 1930)
Leeson was a fool but if you put a twenty-eight-year-old in charge of dealing and the backstage, you've got to expect that to happen, although perhaps not on the scale that it did. The oldest thing in the world is putting contracts in the drawer – OK, it's not a drawer any more, it's an 88888 account in a computer, but it's the same thing. They were crazy. I don't understand the management of Barings in any way whatsoever.

Sir John Craven (b. 1940)
I was very much involved in the ghastly weekend of trying to save Barings. It was absolutely staggering that there were eighteen bank chairmen sitting round the table at the Bank of England, plus the Governor, the Deputy Governor and the Head of Supervision, and the issue that we had to address was, 'What is the potential further loss?' The fact of the matter became very clear and almost laughable in retrospect, but of all this brilliant galaxy of talent, no one had a bloody clue. There just wasn't anybody there who could assess the inherent risks.

At the time there were a lot of people who thought, 'This is going to be the end of London. This is the most terrible thing.' I guess I felt that on the Sunday. On the Tuesday, I got to my normal weekly board meeting in Frankfurt and my colleagues were interested to hear what was going on and I gave them five minutes' dissertation. I said that the Governor of the Bank of England had done the right thing in not seeking to get the Chancellor to use public money to support Barings, which is not part of the central system. The attitude of my German colleagues was, 'Ho, hum. A small bank, a long way away.'

I then went to Tokyo on Tuesday night. Given the fact that a lot of the problems had started in Tokyo with the dealings that Leeson was doing, I thought it would attract a lot of interest there. The next evening I had to make a speech at a reception of a couple of hundred people, a lot of bankers and brokers. After I'd said whatever I was intending to say, I tacked on five minutes on Barings. I must have been the first British banker there since the news had broken. They were politely interested but as I milled around afterwards in the cocktail crowd, no one said, 'I was fascinated by what you said about Barings.' Again it was a very minor event, dwarfed by concerns they had in Tokyo. What had seemed to be terribly important over that weekend in London became a 'Ho, hum' three days later in Frankfurt and Tokyo.

David Verey (b. 1950)

I invited the new Deputy Governor of the Bank of England to lunch and we were chatting away and suddenly he looked at me and said, 'Are you a Mohican?' I took a long pause because I couldn't think what on earth he was talking about. Then he said, 'Mohican as in "The Last of".' There is a group (now a very small group) of so-called British merchant banks who call themselves, apparently, the Last of the Mohicans, and believe that there should be a special place in the sun kept free for this particular type of institution. Quite what it all adds up to I'm not entirely certain, but it's a desire for some sort of implicit guarantee by the Bank of England that they should be allowed to exist. I don't believe in that at all. It's a load of nonsense. You either have a business which can compete or you don't. If you don't, you sell it or merge it or create a business that can compete. Seeking special protection because you are British and you carry a famous name doesn't seem to me a good enough argument to spend tax-payers' money.

David King (b. 1945)

All environments go through an evolutionary process. They go through an agrarian revolution, an industrial revolution and then financial services; that's a natural phenomenon. In the fifties, for example, the UK had a very strong manufacturing base, the car industry was a major generator of net visible income for the UK. We sat back on our laurels probably too much and other countries caught up with us very quickly. In some cases, they were starting without the hangover of heavy union involvement and of environments where there was old machinery. They were starting off with a keen, cheap labour force and little restrictive practices and, in some cases, they protected their domestic markets. This combination brought about the decline of the UK manufacturing industry and in some respects I can see the same thing happening in financial services.

South-east Asia has gone through in, maybe, forty years what we've gone through in four hundred years. They've gone through the agrarian revolution, the manufacturing revolution. Those economies are now looking at financial services and a lot of developing countries in South-east Asia, along with Paris, Germany, Chicago and New York are all keen to pinch some of our business. London is going to have to work far harder than we have in the past to maintain our position.

Although one might lament the decline of certain UK banks, the fact that there are five hundred banks in total in London indicates that the City remains a good place to do business. We have the accounting profession, the legal profession, the infrastructure, the communications, the expertise.

The synergy of insurance, the futures markets and other markets like the Stock Exchange all in the same location is obviously beneficial.

Lord Rothschild (b. 1936)
The most recent years in the City have been a very depressing period, really in terms of the success of British institutions. If you look at the merchant banks that I was most concerned with, in the last couple of years, you've seen Warburgs sold to the Swiss Bank Corporation, you've seen Morgan Grenfell sold to the Deutsche Bank, you've seen Kleinwort Benson sold to the Dresdner Bank, and you've seen Barings sold for nothing, after its crisis, to the Dutch. And most of these firms had histories of two hundred years or so. Just in that very short period of time, you've seen a huge erosion of power and influence of the domestic merchant banking institutions in the City of London. Why?

I'm afraid it's not so very different to the story of other industries, like the British motor-car industry or the British textile industry, or the British motor-cycle industry. I think that there was a failure to compete internationally, a failure of management to come to terms quickly enough with all the changes that have taken place. Now, why was there a failure of management? It's a highly complicated question. Partly to do with skills, partly to do with will, and many of the questions touch on the decline of Britain generally.

I think the owners did care, but I just don't think that they had the management talent, or steeliness of will, to compete with people who cared more and had greater skills. A harder work ethic.

There's been a kind of failure of nerve and resolve. You might have thought that one of the British clearing banks would have decided that it wanted to be a force that would compete with the great big banks of the world – Morgan Guaranty, Deutsche Bank and the big Japanese banks – but none of them succeeded. Why didn't they come forward to acquire the four firms – Warburgs, Morgan Grenfell, Kleinwort Benson and Barings – all of which had great names and businesses? Now, we are, I think, a society which is extremely, in capitalist terms, extremely attentive to short-term results, and you know, you're expected to produce better profits every year. Now, if your competitors will take ten-year views on acquisitions development, that could explain that lack of resolve. But it's still very sad that there isn't a force in England that is there, if you like, competing on equal terms with the Americans, Japanese and Germans.

Perhaps the worst thing of all is that we comforted ourselves by saying that if the chips were down, our qualities of good sense and judgement would prevail. And that was blown out of the water by the Barings fiasco. They, after all, encapsulated all those things that you felt were good and endemic to the British character, and would be there in terrible times; but they weren't.

Sir Brian Corby (b. 1929)

Lloyd's is the nearest thing that the insurance industry has to an insurer of last resort and it provides important capacity to the market. Something like Lloyd's is bound to continue because it is a necessary thing; it's important for the insurance industry and for London that Lloyd's problems be resolved. Quite clearly a business like insurance will only work if people have a sense of security. The one thing that is too often overlooked in the debate about Lloyd's is that, as far as I'm aware, no policyholder has had his claim not met; that's really what insurance is about. If you ask me what is the ethos of the Prudential, for example as an insurer, it is to be there in fifty years when the claims arise. That is the sort of security you've got to provide, not necessarily the cheapest premium but to be there to meet the claim at the right amount at the right time to the right people and speedily.

As an insurer, you have to be a pessimist about every proposition that's put to you but an optimist in total, so in that sense I'm an optimist. As far as London is concerned, I can see no reason that its position should be threatened unless we in Britain take a very inward-looking posture ourselves. There are dangers in that we see things we don't like in the European Community and because we don't like some things we turn against them all. We could find ourselves in an isolated position. That would be a tremendous mistake. We need to question many of our institutions. Are they relevant? Is the way in which they operate relevant? We need to be prepared to think the unthinkable occasionally, to make changes. It's not going to be easy, particularly if businesses are doing quite well. If you have a business that's looking over the edge of the cliff, it's pretty easy to say to everybody that you've got to turn round and go the other way. The skill of management is to persuade people they've got to make significant changes before it's obvious to everybody. That's the skill in a changing environment.

Michael Verey (b. 1912)

Lloyd's is no longer a great flagship for the City. It will take years for it to recover. It's terribly sad that having been regarded all my time as the ultimate in skill and respectability and soundness, that it should have made such an awful mess of its affairs and is now having great difficulty in resolving them. A lot of the people who went in for Lloyd's were very foolish to do so; it wasn't a suitable risk for them to take. It's the old story of a fool and his money are soon parted.

Leonard Toomey (b. 1924)
Half the syndicates in Lloyd's have folded. It's not the place I knew. I don't think there will be many private Names in the future. It will be corporate capital. Can it regain its reputation? I hope and pray so. There are some very clever people at Lloyd's. One of the rotten things is that most of the nice people have gone under.

Dundas Hamilton (b. 1919)
The only thing one can say about Lloyd's is, of course, that every one of them, like every stockbroker, had an unlimited liability. I'm sorry for the people, but they didn't look carefully enough at what they were doing. They thought it was money for old rope but in this life nothing is money for old rope. There's almost always nemesis waiting at the end of it.

Sir Martin Jacomb (b. 1929)
A lot of insurance business came to London through Lloyd's. It's very important that it comes here because there are good lawyers, good loss adjusters, good marine arbitrators and all the ancillary jobs which go with a powerful marine and non-marine insurance market. If Lloyd's packs up or gradually diminishes into insignificance, a lot of those people will depart because most of this business won't come to London. There's no reason why it should come here unless the people with ability and experience are here. We have no divine right to have insurance business in London – it's not written in pounds, it's written in US dollars or D-Marks or yen. The big reinsurance companies are predominantly German, Swiss and American.

Sir Nicholas Goodison (b. 1934)
I remember somebody comparing the old Membership of the Stock Exchange pre-1983 to the cricket team photographed in Edwardian days, a wonderful sunny photograph. You wonder where those people have gone. All those names of Stock Exchange firms have disappeared as a result of the extremely competitive conditions since 1986.

Charles McVeigh III (b. 1942)
None of the leading countries in Europe are particularly happy to concede that their own domestic capital markets will be best traded and developed in London. The reluctance to concede that has meant that in almost every case incentives are being offered to world-class securities firms and banks to participate in domestic markets. Some of these incentives take the form of *quid pro quo* arrangements. For example, the only international securities houses or banks that will be favoured with French privatization

business will be those that have a dramatic commitment to Paris and to France and who meet a certain size and regulatory framework that the French put in place.

One of the main issues right now *vis-à-vis* SEAQ International is that we at Salomon do not believe that the London Stock Exchange's attempt to be the stock exchange of choice for all the European international equity markets has worked. The domestic security markets and their exchanges have increasingly provided more liquidity and better service to those of us who are acting for clients all over the world, making it very difficult to preserve and argue the role of the London Stock Exchange as an international exchange of choice. The labour involved in keeping prices up to date on a screen-based system is really onerous. We have seven traders on the European Equity Desk. Two make strategic decisions, the other five do nothing but input prices into SEAQ International.

At Salomon we are withdrawing from SEAQ International. We'll keep our position with SEAQ in the UK but we're not going to develop our European equity business through the London Stock Exchange any longer. We're the third house to go. UBS withdrew first. NatWest Securities, a very significant force, withdrew last week.

Had the Stock Exchange responded differently, either with different technology or with alliances with local exchanges, they might have been able to preserve it. My guess is that the cracks in the dam are now sufficiently large that it'll be difficult to keep a core group there for ever.

If you fast-forward on your video machine ten years, would Salomon have a greatly diminished position in London and be significantly larger in Frankfurt and Paris and Madrid? I don't think so. The core of risk-taking, of credit analysis, of asset management, will be done by a group of professionals who clearly benefit by each other's presence in one location and they will continue to have satellites in these other cities. There are elements that might make a difference; either an onerous regulatory structure or were there a tax regime that would adversely affect expatriates in this country. A larger tax burden imposed on international individuals would have a profound impact on London's ability to hold a lot of international talent here.

Sir John Craven (b. 1940)

My concern is not for one second that Frankfurt or Paris are going to supersede London as a financial centre. I have no doubt about that whatsoever. Paris is out of it. Frankfurt has nothing approaching our infrastructure and very little in the way of internationally mobile funds under management.

We are assured of being the leading financial centre for the European Union. My concern is that we're now going to make ourselves uncompetitive by signing up for a single currency, a social chapter, minimum wages and all that great superstructure which represents the European project which our friends across the Channel are so keen on. We will become uncompetitive by comparison with our real competitors, who are not Frankfurt or Paris, but New York, Hong Kong and Singapore. That's what frightens me. We risk shooting ourselves in the foot. I'm bound to say my German colleagues don't agree with one word I'm saying, so it's a personal view.

There are journalists who say that a decade ago there were eight purely British merchant banks and now there's only Schroders, Flemings and Rothschilds, and what a national disgrace this is. My view is that it doesn't really matter who owns the shares – indeed Schroder's, Rothschilds, Hambros and Warburgs all started as German firms years ago. What matters is where the jobs are created, where the value is added, where the taxes are paid. When Morgan Grenfell was acquired by the Deutsche Bank in 1990, it was employing about eighteen hundred people making sixty million pounds of profit. Today in the UK it's employing three thousand two hundred people and making two hundred and fifty million pounds of profit. The building we're about to build is going to create a thousand on-site jobs for the next two years in the City of London and a large number of jobs outside. It's right opposite the front door of Morgan Grenfell's present building.

Sir Martin Jacomb (b. 1929)

London is still, by an enormous order of magnitude, easily the most important European financial centre. That's remained so not just because of the time zone, but because of the English language, because people like living in London, because people like dealing with counter-parties who commit themselves over the telephone instead of having to go back and negotiate with their principals. You can still get the business done in London. Morgan Stanley, Goldman Sachs, BZW all want strong positions in Paris and Frankfurt but as of today, there's no diminution whatsoever in the proportion of foreign exchange business done in London or the proportion of insurance done in London.

The old City has gone with the deliberate realization that the international marketplace required internationally owned banks to operate from the City rather than British enterprises. That's been a deliberate policy by the Bank and Government since the early eighties and it's succeeded in spades. But the last act so far, played in 1995, containing the collapse of Barings and the demise of Warburgs absolutely underlines that

British institutions are of incredibly small significance. That has undoubtedly changed life.

I am incredibly sad about Lloyd's and Barings and Warburgs. Every one
of them was a major disaster. I hate seeing what are, in effect, national
assets being chucked away.

Ross Jones (b. 1959)

History makes one cynical about Europe. The whole idea of one Europe
is a load of tosh. What's happening is that we'll obey the rules and they
won't, which has always been the way. It's just a whole load of politicians
on ego trips. They're trying to cause a revolution instead of letting things
evolve. Maybe even the EMU is a good idea, but let it evolve. Why do we
have to do it all by 19XX?

There's an enormous amount of uncertainty around. The City authorities, whether it's the Bank or the DTI, are being slightly wet. They've got
the whole City on hold re. Europe. They should say, 'What are the good
things in London? What have we got as a financial centre?' and then go
out and make sure that other people respect that we've got those things. I
don't think the City is being marketed. The City is in great danger of
losing its pride and place in Europe just by benign neglect.

Dundas Hamilton (b. 1919)

If the Bank of England indicated anything in the City when I joined it, it
was done at once, but as the international markets developed, so other
priorities took place. There's too much money at stake and too many
foreigners that aren't really responsible to the Bank of England, that don't
look to it as the be-all and end-all of things.

The Bank's standing as a regulatory body, and certainly the standing in
the eyes of the politicians, has changed very much. It was a private bank
and people respected its views as the central bank's private views, and it
was totally non-political. Then it was nationalized and became, as everything has to be when it is nationalized, a pawn of the politicians. Although
there is an arm's-length argument between the Chancellor and the
Governor, it doesn't have the same power it had in Montagu Norman's
day.

David Verey (b. 1950)

The European banks respect the Bank of England. There appears to be a
lot of cross-fertilization between central bankers and they're a powerful
group. If you offend the central bank in a particular place, the fact that
you've caused offence will be fed back to your own home base awful
quick.

The Bank of England has led particular exercises; for example, the famous Cooke report which established the ground rules for how much capital a bank should have dependent on its business; people still refer to the Cooke ratios, an internationally agreed standard. Is the Bank of England the big cheese? It's one of the big cheeses, but I wouldn't have said it was *the* big cheese. It's probably the big cheese in certain areas, like foreign exchange, but it wouldn't necessarily be the big cheese in financing bilateral trade. The setting of interest rates for Europe is effectively done by the Bundesbank, whether Ken Clarke or Eddie George like it or not; they can only tweak it slightly.

Nick Durlacher (b. 1946)
The danger to the City comes from Euro-legislation in the sense that there are aspects of Euro-legislation that are quite protective, not only in terms of transactions of physical goods but also in financial services. If the City becomes too protective in a European sense, then the business is incredibly mobile and it will go to somewhere like Singapore where there is an easier and lighter regime.

Haruko Fukuda (b. 1946)
Not very long ago, a senior Japanese stockbroker was quoted in the newspaper as saying that the City of London is like Wimbledon and that we are offering the courts to other nations to come and play in. Just because the courts are in Wimbledon, it doesn't mean that British players dominate it. That is a terribly sad statement and not one I would personally like to make, but unfortunately it is becoming a bit like that.

I'm afraid in my view the fall of Barings had a systemic risk attached to it, that the whole of the merchant-banking industry in Britain came under threat because of that single example and it showed up the low level of the capital base. In the context of investment or merchant banking as opposed to commercial banking, perhaps there is some truth in the statement that the American banks are being global and marching ahead by themselves. The nature of financial activity as an intermediary has become one – probably because the Americans made it that way – which requires rather more capital base than the British firms were able to provide.

I very much doubt that Nikko Europe will move its European head-quarters from London. We had this debate at the end of the 1980s when it was thought that the centre of gravity in the financial markets could move either to Frankfurt or Paris, particularly if there was to be a single market and a single currency. But the infrastructure of the City in terms of the existence of all the international players and the tradition of free trade as well as the physical infrastructure of office space, make it very improbable that the centre of gravity will move either to Frankfurt or Paris.

Singapore is already a very important financial centre in the world and in the Far East it rivals Hong Kong in the volume of activity. But Singapore isn't going to replace activity in London. I think one can be reasonably optimistic about the future of the City itself but that doesn't mean to say that the importance of the British economy within the City is going to remain at the same level as it has been in the past. After all, the City was not just an international market; British companies raised capital through the City and British merchant banks looked after the interests of British industry. Unfortunately, if the Japanese stockbroker whom I was quoting earlier is right – and I fear he probably is – the owners of the institutions in the City will become increasingly foreign, so their priorities will not lie with British industry. To that extent, it's a pessimistic scenario for Britain, but I don't think the City will find itself less important as an international capital market.

Sir Roger Gibbs (b. 1934)
Important institutions coming in from abroad to be based in London re-emphasizes that they believe London will continue to be the financial centre of Europe and one of the three most important financial centres in the world. I am more positive about the future of the Square Mile than I was two years ago. At the Wellcome Trust, when we were diversifying our investments, we bought the Kensington Estate, fifty-four acres of London, for which we paid £283 million. Prices of houses and flats in Kensington over the last nine months have gone up something like eight to ten per cent, which is exactly in the opposite direction to the national trend. One of the reasons for that is that ING executives, Dresdner executives, Deutsche Bank executives and Swiss Bank Corporation executives have got to be in London.

David Verey (b. 1950)
The question is, 'Is there a European threat against large American banks?' Deutsche Bank is a hell of a bank and it is now taking a very active role in the affairs of Morgan Grenfell. The Dresdner Bank and the Swiss Bank and UBS are very powerful. But what none of these yet have is a significant presence in the United States. The next move you will see is one or more of them buying or creating in some form or another a presence in the United States. If they do that and do it well and with credibility, then the American banks will have some competitors on their own turf. It hasn't happened in any major degree so far, but it probably will. The question is whether they are wasting their money, which I think

is more than likely. It won't be many years away (and it may be very few years away) when shares are capable of being traded on the Internet at zero cost. What on earth will be the point in having all these frightfully expensive, highly paid people sitting at desks staring into computer screens? The buyers of shares will be able to trade them between one another. That's probably taking it too far, but the edifices they are creating will probably in ten years' time be seen to have been a huge waste of money.

Personal Postscript

Michael Verey (b. 1912)
Reading the extracts from my interview, I think it shows that the City was quite good fun, quite a worthwhile activity, full of interest, very hard work and long hours. It shows that a good team is what makes it, not just one star; one star is always a danger because if it dips or dies it makes a terrible loss for people. And of course, you have to have a bit of luck, which I had.

Dundas Hamilton (b. 1919)
Thinking back, I suppose one simply thinks that change is the natural order of the day and, certainly, there's been a lot of change in the City of London between the time I first joined and even the time in the nineties when I made my recording. People don't like change. I don't like the changes taking place in the City any more than my father did when he retired from being a partner and I became a partner. He said, 'It's not as good as it was when I joined the Stock Exchange.' In my day, of course, the reliability of individuals and 'my word is my bond' was absolutely sacrosanct. Now, partly because of government regulation and not self-regulation, partly because of the kind of upbringing that children have, there is less ethos and respect and honour in the financial markets than there used to be.

My time in the City is now quite distant, whereas five years ago, when I had only been retired for five years, it would have been quite close. I still act as an adviser to one of the insurance companies and I still chair a company that's vaguely associated with the City, so I haven't totally let go, but the thoughts aren't there any more. Right now, I really don't think of the Stock Exchange ever at all. The change is partly old age, I have quite different interests. I was interested in making money and I'm not interested in making money any more. I'm just interested in enjoying my retirement until the end of my life.

I've always been interested in politics. I was the founding Chairman of the City and Industrial Liaison Council, getting money for the Tory Party and I stood as a Tory Party candidate. Now my contacts with industry and the City are so old and most of them are retired anyway, so that I'm really quite useless for political purposes and can give that up at the end of this year or at the latest by the time the general election takes place. Then I would like to do two or three things. I would like to play golf again. I'd like to look after my little place in the country, three Lutyens cottages that were a stable originally, and a Gertrude Jekyll garden. There I have a studio and a computer and I hope to write plays and maybe a book or two. Every grandfather's life is largely his grandchildren. I don't think it will ever be the same again, because it never is, but if you are saying 'Do I believe my grandchildren will have a good life in Britain?', yes, I do, yes I do indeed.

Leonard Toomey (b. 1924)

At the time of my recording, I was litigating against Stephen Merrett. It was an arbitration and I won. All three arbitrators found for me with costs and interest. After the Merrett case was over, I ended up in the high court in a case against Eagle Star (in 1973 I had reinsured out the whole of our syndicate's business from 1965 back to 1919 with the Eagle Star). The judge was Mr Justice Diamond, who really quite frightened me to death, but he found for me again with costs and interest. With Merrett and Eagle Star I was litigating for eight years. I couldn't retire. Stressful? If I had been a weak man, I'd have been dead. I do have very high blood pressure, I'm a diabetic, I was knocked about in the war (I get a forty per cent disability pension from the army). I always think I'm soft in many ways, but I'm also fairly tough, too. No one's going to run over me. I retired officially on the 31st of December 1990. I was in hospital the next day for surgery, a four-and-a-half-hour operation. I hung on and hung on until the case was over and then I went into hospital.

The money involved in the Eagle Star case was astronomical – the outstandings are about a hundred million dollars. I had the biggest line on the syndicate, my wife had a big line, my son had a big line. We had about two per cent of the stamp. If we had had to find two per cent of a hundred million, the money would soon go, wouldn't it? It frightened me because, coming from the most abject poverty, I've always had a fear of being bust. It was easy for me to make my stand in the case in so far as I had money. If I'd had nothing it would have been much more difficult. Money gives you muscle. It gives you strength. Throughout all this I was very fortunate in my three Leading Counsel, ably assisted by Stephen Moriarty, a barrister, and in my very talented solicitor Patricia Mitchell.

My son became the underwriter of my old syndicate under the aegis of the Chester group, which was a very famous Lloyd's family. I didn't sell the firm, I amalgamated with them. I could have sold the firm, I had about three or four offers but I've never approved of selling firms at Lloyd's. A lot of underwriters flogged their firms, took the money and ran. I don't think Names should be treated as cattle and just flogged. So I joined up with Chesters because I thought it was the best thing for my Names. But they got into trouble and the Names deserted them and the firm went under. You were completely at the mercy of the Members' Agents. If a big Members' Agent leaves you, all the other little ones leave as well.

My son lost his job. Then he got a job with Syndicate Underwriting Management, who were set up by the Committee of Lloyd's. He's now an associate director. He's the liaison man with Equitas. He leaves home at about seven every morning and gets home about nine o'clock at night.

They're all looking over their shoulders all the time. His future? He doesn't think of anything like that. He just lives as he goes along. His salary's not small. He says that in the City of London today, you can't look beyond two years, anybody. I rang my agents today and asked for the man who deals with my affairs: 'Sorry, he was made redundant, Friday, along with two others.' When I was a young man, when you went into that firm you stayed there till you died or retired, you never got the sack.

My wife left Lloyd's in 1989, she's only got two syndicates in run-off, yet she's still got a bill for sixty thousand pounds from Equitas. We will pay it (I'll pay it for her as I've done all the way through) which is what most of us would do. It's the 'no-hopers' and the 'can't-pays' and 'won't-pays' that are causing all the troubles at Lloyd's.

I personally was on some of the worst syndicates. If you listen to the 'won't-payers', we people in Lloyd's were on all the best syndicates and didn't go on the crappy syndicates, et cetera. I was on Gooda Walker 290, Macmillan Syndicate 80, which both lost me a great deal of money. I was on Heath 404. But I didn't litigate. I still don't think they did anything dishonest, they didn't; but they made terrible mistakes.

Of course, those people that have litigated have been treated very handsomely by Lloyd's. If you didn't litigate and paid up, you got very little out of it. I've got to find another three hundred thousand pounds. That's after they've taken all my open-year profits on '93, '94 and '95. And of course, in the last two years, I've had to pay a sixty thousand pounds round-figure levy for those people who won't pay, which I resent. When I became a member of Lloyd's, you were always told, 'You won't pay for anyone else's losses.' It's not worked out that way. As a matter of business, my son bitterly regrets he didn't litigate. We'd have been better treated. They're treating the people that litigated very well indeed. You'd never know it to open your papers, but they are.

I've lost about one point four million. I never let it get me down. It's only money. You come into the world with nothing and as sure as night follows day, you go out with nothing. But when I lose money – like I've got this enormous bill from Equitas, three hundred thousand pounds – I resent it because I'm robbing my children and grandchildren of it. I'm still a millionaire. I've overcome my troubles – all this litigation and the losses at Lloyd's – very well. I'm not happy about it. But I'm lucky. I mean, we had a lovely day today. We went out this afternoon, I drove to Littlehampton, we walked along by the sea and watched the kids on the beach; I'm going to my daughter's on Good Friday; on Sunday I'm driving to Eastbourne to meet my dear friend, Jimmy Archer (who arguably was the most successful underwriter at Lloyd's ever); it will be nice to have lunch with him over at the Grand at Eastbourne. My children come here. It's nice. Where I've been extremely lucky is that all my children have married nice people, that is the most wonderful blessing.

Lloyd's was a lovely place, full of lovely people. I was a lucky boy to walk in there when I was fourteen. I never had a single regret about retiring. Everyone at Lloyd's who knew me well (don't forget, I'd sat in the room for fifty-odd years, I knew their fathers, I knew their grandfathers), they all said, 'You'll never be able to retire.' It's all rubbish! I don't know where the day goes. I do a certain amount of work for the church. And of course I've got shares in about seventy companies. The mail comes in every morning and I have to work. I've always enjoyed that. Stock markets are my life.

Sir Brian Corby (b. 1929)

I ceased to be Chief Executive of the Prudential in 1990 and became Chairman. The Chairmanship is for a five-year term and it is very much a non-executive position. As the Prudential is a major investor in many UK and overseas institutions, I was looking around for something to do whilst I was Chairman that would minimize any conflicts of interest. A colleague of mine on the Prudential board was also on the board of the South Bank Centre, the Chairman of which was due to retire in the course of 1990, and I was invited to become Chairman. The South Bank Centre is the Festival Hall, the Hayward Gallery and the Queen Elizabeth Hall, in all a twenty-seven-acre site. I've always had leanings to be an historian, and anyone who stands on this site can see the sweep of the north bank of the Thames from the Houses of Parliament right through the City to Canary Wharf; one realizes one is in one of the most significant sites in the world. It's a good site but it could be much better and I had the feeling that maybe I could contribute to it. It's quite different from anything else I've done. It's a non-executive chairmanship as well. Initially I was there a couple of hours a week but more recently I've been a lot more often, not least because we are in the course of submitting a major bid for lottery funding to make improvements to the site.

What did I feel when I left the Prudential? I partially left when I ceased to be Chief Executive and became Chairman, which didn't require me going in that often a week. If you've been in a company for forty-three years and been Chief Executive and Chairman, as I had, really the time has to come when you make a break. Of course, I keep up the friendships and connections with people.

The extracts from my recording show that it was pretty clear that we had to make some changes at the Prudential. The 1980s in particular was a pretty go-go sort of period. Undoubtedly it was a bit frenetic on occasions but there are some essential themes running through everything, in particular the attempt to do something about one's distribution system which, for example, led us up the wrong track of estate agency. We decided that estate agency was not in fact the right business for us to be in and that we would get out of it. That occurred more or less when I ceased to be Chief Executive and it was fairly painful because we had to be up-front and admit we got it wrong.

We looked very carefully at the nature of the Prudential's business. We've implemented the sort of changes that were being discussed in the eighties and experimented on in the 1970s in relation to the UK operation. We've cut out some of our general insurance business, where we were not really big enough to be effective in the market. We've made a very significant entry into the United States. We've set on a course of expansion in the Far East, based on Hong Kong, with hopes to get into the Chinese market. So there has been quite a lot of change. When one looks at a company, you seem to see a sequence of important but discrete events. In actual fact, real life isn't like that, there is an essential continuity underlying what happens and it's a continuous process, certainly in a big company.

We also had regulatory problems, including the question of whether or not pensions had been mis-sold in the late 1980s. That put pressure on the then Chief Executive, who had particularly strong views on regulation which clearly didn't conform to the established thinking, and that eventually led to him feeling he should resign. We had to make another appointment as Chief Executive and Peter Davis came in. He is from outside the insurance/financial services sector and I think that's actually a very good thing to have done. There are some remarks in my extracts about how we used to grow our own timber but, looking back on it, the whole financial services sector has been too inbred and has very much benefited from bringing people in with other experiences.

If I were starting my career again, I don't think I would go into the City with the same sort of attitude and approach. In the early 1950s we were tending to look back to try to recreate in Britain the 1930s that we imagined; it was all a myth anyway. We were looking for a degree of stability. We're now moving in a much more uncertain world. I would be much more open-minded about my choice of job now, maybe within the City, maybe outside the City. It was put very well by one of the chief executives of one of the Prudential subsidiaries in addressing his staff a few years ago when he said that he could not guarantee employment for his staff but that he would try and guarantee their employability.

At the time that I ceased to be Chief Executive of the Prudential, I became President of the Confederation of British Industry, which was probably the first time anyone from the financial services sector had taken up that position. I remain a director of a reinsurance company and director of a partially owned Lloyd's management agency. I'm the Chairman of a smallish investment trust and I still have the odd charity that I get involved with. I go back to the City with enjoyment.

Sir Martin Jacomb (b. 1929)

At the moment I am Chairman of the Prudential. When I was asked to do this back in early 1994, I was Deputy Chairman of a competitor company, the Commercial Union. The Prudential is the leading institution for collecting the savings of the population and, since one of my real interests is trying to increase flows of savings and make them work – trying to make sure people save enough and trying to make sure their savings get to work in the right way – I resigned from the Commercial Union in 1993, left a quarantine gap, and then after a decent interval, I went on the board of the Prudential as a non-executive director. I took over as Chairman in May 1995 from Sir Brian Corby.

Brian is a very distinguished life-insurance man who had been at the Prudential all his working life. When he was Chairman, the Chief Executive was a big character, big in every way, called Mick Newmarch, very well known, very strong-minded. Mick Newmarch was the person who personified the Prudential and led it in a very high-profile way, including into a great controversy with the regulators. The Prudential has changed markedly since then. We have a new Chief Executive, Peter Davis, who doesn't have an insurance background. He comes from, principally, a marketing background; his background was first of all General Foods, then Sainsbury's, then Reed Elsevier, the publishers. He is an energetic, intelligent and charismatic leader. Secondly, we've got a new Finance Director, Jonathan Bloomer, and thirdly, a new head of the investment management operations, Derek Higgs.

Although we have experienced Prudential hands as well, we've got a thoroughly fresh team, and that is good because the whole life-insurance industry is going through a bit of a revolution. Two or three big changes are underway; how the industry presents itself to the public (because the public is a great deal more sophisticated than it was ten years ago and understands the products and the price at which they're sold much better than it did, so you've got to be sure you sell people what they really want); secondly, the industry itself is going through a big restructuring programme (a lot of the smaller mutual life insurance companies are not capable of making profits and will have to be taken over or go out of business). Thirdly, there is the information technology revolution which must be mastered if products are going to be sold in the most economical way.

It's a very exciting time to be at what I think is a key position at a key point in the economy, so I feel very lucky to be there. My workload is heavier than ever, which I don't think I do like, but it's what I'm used to and it's the way the chips have fallen or the cookie has crumbled, whatever the metaphor is.

George Nissen (b. 1930)

Reading through the extracts from my interview, I'm surprised to find that so many of the really important issues, which I think are still things which matter, come across quite freshly. Certainly it was a very different world but then that's not surprising because it was all a long time ago. The pace of change is high and rising all the time, particularly since 1993.

I'm finding retirement marvellous, it's really great. I'm pretty busy. I go to the City from time to time. I'm Chairman of an investment trust and I'm on the board of three others. I'm Chairman of the Ethics Committee at the Securities Institute. I've been on a District Health Authority, I'm on the Girls Public Day School Trust. My wife and I have bought the only respectable vanity publisher, the Book Guild, in Lewes. I've become a director of the Ffestiniog Railway – that's really good!

Hugh Peppiatt (b. 1930)

Reading through the extracts from my recording, my life in the City seems very close to me because that was such a central part of my experience and therefore it's very alive in my memory and very real. On the other hand, although I only left in 1990, it does seem long ago because there have been so many enormous changes, not only at Freshfields but also in the City.

I used to be a Whig historian, but I'm not any more and I don't think things progress from less good things to better things. But there's a real sense in which I think something has improved for the better; I have often pulled out files of work we did in the thirties and during the war and immediately after the war and it seems to me that it wasn't that good. By today's standards it was unprofessional or not the sort of standards that we would routinely require in a good firm of lawyers.

Professionally, standards are higher but they are also more meticulous and more particular, which isn't necessarily a move in the right direction. The world is very much more litigious. In any ordinary acquisition of a company, you carry out due diligence, a purely American term. I recall doing a job for Hertz, going to Manchester to buy the leading car-rental company there. I did the deal in the afternoon and went back to my hotel and wrote up the contract in my own hand without any precedents whatsoever. At about half-past-four in the morning, I finished it, had one hour's sleep and we went and signed this document, on my handwriting, off my head, paying maybe a million pounds, a lot of money in those days. It would be unthinkable we'd do that today; the standard form is a seventy-page document.

As I recorded in my interview, the Bank of England had no legal department when I was in the City. All the work came to Freshfields and it was very challenging, everybody loved doing it. Soon after I left, the first steps were taken to employ someone to assist mainly in advising the Bank in respect of regulation. Readily to hand was the ideal person in Peter Peddie, a partner in Freshfields who joined the same day I did and who is a little bit younger than I am. He left Freshfields and immediately went into the Bank as its legal adviser and had a mini-career there before retiring recently. His place has now been taken by an excellent lawyer formerly at Linklaters and the Bank now has what is effectively a legal department with, I believe, a fair number of qualified lawyers working in-house.

I have two sons with law firms in the City, one was at Freshfields and is now at Milbank Tweed, an American firm, and the other is at Stephenson Harwood. My daughter-in-law works at Linklaters. I was delighted that my sons went into the City. The City isn't what it was, but life isn't what it was, nothing much is really. The City, to put it at its lowest, is still the best on offer.

I said in my recording that retirement was traumatic and that was a true statement. My wife said I was incapable of making up my mind about anything for a year afterwards. I would now say that there might be something to be said for leaving a little earlier. I left before I was sixty and if I had left earlier there would have been a better chance of a new mini-career. I've picked up a lot of things and very much enjoy my life. I am Chairman of Moorfields Eye Hospital, which is hard, stimulating work. I'm a director of a large, private reinsurance broker. I'm a director of Hardy Oil and Gas, which I much enjoy. I chair the Appeals Committee for the European Bank of Reconstruction and Development. I'm a trustee of Help the Aged. That's about it.

My work takes me back to the City and I meet friends, but I don't go to Freshfields much. Although I go avidly to excellent dinners and get-togethers, I don't just drop into the office, that's never been Freshfields' way. People have got better things to do than talking to old chaps like us.

Peter Spira (b. 1930)

I retired from County NatWest at the end of March 1991 and I went on as a consultant to the end of 1992. The City is still part of my life, a lot of my contemporaries are still there or have children there. I'm always meeting people I worked with. We often talk about the next generation, the pressure they work under, how much tougher it is for them in a City which is much more run by fear and greed and job insecurity. The pressures we were under were different, the major example being that at Warburgs we were a joke because our lights were on at seven o'clock in the evening; now they work all night.

I'm on the board of directors of a small company called Smithers & Co. and I'm fairly heavily involved with the Société de Surveillance, in Geneva, and at the beginning of last year, 1995, I became Deputy Chairman of their UK subsidiary. Those are my three business activities. I like going to the City, being invited to lunch there and talking over the developments and the gossip and ending up over a coffee saying, 'It's wonderful to hear about all this and not be part of it any more.'

Of my six children, none has so far opted to go into the City; I'm quite pleased but I'm very relaxed about it. There are sides of the City which are great fun and are exciting. If one of my sons wanted to go into the City, I wouldn't deter him.

Retirement is wonderful. Apart from my business activities, I'm getting more and more deeply involved in photography and carpentry and I have more time for travel. For instance, I spent a week in Vietnam and I've been to India recently.

Jack Spall (b. 1930)

I shouldn't think I've been here [at the Kleinwort Benson offices] in five years. It feels strange. It's quite a long time, seven years, since I worked here but it's interesting, walking through the foyer, that there's absolutely nobody that I recognize at all. The only person that I've recognized is the car-park attendant, which is a rather amusing thought. I don't have a feeling of sorrow, gladness, sadness or any other emotion. It seems like quite a big chunk of my past, in fact, because it was eighteen years, the longest I ever worked for anybody. I did fourteen years, nine years, and then eighteen years, so it was a large chunk.

The bullion world has changed since I retired. Sharps Pixley is now Deutsche Morgan Grenfell or Deutsche Sharps Pixley or Deutsche Bank Sharps Pixley, I'm not sure what. Mocatta are still called Mocatta Group but they're very much under the aegis of Standard Chartered. Montagus have gone as a name and are now Hongkong and Shanghai Banking Corp. Rothschilds are still there. Johnson Matthey Bank went some time ago, of course, and are now Republic National Bank of New York.

The American houses have come in. It's not something you can start with small change. The numbers are big, you have to have a big institution behind you. Sharps Pixley was a family firm until 1966. OK, it's thirty years ago but not really that long ago. No way could they possibly have survived into the seventies as a family firm. It's megabuck stuff now.

Reading the extracts from my interview, it sounded like me, it was me. I was a little appalled at some of it; as you said earlier on, it isn't tarted up in any way, it's conversational, not written work and at times I thought, 'Oh, I could have said that in a better way.'

My son now works for Deutsche Bank in Hong Kong. He sent me a tape of a television broadcast he did for *Asian Wall Street Journal*. It was a very odd sensation, seeing him on the screen answering the questions that I was answering fifteen years before on the television. He knows more than I did. He talks about things like options, which in my days were not much of a facet of the market, so it was a little different but the questions were still, 'What do you think the market will do?'

Sir John Craven (b. 1940)

Reading the extracts from my recording, I'm amazed at the detail and the accuracy; I relived things that I'd quite forgotten about. There are one or two things that I feel differently about now and which stuck in my throat as I read it. Did I really think that about Frankfurt in 1990? Did I really think that about the regulatory system in 1990? But I'm sure it's accurately what I felt at the time. A lot has happened in Frankfurt to drag it into the modern financial world; compliance is now known about, there are insider-dealing laws which have got teeth, there's a Take-over Code, defective though it is. German companies are now beginning to conduct their affairs with an eye to their shareholders rather than simply to those of the management and the labour force. They are being forced to do so because such a large portion of the equity of many German companies nowadays is held by institutions in London and New York and therefore they are having their feet held to the fire in the same way that British and American companies have done for years.

Regulation is much more effective today than I would have given it credit for five years ago. I exited from the SIB just after Andrew Large, an old friend, came on board and I think he has taken a much more proactive and rigorous approach to the whole question of regulation and he's certainly put his imprint on it and been rather successful. I'm still concerned. Regulation is hugely expensive and creates for us a competitive disadvantage, particularly *vis-à-vis* our competitors in South-east Asia and probably in the United States. When we last talked I had only been to South Africa twice since I left as a schoolboy whereas I have been back at least half a dozen times in 1995. South Africa has been undergoing its own Big Bang and in the last eighteen months or so I and my colleagues in Morgan Grenfell felt this was an opportunity. Two weeks ago, we clinched a transaction where we will own a fifty-per-cent interest in probably the best stockbroker in South Africa. We've also become more and more involved in corporate work in South Africa.

I was in China last week. The Deutsche Bank has a rep office with about ten people in Beijing. Deutsche Morgan Grenfell is opening an office in Shanghai next year. I'm not at all sure that China is yet a place where you have to be as a bank or an investment bank. There's relatively little quality business there yet, but eventually it's going to be vastly important because it's one point two billion people. We are putting much more effort at the moment into India than we are into China. A debureaucratization has taken place in India.

When we last spoke we might have had two or three hundred people in South-east Asia, today we've got getting on for a thousand. We are represented in a significant way in all the so-called Tiger economies, doing stockbroking, merchant banking, fund-management business, development capital. There's a Deutsche Bank commercial banking network with seventy branches throughout Asia.

Even when we last talked it was true, but it's truer now that when you're over fifty, you're getting very old in the City. I'm fifty-five. I'm one of only three directors of Morgan Grenfell over fifty, out of ninety or a hundred people. The way the City has evolved over the last three or four years, I should think it's very normal now to find people aged twenty-nine or thirty – which is what I was when I went on the board of Warburgs – in similar positions. This year, 1995, we've had 3,279 applications from perfectly well-qualified graduates. Next year we will probably take in seventy-five graduate trainees because the business is expanding so fast.

In 1990 when the Deutsche Bank acquired Morgan Grenfell, I and my German colleagues were concerned that if we didn't handle things very carefully, trying to bring a very old-line, relatively small British merchant bank with an Anglo-Saxon linear management structure together with a very large, powerful, commercial-investment, universal bank employing at that time about seventy thousand, with a very different horizontal and hierarchical management structure, we would lose an awful lot of people. I negotiated with the buyers, who became my colleagues, an arrangement whereby we would effectively preserve the independent identity and independent management structure of Morgan Grenfell until such time as it seemed to make sense from all our points of view to integrate the two activities.

We ran Morgan Grenfell almost as a wholly independent unit for five years – five extraordinarily successful years in that the profits went from about sixty million pounds pre-tax in 1989 (the last year of independence) to an average of about two hundred and twenty millions pre-tax in 1992–1994, the last full year that we've reported on. We continued with all the activities that had been at Morgan Grenfell at the time of the acquisition. We added a couple more highly profitable businesses – one was a development capital business, where we attracted a team from Charterhouse Japhet, and the other was an emerging markets business where we attracted an extremely talented group of people. From 1990 through to early 1995 we didn't lose a single director from Morgan Grenfell to a mainstream competitor, which is quite extraordinary; two retired – one went to teach at Oxford and one went to look after the finances of the Hong Kong Airport Authority.

In the middle of 1994 my colleagues and I on the board of the Deutsche Bank began to think that the time had come to integrate the investment banking activities of Deutsche Bank and Morgan Grenfell. After many hours of discussion, we announced the bringing-together of about 7,500 people operating in about fifty different countries, covering eight global products into a single organization.

What we are going through at the moment is the third determining point in the thirty-five years I've been in the investment banking industry. The first determining point was May Day in New York in 1974 when commissions became negotiable and outside ownership became possible and so on. What happened then was that the men were separated from the boys. A few firms realized that life had changed, that they needed more capital, that they had to diversify their activities and could no longer rely on a flow of rich commission business from Stock Exchange business. They organized themselves appropriately, changed their strategies and have survived and prospered to the names you know today, Goldman Sachs, Morgan Stanley, Merrill Lynch and so on. A few firms were small enough to shrink into niches and find perfectly profitable futures. Then there are the ones in the middle who were too small to play in the big league, too big to shrink – most of them went out of business. Whoever remembers them now?

The second determining moment was Big Bang in London in 1984–5. The same impulse, the Stock Exchange being threatened with legal action by the Monopolies Commission, being forced to open Membership to outsiders and to accept negotiable commissions and as a *quid pro quo* being allowed to go dual capacity. The same thing happened, a few major firms realized the need to change their strategies and those have survived and prospered. Wedd Durlacher and de Zoete's both operate under a different name but both got the right strategy and the right partner and survive as the very successful BZW. Again, Rowe & Pitman and Akroyd & Smithers are another two successful ones, they don't trade under their old names, but together they made up the nucleus of Warburg Securities. Again the small firms were small enough to shrink into niches but the whole middle level of the cake went out of business. What happened to Sebags? What happened to Messels? The ones who got it wrong have disappeared. The ones who got it right have survived.

We come to 1995. There's a battle of the Titans going on. The battle is for a place at the table in the new superleague of globally integrated investment banks. There's probably only room for five or six of them. At that table there will certainly be three major Americans, Goldman Sachs, Morgan Stanley, Merrill Lynch, possibly J. P. Morgan. There's going to be an almighty scramble for a place at that table amongst the Europeans. We shall see who is going to survive and prosper.

I'm still on the main board of the Deutsche Bank and I have to spend on average a day a week in Frankfurt, which works out to about three hundred and fifty working-trips over the last six years and as many nights in a hotel there. The challenge and interest of being the only foreigner ever to sit on the board of an institution like the Deutsche Bank was a huge privilege, but I've paid for it heavily in personal disruption, time away from home and all the rest of it.

John Wolff (b. 1940)

I left Rudolf Wolff at the end of 1990 in order to set up my own consultancy business. It was mainly because Rudolf Wolff was part of a very large (and very good) organization called Noranda Mines, a multinational company and although I was quite an important cog in a large machine, it was restrictive. I began to feel more and more that I wanted to be a freer spirit. Time was passing by, so if I was going to make a move, I had to get on and do it. Most people were surprised when I resigned. It was a difficult decision and became more so after I'd made it because a lot of people couldn't understand it and were shocked because my name was

Wolff and the company was called Rudolf Wolff. I knew it was the end of an era. I was the fourth generation and now there's no family member left in the firm. It was very tough.

I'm not divorced from the firm, I probably speak to them several times a week but it's obviously a much more distant relationship. I wasn't in a position to retire; I've got a vast family and still two children to educate. The ultimate risk in setting up on my own isn't quite so big as it might seem because I could probably go back and get a job with quite a number of companies, not necessarily in a job I would want.

The new company is called John Wolff International and it's a consulting business; I sell my brain and experience. I'm a one-man band but I've got a network of people that I can sub-contract work to if I need to, but I don't often do that. I rent offices in the City almost next to the Guildhall. I wanted something with more character than just a box and was able to rent furnished accommodation in an older building. For example, the lift is about ninety years old and has a preservation order on it. Originally, it must have been hand-pulled and it's got lovely wrought-metal work all round it and glass and wood inside. Visitors can't work it on their own, so a factotum who works for the firm of lawyers in the building comes to operate it for them.

What you have is freedom but you don't have security. You do wonder sometimes where the income's going to come from in six months' time. I work approximately the same hours as I did before and I also do some Merger and Acquisition work and I'm on a few boards and I do some charitable work. I'm not in the hierarchy of the LME any more but I have to follow the market closely because of my job so I'm in touch with the people there all the time.

Charles McVeigh III (b. 1942)
When we made the original recording, I was one of three senior executive people left out of the seventy-seven partners in 1981. Through the difficulties of last year another couple have left of the original gang, so I'm the last.

David King (b. 1945)
The LME has grown sevenfold in seven years and last year we grew just as much as ever. This year we've consolidated a little but our global dominance appears more and more secure. Last year we turned over two trillion US dollars (two thousand billion US dollars). The Chancellor opened our new premises in November 1995 and in his speech said the LME had estimated earnings of about two hundred and fifty million sterling invisible earnings for the UK, a net figure which is quite an

achievement against a background of other areas of the City where the strength of the UK seems to be in decline.

The LME is a hundred and eighteen years old. For the first ninety-nine years, the LME was in Leadenhall Market and it was in the second building, Plantation House, for fourteen years. We've now moved to Leadenhall Street, less than a mile away from our original home. Our part of Plantation House is empty (Rudolf Wolff is still there but their lease will be expiring in due course) and my view is that it will be pulled down in a couple of years because it's a fairly large ground area which could make an attractive proposition to somebody in the future. There has to be a point when a building is more attractive if it's pulled down and rebuilt; the occupancy level of Plantation House could be trebled. It was built in the 1930s with old-fashioned wide corridors, high ceilings and no infra-structure for cabling. Just about every new building in the City now has raised floors for cabling; where we are now, I could within half an hour get a link to any other part of the building just by lifting up the carpet tiling.

The technology we had when we moved in only twelve months ago was state of the art, but by the time it gets dust on it, it becomes obsolete. Our brief to the architect who converted the building was to create a world-class environment with a slightly clubbish atmosphere. The room in which we sit at the moment has panelled walls, for example. The Chairman's office and the board room have panelled walls. Behind the neo-Classical exterior with the colonnades and the marble and panelled walls, there are millions of pounds' worth of technology, tucked away under floors, in the basement, et cetera. We wanted flexibility for an element of growth and, for example, we have spare capacity for double the number of staff.

We have a thirty-year lease on this present building but we have five-yearly break clauses. The most valuable asset that we have in this building is the capacity to walk away from it every five years without losing a great deal of money. Who knows – maybe not within five, but certainly within ten years, the way we trade will probably have changed. We may be screen-trading totally, there may be nobody on the floor. At the other extreme, we may be trading twenty-four hours a day on the floor because our market operates twenty-four hours a day. Technology doesn't sleep.

My office has a balcony on the outside and I overlook the trading floor. I can see and hear through the course of the day people trading on the floor and to the left of my desk I have a computer which shows me the prices being traded on the floor and also the prices being traded twenty-four hours a day so I perpetually can see what's going on in the market. The brokers are trading on the floor at the moment – there are about a hundred and eighty-five people down there which is why the noise levels of voices and bells has been changing while we speak. Our daily volume of trading is ten thousand million dollars, so a lot of the noise was generating my salary, amongst other things, so I don't mind it! I notice it when the volume changes because you expect it to go in waves towards the end of each trading session. I would know if the volume had risen higher than usual and then I would look to the screen to see what was happening in the market. I'm aware of what's going on. They also know I'm up here, of course.

I have a fairly plush office, not because I feel I deserve one but because we need an environment appropriate for senior visitors to come to the Exchange. We have an ongoing trail of visitors. We had Chinese in yesterday. We've had Taiwanese, we had a meeting with the Koreans. One of the major watersheds of recent times was the breakup of the Soviet Union because it appeared to be the catalyst for what was previously perceived to be impossible to become possible – for the Cold War to end and the Berlin Wall to come down and, notwithstanding the Tiananmen Square hiccup, the opening up of China.

In my diary for next year there are about fifty conferences around the world and that includes China and Russia, which a few years ago, although they both used our market for many years, would have been too hard to visit. The importance of Russia and China probably remains the same; we previously dealt with the state organizations but we now deal with commercial organizations. In some respects they're suffering right now the worst of both worlds in that there's a large element of corruption and they are a little like the Wild West. They're going through the learning process. These countries are also trying to set up their own Exchanges and some of them have copied the LME. I don't believe it's a threat. It may be in the very, very long run, twenty or thirty years, but they have to go a long way in sorting out the infrastructure – they need a legal system, a communications system, a regulatory system – which they are developing, but these things take time.

Haruko Fukuda (b. 1946)

I'd forgotten a lot of what I had said in the recording but if I was asked the same questions now I would answer them in similar terms.

A couple of years ago I was promoted to Vice-Chairman of Nikko Europe, but in substance the work I do has not changed very greatly. I still run, on a day-to-day basis, the Corporate Finance Department, which is involved in Mergers and Acquisitions and Project Finance Advisory Work and that sort of thing. And of course, I have all the duties of being a director of the company.

I tend to travel to countries where we think we may be able to develop corporate finance businesses. In the recent past we have gone further afield. In the earlier years we concentrated very much on the European region, including the peripheral areas, such as Southern, Eastern and Central Europe. With the demand being made for Japanese companies to collaborate with European companies in third countries, such as in the Asian region or the Far East, it's become more necessary for us to have understanding, knowledge and contacts in Asia and the Pacific as well as in Europe. Again, the Middle East is becoming rather more interesting because of the peace initiative. Also, some African countries. We have been working on a major project in Zambia to develop one of the world's biggest copper mines. Recently I've been to India and also Malaysia, Thailand, Singapore, Hong Kong, China.

It's quite different from my days at James Capel. Competitive forces have changed, alignment of forces has changed. About the time I left James Capel the Japanese institutions were probably at their peak. They were very big and they dominated everything in terms of numbers. In the last five years the presence of the Japanese in financial activities has somewhat declined and instead so-called Asian Tiger nations have become very much more present. European investors' interest in emerging markets has increased tremendously.

The profitabilty of Japanese financial institutions has been at a very low ebb for the last five years. Last year Japanese securities companies posted operating losses, which were very serious. Companies are making every effort to rationalize and produce greater efficiency. We have been dedicating our time to doing that ourselves and at the same time generating new sources of revenue. Japanese companies have some reserve in that the Japanese economy is mature – it's not a bankrupt economy – and has a lot of inner resources and latent assets.

The pleasure I get out of working is quite different from the pleasure I get out of my house in the country. They are two sides of the same coin and they complement each other. I don't think I would be happy doing either one or the other exclusively. The time constraint is a problem but one just has to be terribly well organized and be completely in control of one's own diary. I'm terribly lucky because I've got very good support with two personal assistants and my driver and so on. At home I also have very good support. If I didn't have those kind people around me, my life would be totally impossible.

David Verey (b. 1950)
The events which have taken place since my interview confirm that Lazards' decision not to buy a broker and a jobber at the time of Big Bang was the right one. As with Warburgs and Kleinworts, once you get into businesses that demand capital usage, there is no amount of money that

you can't use. Once you have a great demand for money, it means you have to find people to provide that money for you, which usually leads to a loss of independence of one form or another. The Lazard philosophy is to say that captial is 'bad' and therefore we should have as little of it as we possibly can get away with and concentrate on remaining small but having clout at the same time; that means powerful people. We last spoke in 1992, which was a dreadful year (we made money but didn't make very much), but since then we've had pretty much a straight line of profits going upwards and this last year was probably the most successful ever.

As far as my personal life is concerned, it is certainly possible to combine family life with City life. Of course, it's not easy and the tensions between what is expected of you in the process of earning your crust and family life, children and all that is bound to continue to exist. Wives and husbands need to choose one another very carefully, which is clearly platitudinous, but there has got to be a level of understanding that says you can prioritize in certain circumstances.

Davina Walter (b. 1954)
There's been a huge amount of change in the City over the past few years and I suspect it's unrealistic to say that there are that many happy places left to work. It's a result of a huge amount of change in a short space of time and the pressures and demands put on people. I still very much enjoy working in the City but you have to be realistic – not quite expect that each day is your last working in the City, but you have to realize that you don't have a job for life.

I'm now on the fund-management side of Morgan Grenfell, having joined in August 1995. When we last spoke, I was looking at my options because I wasn't happy. There'd been a huge amount of change at Henderson, especially in terms of the people who employed me. Richard Henderson, who was my boss, had decided to retire just before he was fifty. There was also speculation that Hendersons was going to be taken over and that's debilitating on morale. A new head of investments came in at the end of 1992 and he brought about a lot of change within the company, for better or for worse (a lot of it was for better). I was well plugged-in in terms of seniority and my position but therein was another frustration because I was classic marzipan layer, i.e. senior on paper but not in a position to have a voice. I thoroughly enjoyed my job in terms of the funds that I ran and it was a dream ticket that I knew I would never be able to replicate anywhere else, but my morale was pretty low.

I didn't want to walk away from something I'd built up over twenty years, so I looked at the type of institution that I'd like to go and work for if it wasn't going to be at Hendersons. I thought I'd be most attuned in a merchant bank. Not many merchant banks manage their US money still in the UK, most of them have sent it out. I didn't think I was a Warburg-type of fund manager. My options were few and far between. Morgan Grenfell had always struck me as one place that would be great to work. It was the only option on paper that I wanted. They're incredibly successful.

I couldn't believe it when I was offered the job because I had to overcome a lot of hurdles. I was interviewed by the Chief Executive and by the person who runs the pension-fund side. I'd definitely got the experience but on paper I came from a negative standpoint because I hadn't been to university and in this day and age people wouldn't walk in the door if they hadn't been to Oxford or Cambridge.

My boss is actually a thirty-four-year-old and she's a woman. I have no problems about it. She has the utmost respect of her team. They are mostly around her age and there are a few mid-forties. I work for MGIM which is Morgan Grenfell Investment Management, which covers the pension funds. We're a team of about forty-five.

Valerie Thompson (b. 1956)
I've been gone from Salomon for nine years now and that seems a long time. A few weeks ago, I went to Charlie McVeigh's twenty-fifth anniversary with the firm; that was wonderful. That was the first time I had been back to the company since resigning; I never set foot in there until that evening. I actually thought I was going to burst into tears, but I didn't. It was lovely to see some of the old faces. There was a small dinner party afterwards, which I was honoured to be invited to. Eddie Aronson, who first hired me into the firm, was there and that was tremendous.

I consciously didn't want to go back to Salomon before now. I find it very hard to walk away from anything and to let go and sever ties. I had actually tried four times in my career to resign from Salomon Brothers and in the extracts from the recording I say 'Salomon were my family' and they were. It was only within the Salomon environment that I learned how normal people behave, how they dress, how they speak to each other, how they interact; they were very accommodating of me in many ways, given my background. We've all got our baggage, but I don't recall working with anyone that was as fucked-up as I was. My best times of my life were with Salomon and some of the worst times, but in terms of being in that fortunate position where you've learned a trade and you're doing it successfully and it's working and you're absolutely gripped to bits by it, that's a lovely feeling.

In the end, I was very bored with the job I was doing. I could price deals very well but I didn't love doing it. There was a blandness to it, not a great thrill. I was most happy trading, fast-paced trading. That was when I was really in my element. If I'd been running an illiquid trading unit, which is what I wanted to do, I could have stayed on.

It was almost time to leave home. That sounds a very childish thing to say, but actually it was time to go out on my own and learn a lot about myself and to test whether I could do the things I wanted to do. I wanted to sow the seeds so that I could build a life that was not going to be dependent on Salomon Brothers because I've always had this big fear of being dependent. That probably comes because when we were very young, as children, you become dependent on your parents – and, guess what, they're not there. That shocked me so much that the fear of actually ending up dependent ensured that I'd always said to myself, 'I'll never wait till I'm kicked out, I'll never wait till the rug's pulled from under my feet. I will never get to the point where I am dependent on a company or, probably, anyone.' I just didn't like that feeling of vulnerability and insecurity. I wanted more freedom.

The other consideration was that I had been divorced for eighteen months and I did want to get to know my children. We are very close now. I'm not sure it would have been like that if I'd stayed. A lot of women carry that guilt around. I'm not so sure that they needed me as much as I feel there's an inherent need in mothers to be close to their children. After I left Salomon, I worked very hard in the early days and then I had a period when I didn't work so hard about three or four years ago and that was quite nice. I still worked every day but not quite so hard. I'd been doing a lot of spiritual work. I just slowed down and took out more time for playing, but it didn't last very long because the responsibility is there. I was still running the business. There's a direct correlation, if you don't work so hard, you don't make so much money. I'm the breadwinner. The children's livelihood depends on me and so does my own; there isn't anyone to go to. So you have to continue working.

I could have done with another couple of years at Salomon but that would have been too stiff a trade for me, to give up all of my longings for another two years was too heavy, it wasn't worth the money. So far, I haven't made as much money as I did at Salomon but it's been a building process and we're now starting to make very good money. I don't have extravagant needs, thank God. Most of the money I need is to support the family and the mortgage.

After being on my own for nine years, I did remarry a second time but sadly it didn't work. There were too many differences in terms of what we wanted and were willing to give, and the trust wasn't there. Without trust, you're dead, nothing can grow. But I've learned loads and now I'm coming to terms with the hurt and everything, I'm actually grateful for the whole experience as it helped me in a lot of ways.

Euromarket Trading Consultants was formed in 1987. We started off running a few workshops for people that were working in the business, on the maths and some of the soft skills (the interaction between trading and sales people) and we were doing a little bit of recruitment. Training is pretty new because it's never been required in years gone by, because everything moved at a very slow pace, it was all very basic. You got a book or you chatted to someone and eventually you grasped what it was; but with all this proliferation of product and so on, it became quite urgent for some companies and they did invest in training. But the City has seen quite a few bad times over the last five years and the first thing to be cut is training. I realized companies are much happier paying for head-hunters than training.

I wouldn't say any company loves to pay head-hunting fees (although by the unscientific way some come at hiring people and firing them, you'd think they did), but the fact is, it's a panic thing; they want someone and they'll pay the fee and they'll hire them. In the eighties, when firms were really expanding, a lot of head-hunters raped the City firms. Some, I believe, were being paid peace money for not touching a company's people. The City felt exploited but the whole City is about exploitation, isn't it, in a way? Someone once said to me, 'Head-hunters are parasites.' I said, 'What's the City then? We're all parasites.' It's a matter of degree. Nothing's whiter than white. Everyone's trying to make a living. In every profession there are people that do it with a bit more sense of ethics than others.

For certain jobs, certain companies like to use search firms and have beauty parades and have twenty-seven-page glossy reports presented to them about what they're doing. We don't run like that. We will cut through the crap. There's a certain type of client that is drawn to Euromarket Trading and it's not the client that wants to interview fifty people. Our clients know how to use us. We share the same philosophy and approach. They want to interview the best two or three people and they want us to go out and do all the work. They trust us. Once you assess the needs and wants of both sides, the universe of potentially suitable candidates for any one position is extremely tiny. It's never been any different and it never will be any different. That's the way people work. At the end of the day, there's going to be one or two people you'd feel more comfortable working with than the rest of the world. There is that chemistry element.

I've written a book on the international bond markets, a practical guide designed to educate and inform. That's taken a big chunk out of the last eighteen months. I had the idea about eight years ago, but in my heart of hearts, I knew I wasn't ready. It's coming out in about four weeks. It's called *Mastering the Euromarkets*, which is not my title. My title was *Street Smart*.

I'm glad I've become resourceful, because if you're one step ahead of the game you'll always have an edge. These days there isn't the security but there isn't the resourcefulness either. This country has traded for too long on the achievements of its ancestors. The younger children are not in search of the same excellence. A lot of people have grown up over the last twenty years that don't grasp the concept that you have to give something to get something. We've bred a generation of people that say, 'These are my rights. I want. I want. I expect. I expect.' They're going to have a very hard time coming to grips with poverty and real hardship, with the fact that when the health service crumbles and all the money goes, there'll be no waiting-lists to complain about, the country'll be frigging broke. A lot of people are going to be really shocked. There's that old saying, 'It takes two generations to make it and one to lose it', and maybe we're going through a phase that we're not even aware of, where this is the generation that's going to lose it all and then we'll be back to square one and have to build it up again. Maybe that's the way life works, I don't know.

Philippa Rose (b. 1958)
The extracts from my recording are very much about the beginning of the company. The company has changed a lot since then. I would now regard us as one of the leading head-hunters in the field of investment banking in Europe, with an outstanding representation in corporate finance. We have got a fantastic client list. We're now the lead head-hunter in corporate finance for BZW and J. P. Morgan and Lehman Brothers. Although we no longer work for Goldman Sachs, we worked for them consistently over the last eight years and placed over forty people with them.

We now employ fourteen people and have three partners. We are looking for five more professionals. We're very understaffed for the amount we have on our plate. Our systems are state of the art and for the past two years we have employed our own programmer, which I think is unique in the head-hunting profession. We have four interrelated data-bases with, roughly, forty thousand files on people round Europe.

About forty-five per cent of our work is overseas, so we travel a lot. That's going to increase as the demand for people with sector expertise as opposed to geographic expertise increases. We're running at the moment about nine different sector searches – for example, for a pharmaceutical specialist, a telecoms specialist, we are just about to start an oil and gas specialist; they're all corporate finance assignments. These are searches which you can't conduct in one country. Such a person could be based anywhere in Europe. There is much less interest in purely geographic sites.

In the extracts, I mentioned that we were having a period of stability, but now it's turmoil once again. There is an enormous amount of movement in the City, people are very mobile again. I'm not having a problem either finding work to do or fulfilling the assignments. This destabilization is largely because of the bank mergers and because of the increasing rarity of the independent banks; Schroders, Hambros and Robert Fleming are the only three independent UK banks. I don't remember a few years ago these endless discussions of 'Who's going to own this bank?' Any bank that's independent is viewed as a more risky prospective employer as people don't believe that independent banks are going to survive. On the other hand, some people are not suited to the huge institutions that are being created by mergers – they feel swamped. People's views have polarized quite dramatically; there are those who are completely devoted to the integrated bank concept, who want to be able to offer their clients every single product, and who are therefore susceptible to an approach from BZW or Deutsche Bank Morgan Grenfell; there are those who are more drawn to the boutique approach, the more focused product range, the firms who are not trying to be all things to all men, and for those sort of people Schroder Wagg is very appealing.

I feel very, very deeply involved in the firm. The problem is that I also feel a very strong pull to a more balanced way of life. Having now spent fifteen years of my life devoted to this company in a slightly obsessive way – it's completely dominated my life and pervaded my free time at weekends and in the evenings – I now want more space and more time for my children. I also want more time to develop other interests. I feel I've got other talents which are lying dormant at the moment and I want to develop them. I'd like to do much more in the music world, both learning instruments and listening to music. And also dancing, which I love and find incredibly liberating – rock and roll, and I want to learn salsa.

I've already gone down to a four-and-a-half-day week and I work from home on Tuesday morning. Tuesday afternoon is strictly to be with my children. I virtually never work at weekends now, although there are odd exceptions. I'm also taking much more holidays, probably in total eight weeks a year although, sadly, the business calls rarely allow me a complete break. I now have passed on to other people a lot of the work that I don't strictly need to do myself. I spend most of my time talking to clients, interviewing senior candidates and training people who are at an advanced stage of learning within the company. Luckily, I don't have to spend a great deal of time pitching for business because, once we've established a relationship with a client, we tend to be given all their business. Despite all this, my workload doesn't seem to have eased at all, and I still do work under an enormous amount of pressure during the time that I am in the office. Our clients continue to be extremely high quality and, rightly, very demanding. The problem of juggling all the balls in one's life shouldn't become apparent to them.

So, I haven't got the balance quite right, but I'm still working on it. It's less usual for men to want to withdraw from work pressure quite as early as me. There are a lot of men aged forty-five stating a desire to spend less hours in the office, but at my age (thirty-seven) most men are at the peak of their career and still working incredibly hard, often at some cost to their marriages and their family life. I've already screwed up my marriage and that's been a very sobering experience and has forced me to stand back and actually look critically at the balance in my life.

Ms A (b. 1959)

I am now an eighteen-months-qualified solicitor working as a corporate assistant for a medium-ranked City firm. Ironically, I was persuaded to do corporate work because of my City background and so find myself on occasion working very long hours which was something I had hoped to avoid. What I do is considerably more interesting than dealing (in terms of tickling the grey matter) not least because of the variety of work that I encounter.

Working for a law firm has inevitably brought its own set of challenges – time-sheets, operating in a partnership (all the partners are 'the boss'), the need to provide for oneself in terms of medical insurance and a pension. I still encounter sexism ranging from the tedious and unimportant 'male-bonding' type behaviour which involves jokes in bad taste, to the more alarming institutional attitude to women who become pregnant, for example. Lawyers are more conservative than brokers so the attitude is generally more 'little woman should be at home' than 'it's wearing a skirt, let's make a play'. The lawyers are more charming and intelligent but also more coarse and on occasion viciously Machiavellian. The brokers were easier to read.

Reading back through the interview extracts, it is clear that an unhappy affair with a client crystallized my feelings of impatience and frustration with the City, which I suspect I regarded as very much my 'woman in a man's world' problem. With hindsight, I may have been hasty in leaving; my final position was as a director and I would have been on a six-figure salary – I had made it. Emotionally, however, I am not sure I would have coped, so ultimately leaving was my only choice. Law school provided me with the emotional space to take stock but I still hung on to the City and to an immature dependency on a man who was very bad for me for a long while afterwards.

Confidence does not come from making a lot of money and achieving status if it is in a world which it is difficult to respect. Not for me, anyway. The law has offered part of the solution – I like myself a lot better. I think this has meant I have finally grown up and was open this time last year to meeting a wonderful man on holiday. Further irony: he works in the City! But in a wholly different area from those I have previously encountered. He comes home at five-thirty, his colleagues are thoughtful, sane and love their spouses, have a life . . . and a lot of them are women. We are getting married in the autumn and are discussing children soon. He feels (and I think he is right) that to make sense of my career and my life with him I should work as an in-house lawyer for a City institution advising on compliance with the Financial Services Act and institutional regulators. This will be interesting, well-paid and I will be able to go home at five-thirty to see my children. We'll see!

Ross Jones (b. 1959)
Gerrard & National has moved from Lombard Street to Cannon Bridge, where the futures markets are. It's a much more dynamic environment – you get to work at the same time, but you don't leave the office during the day. At Lombard Street you worked hard but were much more relaxed. Cannon Bridge is very open-plan, very visible and much more productive in the sense that you go to many more meetings and are seen to be doing much more work, but I don't know that means I'm any better at my job. My job title has changed in name – I'm now Chief Executive of Gerrard & National Limited, which is the discount house which we're merging with the Stock Exchange money-broker, but in terms of what I do on a day-to-day basis my job hasn't changed that much.

I've lost my two great mates in the company. Henry Askew has retired – he would hate the modern world. The business has changed. We're much more short-termist now. I've got people working with me that I like and I trust but I do not have a great mate in the company that's sharing responsibility with me. I'm on my own.

Since our interview, the City has changed enormously. I was hoping for stability and, hopefully, a move back to the old world and it has gone the other way. When we talked last the world which I was in was still very much word-of-mouth and non-legal agreements. We are now in the process of totally legalizing that market – everything will be done under legal agreement with annexes; you have to sign documents before you can deal. Absolute nightmare. The markets have become much more sophisticated and people have legal agreements in place. I think it's destroyed the whole fabric of the City.

The City world I came into in 1977, certainly at Gerrard & National and the type of institution we dealt with, was everything that I believed was important in life in terms of loyalty, the way things worked, the people. I was becoming disillusioned when we did the recording three years ago. I would say my disillusionment was almost fulfilled now. Yet I still love the City, I still want to work there. If I won ten million quid on the Lottery, I would still carry on working there.

Glossary

Accepting Houses Committee The Committee was established to supervise accepting houses and dealings in fine bills generally and to ensure maximum collaboration between them. Membership was normally reserved for the major merchant banks and leading accepting houses whose bills were freely taken by the Bank of England.

Big Bang The name given to the changes in securities trading rules which took effect in 1986. Foreign Securities firms were admitted. London's Minimum Commission Rules were abandoned, and trading started on automated screens in traders' offices. The distinction between jobbers and brokers was abandoned.

Box In the old Stock Exchange, small sub-offices located around the trading floor, used by brokers for the receipt and processing of orders. Also the place at Lloyd's of London where the underwriters sit and where the brokers queue to place their risks.

Court of the Bank of England The governing body of the Bank, consisting mainly of non-executive members drawn from different parts of the financial community.

Discount House A London financial institution authorized by the Bank of England to participate in the weekly offering of Treasury Bills by the Bank, and to deal in these and other bills.

Eurobond Market The market for transactions in bonds denominated in foreign currencies, mostly US dollars. The participants are principally international securities houses and banks, and deal on the telephone.

Gilt-edged Market The market, and participating organizations, in which transactions in stocks issued by the UK government and local authorities are undertaken.

LIFFE The London International Financial Futures and Options Exchange. Established in 1982, this exchange, independent of the Stock Exchange, was set up to deal principally in financial futures, but also in options, primarily in government stocks, but also in equities and indices.

Rostrum The focal point of the room at Lloyd's of London and the site of the Lutine Bell, originally taken from *HMS Lutine*, which is rung when the attention of the whole community is needed for a dramatic announcement.

SEAQ The Stock Exchange Automated Quotations system. A computerized screen system allowing market makers' quotes to be available to dealers' offices throughout the UK. The system eliminated the need for a trading floor.

SIB The Securities and Investment Board is the senior arm of the regulatory system set up under the Financial Services Act of 1986. Although financed by the organizations it was set up to regulate, it could otherwise be described as London's SEC. It is not staffed by civil servants.

Taurus A complex automated system which was intended to computerize the transfer and registration of stock and shares following any deal on the Stock Exchange. Its complexity and cost led to its abandonment in 1994.

Stock Exchange Council The ruling body of the old Stock Exchange, whose members were elected for three-year terms by the members of the Exchange.

National Life Story Collection
'City Lives' recordings

Interviews completed or in progress
(job titles apply to position at time of the recording):

Jeremy AMIAS	Managing Director, Fixed Income Sales, Salomon Brothers International Ltd
Henry ASKEW	Managing Director, Gerrard & National
Hermann ABS	Hon. President, Deutsche Bank
Sir John BARING	Chairman, Barings plc
John BARKSHIRE	Director, LIFFE
Professor Gerald BENNEY	Goldsmiths' Company
Lord BENSON	Former Senior Partner, Coopers & Lybrand
Sir Timothy BEVAN	Former Chairman, Barclays Bank PLC
Win BISCHOFF	Group Chief Executive, Schroder plc
Sir George BLUNDEN	Deputy Governor, Bank of England
Lord BOARDMAN	Chairman, National Westminster Bank
Peter BRANDT	Formerly of William Brandt's Sons & Co.
Ian BRINDLE	Senior Partner, Price Waterhouse
David BURTON	Formerly Chairman, LIFFE
Stephen CARTER	Chief Executive, BIFFEX
John CASTLE	Former Beadle, Drapers' Company
Arthur CHAMBERLAIN	Former Clerk, the Corn Exchange
Ferrier CHARLTON	Former Senior Partner, Linklaters & Paines
Christopher CLARKE	Former Senior Partner, Slaughter and May
Sir Robert CLARKE	Former Partner, Slaughter and May
Hilton CLARKE	Former Principal, Discount Office, Bank of England

William CLARKE	Chairman, ANZ Merchant Bank
Laurie CONNER	Director, Hoare Govett
Lewis COOKE	Former General Manager, National Westminster Bank
Sir Brian CORBY	Chief Executive, Prudential Insurance
Sir John CRAVEN	Chief Executive, Morgan Grenfell
Lord CROMER	Former Chairman, Barings plc
Sir Peter Averell DANIELL	Former Master, Drapers' Company
Lady DAVIS	Former Clerk, Bank of England
Monika DAY	Underwriter, Lloyd's of London
Nicholas DURLACHER	Chairman, LIFFE
Jeremy EDWARDS	Joint Managing Director, Henderson Administration Group
John FAIRBAIRN	Director, M & G Group
Lt Colonel John FARR	Former Director, Federation of Commodity Associations
Haruko FUKUDA	Director, Nikko Europe plc
Audrey GARNHAM	Secretary, Slaughter and May
Sir Roger GIBBS	Former Chairman, Gerrard & National Holdings plc
Graeme GILCHRIST	Former Chief Executive, Union Discount of London Ltd
Sir Nicholas GOODISON	Former Chairman, Stock Exchange
Arthur H. GORDON	Hon. Chairman, Kidder Peabody
Martin GORDON	Chairman, SBC Warburg Asia Holdings
Arthur GRIMWADE	Former Prime Warden, Goldsmiths' Company
Victoria HAHN	Underwriter, Willis Faber & Dumas Ltd
Charles HAMBRO	Chairman, Hambros Bank Ltd
Dundas HAMILTON	Former Deputy Chairman, Stock Exchange
Susan HARE	Librarian and Archivist, Goldsmiths' Company
Edwina HART	President, BIFU
John HENDERSON	Chairman, Henderson Administration
Olive HERN	Former secretary, Hoare Govett
Terence HIGGINS	Lloyd's of London
Francis HOLFORD	Chairman, Rudolf Wolff
David HOPKINSON	Chairman, Harrisons & Crosfield
Sir Martin JACOMB	Formerly Deputy Chairman, Barclays Bank

Michael JENKINS	Chief Executive, LIFFE
Peter JOHNSON	Former General Manager, Gerrard & National Holdings plc
Ross JONES	Managing Director, Gerrard & National Holdings plc
John KENNEDY	Partner, Allen & Overy
David KING	Chief Executive, London Metal Exchange
Lord KINGSDOWN	Former Governor, Bank of England
Sir Kenneth KLEINWORT	Director, Kleinwort Benson Group
Nick LAND	Senior Partner, Ernst & Young
Peter LANGLEY	Senior Partner, Slaughter and May
Andrew LARGE	Chairman, SIB
Murray LAWRENCE	Chairman, Lloyd's of London
Gareth LEWIS	Director, Berkeley Insurance
Gwilym LEWIS	Former Chairman, Arbon Langrish
The Earl of LIMERICK	Director, Kleinwort Benson Group
Hon. James MACKAY	Secretary, Cuthbert Heath Names Association
George MALLINCKRODT	Executive Director, Schroder PLC
Tony MALLINSON	Former Senior Partner, Slaughter and May
Charles MCVEIGH III	Chairman, Salomon Brothers International Ltd
Sir Peter MILLER	Former Chairman, Lloyd's of London
Sir Jeremy MORSE	Chairman, Lloyds Bank
Iain MURRAY	Partner, Linklaters & Paines
Julius NEAVE	Former Managing Director, Mercantile & General Reinsurance
George NISSEN	Consultant, Morgan Grenfell, Chairman, IMRO
Eddie NUTT	Almoner, Kleinwort Benson Group
Lord O'BRIEN of Lothbury	Former Governor, Bank of England
John OLIVER	Lloyd's of London
Hugh PAINE	Former Partner, Linklaters & Paines
Bill PARK	Partner, Linklaters & Paines
Jane PARTINGTON	Stockbroker, UBS Phillips & Drew
Sir Bruce PATULLO	Governor, Bank of Scotland
Hugh PEPPIATT	Former Senior Partner, Freshfields
Michael PESCOD	Partner, Slaughter and May
John PHIPSON	Partner, Linklaters & Paines
Henry PICKTHORN	Former Partner, Linklaters & Paines
Dennis PRESLAND	Lloyd's of London

Sir John PRIDEAUX	Goldsmiths' Company
Walter PRIDEAUX	Former Clerk, Goldsmiths' Company
Sir John QUINTON	Chairman, Barclays Bank
E. E. RAY	London Society of Chartered Accountants
Sir John READ	Former Chairman, Trustee Savings Bank
Mavis REES	Personnel Manager, Linklaters & Paines
Lord REMNANT	Chairman, National Provident Institution
Lord ROLL	President, S. G. Warburg Group plc
Philippa ROSE	Philippa Rose & Partners
Lord ROTHSCHILD	Chairman, St James's Place Capital plc
David ROWLAND	Lloyd's of London
Sir David SCHOLEY	Chairman, S. G. Warburg Group plc
Bruno SCHRODER	Director, Schroder PLC
Colin SHARMAN	Chairman, KPMG Peat Marwick
Lord SHAWCROSS	Former Chairman, Panel on Take-overs and Mergers
Mark SHELDON	Joint Senior Partner, Linklaters & Paines
Ms A. SMITH	Former stockbroker
Jack SPALL	Former Deputy Chairman, Sharps Pixley
Peter SPIRA	Former Deputy Chairman, County NatWest
Sir David STEEL	Former Director of the Bank of England
Lord SWAYTHLING	Former Chairman, Samuel Montagu
Valerie THOMPSON	Managing Director, Euromarket Trading Consultants
Leonard TOOMEY	Lloyd's of London
David VEREY	Chief Executive, Lazard Brothers & Co.
Michael VEREY	Former Chairman, Schroder Ltd
G. H. VEILER	LSCA
David WALKER	Former Chairman, SIB
Derek WALKER	Baltic Exchange
Davina WALTER	Investment Manager, Henderson Administration

The NLSC is extremely grateful for the help of its Trustees and Advisers in seeking sponsorship for 'City Lives'. The project has been made possible through support from ANZ, Allen & Overy, The Baltic Exchange, The Bank of England, The Bank of Scotland, Barclays Bank plc, The Baring Foundation, James Capel, Sir John Craven, The D'Oyly Carte Charitable Trust, The Daiwa Anglo-Japanese Foundation, The Drapers' Charitable Company, The Ernest Kleinwort Charitable Trust, The Esmee Fairbairn Charitable Trust, Euromarket Trading Consultants Limited, Freshfields, Gerrard & National Holdings plc, The Goldsmiths' Company, Hambros plc, Henderson Administration Group plc, The Joint Exchanges Committee, KPMG Peat Marwick, Lazard Brothers & Co. Ltd, LIFFE, Linklaters & Paines, Lloyds Bank plc, Lloyd's of London, M&G, National Westminster Bank plc, Nikko Europe, George Nissen, PosTel Investment Management Ltd, Price Waterhouse, Prudential Insurance, The Rose Partnership, S. G. Warburg Group plc, Salomon Brothers International, Schroder PLC, SIB, Slaughter and May, The Rt. Hon. Lord Swaythling, TSB Group plc, The Stock Exchange, The Wellcome Trust, Mr and Mrs T. R. Winser.

The recordings for 'City Lives' were carried out by:

Rebecca Abrams, Dr Bernard Attard, Louise Brodie, David Burgoyne, Professor Kathleen Burk, Dr Richard Cockett, Cathy Courtney, Ray Davies, Carol Freeland, Patricia Mendelson, Dr Robert Perks, David

Philips, Dr William Reader, Dr Kay Sanderson, Dr Judy Slinn, Katherine Thompson, Professor Paul Thompson, Jane Westlake and Jennifer Wingate.

City Lives was established by Professor Paul Thompson and Jennifer Wingate. They and Dr Robert Perks, the NLSC's Deputy Director and the Curator of Oral History for the British Library's National Sound Archive, have overseen the project throughout its development. At its outset, City Lives was administered by Carol Freeland and latterly by Jean Rigby, who became the NLSC's Co-ordinator in 1991. We are enormously grateful to Audrie Mundy, Katherine Thompson and Carol Haskel for the generous hours they have given to the NLSC as volunteers and for their commitment to our work.

Index